Chri
Clive Oxenden
Paul Seligson

ENGLISH FILE

Pre-intermediate Student's Book A

Paul Seligson and Clive Oxenden are the original co-authors of *English File 1* and *English File 2*

Contents

G word order in questions
V common verb phrases, spelling and numbers
P vowel sounds, the alphabet

What do you do?

I'm at university.

1A Where are you from?

1 VOCABULARY & SPEAKING common verb phrases

1 HOME AND FAMILY

- Where ________ you from?
- Where ________ you born?
- Where do you ________?
- Do you ________ in a house or flat?
- Do you ________ any brothers and sisters?
- Do you ________ any pets?

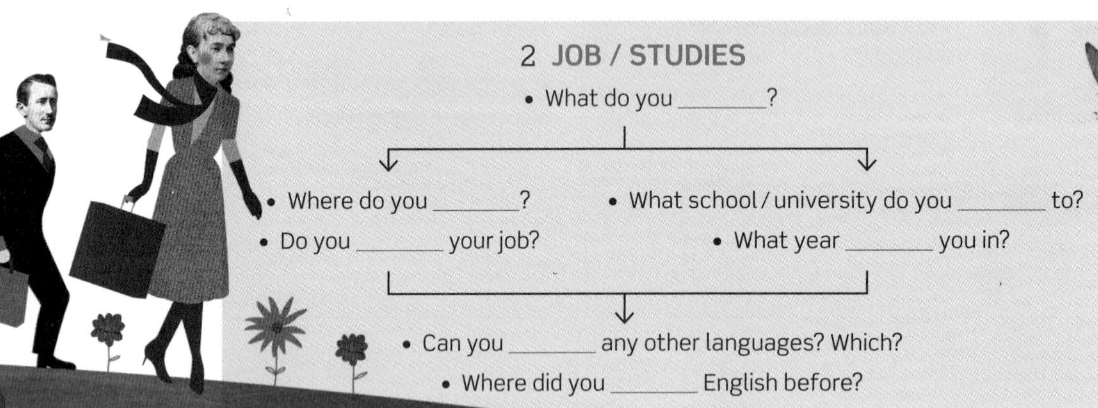

2 JOB / STUDIES

- What do you ________?
  - Where do you ________?
  - Do you ________ your job?
  - What school / university do you ________ to?
  - What year ________ you in?
- Can you ________ any other languages? Which?
- Where did you ________ English before?

3 FREE TIME

- What kind of music do you ________ to?
- Do you ________ a musical instrument? Which?
- What TV programmes do you ________?
- Do you ________ any sport or exercise? What?
- What kind of books or magazines do you ________?
- How often do you ________ to the cinema?
- What did you ________ last weekend?

a Complete the questions with a verb.

b 1 2))) Listen and repeat the Free Time questions. Copy the rhythm.

> **Sentence stress**
> Remember that we usually stress the important words in a sentence (the ones that carry important information), and say the other words less strongly, e.g. **Where** are you **from**? **What** do you **do**?

c In pairs, ask and answer the questions. Can you find at least **one** thing from each section which you have in common?

We live in the city centre.

2 GRAMMAR word order in questions

a Re-order the words to make questions.

1 born where your parents were ?
2 where from teacher our is ?
3 name your how you do spell ?
4 did last you go night out ?

b ➤ **p.126 Grammar Bank 1A.** Learn more about word order in questions and practise it.

c Stand up and ask different students the first question until somebody says *yes*. Then ask the follow-up question. Continue with the other questions, asking different students.

Do you drink a lot of coffee? *Yes, I do.*

How many cups of coffee do you drink? *Five cups a day.*

Present
/ drink a lot of coffee (or tea)? How many cups...?
/ go to bed early during the week? What time...?
/ spend a long time on Facebook every day? How long...?

Past
/ have a big breakfast today? What...?
/ go somewhere nice on Saturday? Where...?
/ see a good film last week? What film...?

3 PRONUNCIATION vowel sounds, the alphabet

a 1 5 Look at the sound pictures. What are the words and vowel sounds? Listen and check.

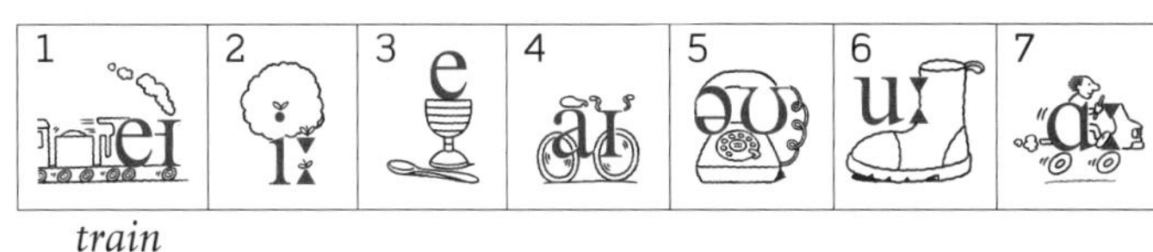

b ➤ **p.166 Sound Bank.** Look at the typical spellings of these sounds.

c Add these letters to the circles.

E G H J M O R W X Y

d 1 6 Listen and check. Practise saying the letters in each circle.

e Ask and answer with a partner.

- Do you normally get in touch with your friends by phone, email, or Facebook?
- Do you have an iPod or MP3 player? What kind?
- Do you often watch DVDs? What kind?
- Do you watch the BBC, CNN, or MTV?
- Do you have any friends from the UK or the USA?

4 SPELLING & NUMBERS

a 1 7 Listen and write six first names.

b ➤ **Communication** *What's his name? How do you spell it?* **A** *p.100* **B** *p.103.*

c How do you say these numbers?

13 30 76 100 150 375 600 1,500 2,000 10,500

d 1 8 Listen and write the numbers.

1 Gate ________ 3 Tel: ________ 5 £________
2 ________ miles 4 Population: ________

e Interview your partner and complete the form.

Student information

first name
surname
address

phone number
email

G present simple
V describing people: appearance and personality
P final -s / -es

I like good books.

He doesn't like sport.

1B Charlotte's choice

1 VOCABULARY describing people

a 1 9))) Listen to a man describing his girlfriend and tick (✓) her picture.

b Listen again. What two questions does Luke's friend ask him? How does Luke answer the second question?

> ***What does she look like? What is she like?***
> *What does she look like?* = Tell me about her appearance (Is she tall / short? What colour hair does she have?).
> *What is she like?* = Tell me what kind of person she is (Is she friendly? Is she shy?).

c ➤ **p.150 Vocabulary Bank** *Describing people.*

2 READING

a Who do you think knows you better, your mother (or father) or your best friend? Why?

b Read the introduction and the first paragraph of the article.

1. What is the idea of the experiment?
2. Who is Charlotte?
3. Who are Alice and Katie?
4. What do Alice and Katie have to do? Then what happens?

c Now read what Charlotte says. With a partner guess the meaning of the highlighted words and phrases.

d Cover the text. Can you remember?

1. What does Charlotte like doing?
2. What's she like?
3. What kind of men does / doesn't she like?
4. Who does she think is going to choose better? Why?

Who knows you better – your mother or your best friend?

In our weekly experiment, single people who are looking for a partner ask their mother and their best friend to help.

This week's single person is Charlotte Ramirez, a 25-year-old web designer. Her father is Spanish and her mother is English. She lives in Brighton and she doesn't have a partner at the moment. Her mother, Alice, chooses a man she thinks is perfect for her daughter and her best friend, Katie, chooses another. Then Charlotte goes on a date with each man. Which one does she prefer?

'I love going to the cinema, but I often feel like staying at home with a good book,' says Charlotte. 'I'm quite friendly and sociable and I get on well with most people. I think I have a good sense of humour.'

'What kind of men do I like? Well, I like interesting men who can make me laugh. Physically, I prefer men with a really nice smile who are taller than me. And I don't usually like men with beards! I like men who are into literature and art, and classical music.'

'I'm not sure who is going to choose better for me. Both my mum and my best friend know me very well. Perhaps Katie could find me a guy who is physically more compatible, but my mother has known me for longer!'

3 GRAMMAR present simple

a From memory, try to complete the sentences using the present simple.

1 She ________ have a partner at the moment.
2 She ________ on a date with each man.
3 Which one ________ she prefer?
4 What kind of men ________ I like?
5 I ________ usually like men with beards.

b In pairs, answer the questions.

1 Which letter do you add to most verbs with *he*, *she*, and *it?*
2 How do the verbs below change with *he, she,* and *it?*
watch | study | go | have
3 What auxiliary verbs do you use to make questions and negatives with...?
a *I | you | we | they* **b** *he | she | it*

c ➤ **p.126 Grammar Bank 1B.** Learn more about the present simple and practise it.

d Can you remember the kind of men Charlotte likes and doesn't like?

e Look at the photos of Alexander and Oliver. Find out about them. ➤ **Communication** *Alexander and Oliver* **A** *p.100* **B** *p.103.*

f Which man do you think is better for Charlotte? Why?

4 LISTENING

a **1 14** Listen to Charlotte talking about what happened when she met Alexander. What did she think of him? Does she want to see him again?

b Listen again and write down any adjectives or expressions that Charlotte uses to describe his appearance and personality.

c **1 15** Now repeat for Oliver.

d What does Charlotte decide in the end? Do you agree with her?

5 PRONUNCIATION final -s / -es

a **1 16** Listen and repeat.

snake	She likes cats. He works with his parents.
zebra	He has brown eyes. She wears jeans.
/ɪz/	She relaxes with boxes of chocolates. He uses glasses to read.

Pronunciation of final -s / -es: verbs and nouns
The final **-s** is pronounced /s/ or /z/. The difference is quite small.
The final **-es** is pronounced /ɪz/ after *ch, c, g, sh, s, z,* and *x*.

b **1 17** How do you say the *he | she | it* form of these verbs and the plural of these nouns? Listen and check.

verbs: choose cook go live stop teach
nouns: boy class date friend language parent

6 SPEAKING & WRITING

a Look at the form below and prepare to give this information about your friend.

Do you have a friend who is looking for a partner?
Help him / her to find one!

Name
Relationship: Single / Divorced / Separated
Age
Job
Appearance
Personality + / –
Likes
Doesn't like
Search

b Work in pairs. Ask and answer about your people. Compare the information. Do you think the two people are compatible?

What's his (her) name?

c ➤ **p.111 Writing** *Describing a person.* Write a description of a person you know.

7 1 18 SONG *Ugly* ♫

G present continuous
V clothes, prepositions of place
P /ə/ and /ɜː/

1C Mr and Mrs Clark and Percy

What's the woman doing?

She's standing in front of the window.

1 VOCABULARY clothes

a Look at the pictures. What are the models wearing? Match the words and clothes.

- ☐ boots
- ☐ shirt
- ☐ shoes
- ☐ skirt
- ☐ top
- ☐ trousers

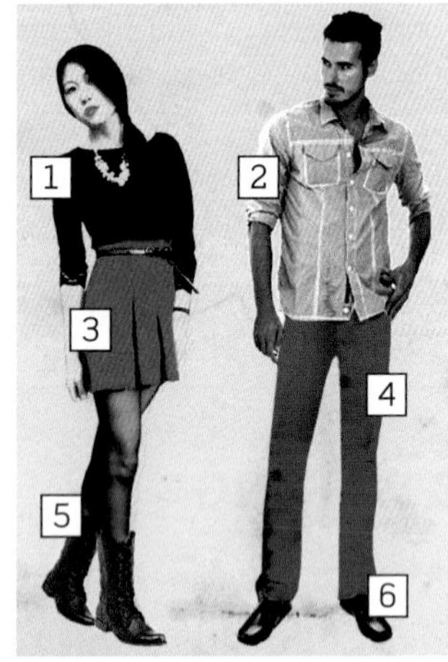

b ➤ **p.151 Vocabulary Bank** *Things you wear.*

2 PRONUNCIATION /ə/ and /ɜː/

a **1 20** Listen to these words and sounds. Practise saying them.

1 computer	trousers trainers sandals sweater cardigan
2 bird	shirt skirt T-shirt

b Underline the stressed syllable in the words below. Which sound do they have, 1 or 2?

actor cinema first painter third
arrive fashion world university
picture working prefer

c **1 21** Listen and check.

d ➤ **p.166 Sound Bank.** Look at the typical spellings for these sounds.

e Ask and answer the questions with a partner.

What clothes do you usually wear…?
- at work / university/ school
- when you go out at night
- when you want to relax at the weekend

3 GRAMMAR present continuous

a Look at the painting on p.9 by the British artist David Hockney (1937–). In pairs, describe the man and the woman.
- What do they look like?
- What are they wearing?
- What are they doing?

b Underline the correct form of the verb, present continuous or present simple.

1. In the painting the man *isn't wearing* | *doesn't wear* shoes.
2. In the UK women often *wear* | *are wearing* big hats at weddings.
3. In the painting a white cat *sits* | *is sitting* on the man's knee.
4. My son usually *sits* | *is sitting* at the back of the class so that the teacher can't see him.

c ➤ **p.126 Grammar Bank 1C.** Learn more about the present continuous and practise it.

d Look at the pictures on page 4. What are the people wearing? What are they doing?

4 LISTENING

a **1 24** Look at the painting of *Mr and Mrs Clark and Percy* on p.9 and listen to the audio guide. Focus on the people and things in the painting as they are mentioned.

b Listen again. Mark the sentences **T** (true) or **F** (false).

1. Percy is the name of the cat.
2. Mr and Mrs Clark made clothes for famous people.
3. The painting shows their living room.
4. The painting is quite small.
5. Celia is pregnant in the painting.
6. Ossie is putting his feet into the carpet because he is cold.
7. The position of the couple in the painting is unusual.
8. The open window is a symbol of the love between them.
9. The cat is a symbol of infidelity.
10. Celia and Ossie later got divorced.
11. Celia doesn't like the painting.
12. Ossie Clark died in 1995.

Celia today.

Mr and Mrs Clark and Percy (1970–71) by David Hockney in the Tate Gallery, London

5 VOCABULARY prepositions of place

a Look at some sentences which describe the painting. Complete them with a word or phrase from the list.

in (x2) on (x2) under in front of be<u>hind</u> be<u>tween</u> next to on the right on the left in the middle

1 There are two people ________ the room.
2 The woman is standing ________, and the man is sitting ________.
3 ________ of the painting, ________ the man and the woman, there's an open window.
4 A white cat is sitting ________ the man.
5 There's a carpet ________ the man's chair.
6 There's a telephone ________ the floor ________ the man's chair.
7 ________ the telephone there's a lamp.
8 ________ the woman there's a table, and a vase with flowers ________ it.

b 1 25 Listen and check. Then cover the sentences and look at the painting. Say where the things and people are.

6 SPEAKING

Describing a picture (a painting or photo)
When we describe a picture we normally use:
- *There is / There are* to say what is in the picture, e.g. *There is a table and a vase with flowers in it. There are two people.*
- The present continuous to say what the people are doing, e.g. *The woman is standing and the man is sitting.*
- Sometimes we combine *There is* and the present continuous, e.g. *There is a woman standing near the window.*

a ➤ **Communication** *Describe and draw* **A** *p.100* **B** *p.106.* Describe your picture for your partner to draw.

b In small groups, ask and answer the questions.
1 Which of the three paintings in this lesson do you prefer? Why?
2 What pictures or posters do you have on the wall in your bedroom or living room?
3 Do you have a favourite painting? What? Can you describe it?
4 Do you have a favourite painter? Who?
5 Do you (or did you) paint or draw? What kind of things?

Practical English Hotel problems

EPISODE 1

1 INTRODUCTION

a Look at the photos. Describe Jenny and Rob.

b 1 26 Watch or listen to Jenny. Number the pictures 1–6 in the order she mentions them.

c Watch or listen again and answer the questions.

1 What does Jenny do?
2 Where did she go a few months ago?
3 Who's Rob Walker?
4 What did they do together?
5 What does she think of Rob?
6 What's Rob's one negative quality?
7 How long is Rob going to be in New York?

A *1*

B

C

D

E

F

2 CALLING RECEPTION

a 1 27 Cover the dialogue and watch or listen. Who does Rob call? Why?

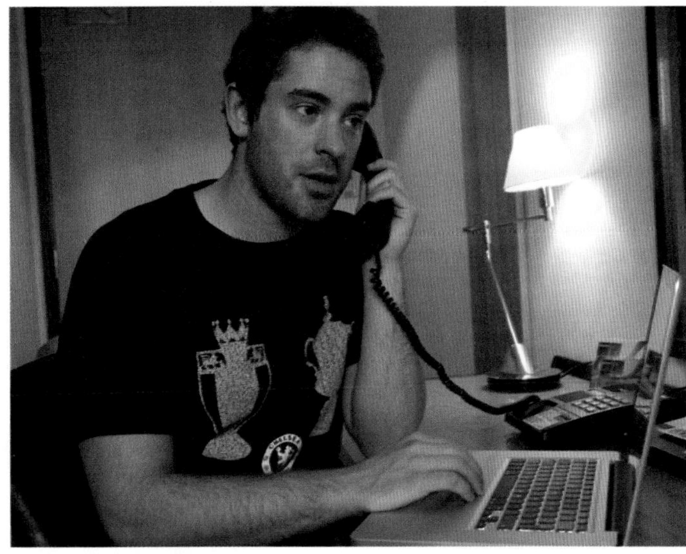

b Watch or listen again. Complete the **You Hear** phrases.

You Hear	You Say
Hello, reception.	Hello. This is room 613.
How can I ________ you?	There's a problem with the air conditioning. It isn't working, and it's very hot in my room.
I'm sorry, sir. I'll ________ somebody up to look at it right now.	Thank you.
Good ________, reception.	Hello. I'm sorry to bother you again. This is room 613.
How can I help you?	I have a problem with the Wi-fi. I can't get a signal.
I'm sorry sir. I'll ________ you through to IT.	Thanks.

c 1 28 Watch or listen and repeat the **You Say** phrases. Copy the rhythm.

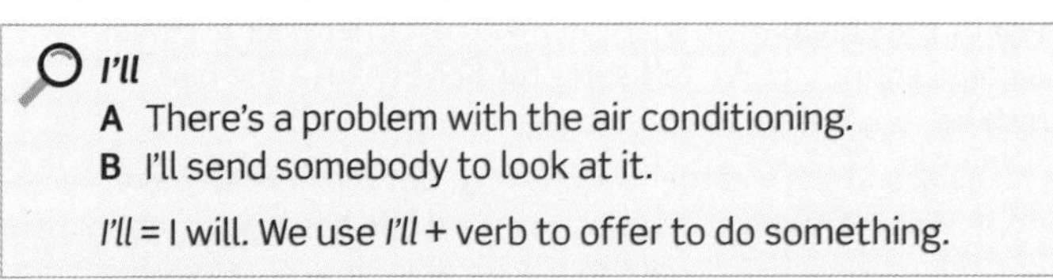

I'll

A There's a problem with the air conditioning.
B I'll send somebody to look at it.

I'll = I will. We use *I'll* + verb to offer to do something.

d Practise the dialogue in **2b** with a partner.

e In pairs, roleplay the dialogue.

A (book open) You are the receptionist. **B** (book closed) You are a guest. You have two problems with your room (think about what they are). **A** Offer to do something about **B**'s problems. You begin with *Hello, reception.*

f Swap roles.

3 JENNY AND ROB MEET AGAIN

a 1 29 That evening Jenny goes to the hotel to meet Rob and they go out for a drink. Watch or listen and mark the sentences **T** or **F**.

1 Rob says he doesn't like the hotel.
2 Jenny is going to show him round the city tomorrow.
3 Barbara is Jenny's boss.
4 Rob is hungry.
5 It's four in the morning for Rob.
6 They're going to meet at eleven.
7 Jenny thinks that Rob is going to get lost.

b Watch or listen again. Say why the **F** sentences are false.

c Look at the **Social English phrases**. Can you remember any of the missing words?

Social English phrases

Jenny Here you ________ at last.
Rob It's ________ to be here.
Jenny Do you have a ________ view?
Jenny Barbara's ________ forward to meeting you.
Jenny You ________ be really tired.
Rob I guess you're ________.
Rob By the ________...
Jenny It's ________ to see you too.

d 1 30 Watch or listen and complete the phrases.

e Watch or listen again and repeat the phrases. How do you say them in your language?

Can you...?

- [ ] tell somebody about a problem (e.g. in a hotel)
- [ ] offer to do something
- [ ] greet a friend who you haven't seen for a long time

G past simple: regular and irregular verbs
V holidays
P regular verbs: *-ed* endings

Where did you go on holiday?

I went to Venice with some friends.

2A Right place, wrong person

1 VOCABULARY holidays

a In one minute, write down five things you like doing when you're on holiday, e.g. *relaxing, going to museums*. Then compare with a partner.

b ➤ **p.152 Vocabulary Bank** *Holidays*.

c In pairs, interview your partner with the holiday questionnaire. Ask *Why?*

My perfect summer holiday

Which do you prefer...?

going abroad **or** going on holiday in your country
going by car, bus, plane **or** train
going to the beach **or** going to a city
staying in a hotel (or apartment) **or** going camping
sunbathing, going sightseeing **or** going for walks
hot, sunny weather **or** cool, cloudy weather
going with friends **or** going with your family

2 READING & SPEAKING

a Work in pairs. **A** read about **Joe's** holiday. **B** read about **Laura's** holiday. Find the answers to questions 1–5.

1 Where did he / she go on holiday?
2 Who did he / she go with?
3 Where did he / she stay?
4 What was the weather like?
5 Why didn't he / she enjoy the holiday?

b Now tell your partner about the holiday you read. Use questions 1–5 to help you.

c Read your partner's text. In pairs, guess the meaning of the highlighted words and phrases. Whose holiday do you think was worse? Why?

d Have you ever had a holiday that you didn't enjoy very much? What happened?

The place is perfect, the weather is wonderful,

but if you're with the wrong person, a holiday can be a disaster...

Joe 28, a flight attendant

Last October I went on holiday to Thailand for two weeks with my girlfriend, Mia.

The holiday began well. We spent two days in Bangkok and saw the Floating Market and the Royal Palace. But things went wrong when we left Bangkok. I wanted to stay in hostels, which were basic but clean, but Mia said they were too uncomfortable and so we stayed in quite expensive hotels. I wanted to experience the local atmosphere but Mia just wanted to go shopping. I thought I knew Mia very well, but you don't know a person until you travel with them. It was awful! We argued about everything.

For our last four days we went to Ko Chang, a beautiful island. It was like being in paradise. The weather was lovely and the beaches were wonderful, but we just sunbathed without speaking. We spent our last night back in Bangkok and we went for a drink with some Australians. They were really friendly and Mia started flirting with one of the boys. That was the end.

> ❛ you don't know a person until you travel with them ❜

When we arrived at Heathrow airport the next day we decided to break up.

I took hundreds of photos, but when I got home I didn't show them to anyone.

Laura 26, a nurse

> ❛ I'd love to go back to Venice one day... but without Linda. ❜

Last spring my best friend Isabelle and I booked a holiday in Venice. We rented a small apartment for a week with a fantastic view of the canals. At the last moment another friend, Linda, asked if she could come too. We felt sorry for her because she had problems with her boyfriend, so we said yes.

Venice was magical and the weather was perfect, but the holiday was a disaster for one simple reason: Linda was so mean! She has a good job so she's not poor, but she just didn't want to pay for anything. When we went sightseeing she didn't want to go to any museums or galleries that cost money. When we went on a gondola she complained that it was very expensive. When we went to have lunch or dinner she always wanted to go to cheap restaurants or she bought pizzas and ate them in the flat. But the night I invited her and Isabelle out on my birthday she chose the most expensive things on the menu! The worst thing was that although Isabelle and I paid for the apartment, Linda never once bought us a coffee or a drink.

I'd love to go back to Venice one day...but without Linda.

3 LISTENING

a 1.34 You are going to listen to Mia and Linda talking about the holidays. First listen to Mia. Does she agree with Joe about the holiday?

b Listen again. What does Mia say about...?

1 her relationship with Joe before they went
2 the places where they stayed
3 talking to other travellers
4 photos
5 going on holiday with a boyfriend

c 1.35 Now listen to Linda. What's her opinion of the holiday? Then listen again. What does she say about...?

1 Venice
2 what they did there
3 the cost of her holiday
4 her next holiday

d Who do you sympathize with most, Joe or Mia? Laura or Linda?

4 GRAMMAR past simple: regular and irregular verbs

a What is the past simple of these verbs? Are they regular or irregular? Check your answers in **Joe's** text.

go ______	begin ______
spend ______	leave ______
want ______	be ______ / ______
stay ______	think ______
know ______	argue ______
sunbathe ______	take ______

b Now underline the past simple [+] verbs in **Laura's** text. What are the infinitives?

c Find and underline two past simple [-] verbs in the two texts. How do you make [-] and [?] in the past simple...?

- with normal verbs
- with *was / were*
- with *could*

d ➤ **p.128 Grammar Bank 2A.** Learn more about the past simple and practise it.

5 PRONUNCIATION regular verbs: *-ed* endings

a 1.37 Listen and repeat the sentences.

tie	We booked a holiday. We walked around the town.
dog	We sunbathed on the beach. We argued about everything.
/ɪd/	We rented a flat. We decided to break up.

b Say the past simple of these verbs. In which ones is *-ed* pronounced /ɪd/?

arrive ask end invite like love need park start stay

c 1.38 Listen and check.

Regular past simple verbs
Remember that we don't normally pronounce the *e* in *-ed*.
The *-ed* ending is usually pronounced /t/ or /d/. The difference between these endings is very small.
We only pronounce the *e* in *-ed* when there is a **t** or a **d** before it, e.g. *wan**t**ed*, *en**d**ed*. With these verbs *-ed* = /ɪd/.

6 SPEAKING

a Look at **Your last holiday** below. What are the questions?

b Think about your answers to the questions.

YOUR LAST HOLIDAY
1 Where / go?
2 When / go?
3 Who / go with?
4 Where / stay?
5 What / the food like?
6 What / the weather like?
7 What / do during the day?
8 What / do at night?
9 / have a good time?
10 / have any problems?

c Work in pairs. Ask your partner about his / her holiday. Show interest in what he / she says, and ask for more information. Then swap roles.

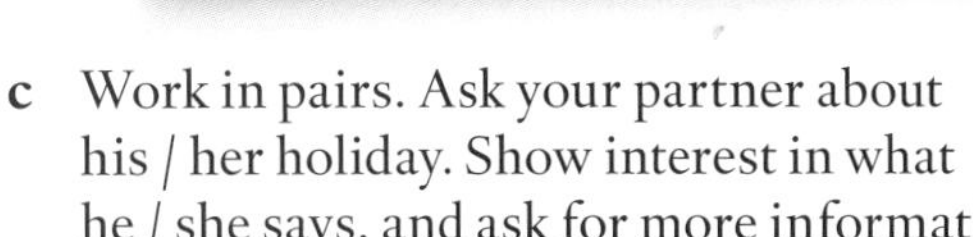

Useful language for showing interest
[+] *Really? Wow! Fantastic! Great!* etc.
[-] *Oh no! How awful!* etc.
[?] *Was it expensive? Why? What happened?* etc.

G past continuous
V prepositions of time and place: *at*, *in*, *on*
P sentence stress

What was happening?

People were waiting for the results.

2B The story behind the photo

1 READING

a Look at a photo which news photographer Tom Pilston took in 2008. What do you think is happening?

b Read Tom's description of what happened on the night he took the photo. Were you right?

c Read it again and answer the questions.

1 Why did Tom Pilston go to Chicago?
2 Why couldn't he take a photograph of Obama?
3 What was the weather like?
4 Where did he take this photo?
5 Where could the people see the election results?
6 Was he sorry that he couldn't go inside the center?
7 What happened when Obama won?

d Why do you think the photographer thought his photo was better than a photo of Obama himself? Do you agree?

A moment in history

On 4th November I arrived in Chicago late in the evening. I wanted to photograph Barack Obama and his family in the Convention Center, but when I got there I discovered that I didn't have my press pass and I couldn't go inside. I walked around the park outside the center. Although it was November, it was a warm night. The atmosphere was wonderful. When I took this photo everybody was looking at the TV screens waiting for the election results. Some people were quietly holding hands and smiling – others were tense and nervous. They felt that it was their moment. Suddenly I realized that this was a better place to be than inside. I was watching Obama's victory through the faces of all these people, African, Hispanic, Chinese, white. At about 11 o'clock the results were announced, and everybody went mad. People started laughing, shouting, and crying. But when Obama made his speech they all became quiet and emotional. There was only one place to be on the planet that night – and I was there.

2 GRAMMAR past continuous

a Look at the highlighted verbs in an extract from the text. Do they describe actions that happened…?

a after he took the photo
b at the same time as he took the photo

> When I took this photo everybody was looking at the TV screens waiting for the election results. Some people were quietly holding hands and smiling – others were tense and nervous.

b ➤ **p.128 Grammar Bank 2B.** Learn more about the past continuous and practise it.

c 1 41 In pairs, listen to the sounds and make a sentence using the past continuous and the past simple.

They were playing tennis when it started to rain.

3 VOCABULARY *at, in, on*

a Which preposition do you use before…?

1 a date (e.g. 4th November) _____
2 a time (e.g. 11 o'clock) _____
3 the morning, the afternoon, etc. _____
4 a room or building (e.g. the Convention Center) _____

b Check your answers to **a** in the text. What preposition do you use with…?

1 a month (e.g. January) _____
2 the weekend _____
3 home, work, school _____

c ➤ **p.153 Vocabulary Bank** *Prepositions.* Do part 1.

d ➤ **Communication** *at, in, on* **A** *p.100* **B** *p.106.* Answer the questions with a preposition and a time or place.

4 PRONUNCIATION sentence stress

a 1 43 Listen and repeat the dialogue. Copy the rhythm.

A **Where** were you at **six o'clock** in the **evening**?
B I was at **work**.
A **What** were you **doing**?
B I was **having** a **meeting** with the **boss**.

b In pairs, take turns to answer the questions about yesterday.

6.30 a.m. 11.00 a.m. lunchtime 4.00 p.m.
6.00 p.m. 10.00 p.m. midnight

Where were you at 6.30 in the morning?
I was at home.
What were you doing?

5 LISTENING

a Look at a famous photo which was on the cover of many magazines around the world in the 1960s. Where do you think the people are? What do you think is happening?

b Read the beginning of a newspaper article. Why do you think it is called '*The image that cost a fortune*'?

c 1 44 Now listen to the woman in the photo talking about it. Were you right?

d Listen again. Choose a, b, or c.

1 In 1968 she ____.
   a wasn't interested in politics
   b was a communist
   c was an anarchist
2 She loved the atmosphere because all the students were fighting for ____.
   a peace b democracy c freedom
3 She was sitting on a friend's shoulders ____.
   a because she was tired
   b to take photos
   c so that she could see better
4 She was carrying the flag because ____.
   a she was a leader in the demonstration
   b somebody gave it to her
   c she brought it with her
5 Her grandfather died six ____ later.
   a days b weeks c months

e Do you think she is sorry that she was in that photo?

6 SPEAKING & WRITING

a Talk to a partner. Give more information if you can.

1 Do you have a photo you really like? Who took it? What was happening at the time?
2 Do you upload photos onto Facebook or other internet sites? What was the last photo you uploaded?
3 Do you have a photo as the screen saver on your computer or phone? What is it of?
4 Do you have a favourite photo of yourself as a child? Who took it? What was happening when they took it? What were you wearing?
5 Do you have any photos in your bedroom or living room? What are they of?
6 Do you know any other famous historical photos? Who or what are they of?

b ➤ p.112 **Writing** *My favourite photo*. Write a description of your favourite photo.

The image that cost a fortune

Caroline de Bendern was born in 1940. She was the granddaughter of Count Maurice de Bendern, a rich aristocrat who owned a lot of property in Paris and Monaco. Although he had other grandchildren, the Count decided to leave all his money to Caroline. 'I never knew why,' says Caroline. 'Perhaps because I was pretty.' He paid for her to go to very expensive schools in England, and he hoped that she would marry well, perhaps a member of a European royal family. But Caroline was a rebel. She went to New York and worked there for a short time as a model. Then, in 1968 when she was 28 years old she returned to Paris...

Adapted from a British newspaper

iTutor

G time sequencers and connectors
V verb phrases
P word stress

Why was she was going very fast?

Because she was in a hurry.

2C One dark October evening

1 GRAMMAR time sequencers and connectors

a 1.45 Read the story once. Then complete it with a word or phrase from the box. Listen to the story and check.

After that	Next day	One evening in October
Suddenly	~~Two minutes later~~	When

b With a partner, answer the questions.

1 Why did Hannah go and speak to Jamie?
2 Why did Jamie play *Blue As Your Eyes*?
3 What happened when Hannah left the club?
4 What was the restaurant like?
5 Where did they go every evening after that?
6 What was the weather like that evening?
7 Why was Hannah driving fast?
8 Why didn't she see the man?

c From memory complete these sentences from the story with *so*, *because*, or *although*. Then check with the story.

1 She was going very fast ______ she was in a hurry.
2 ______ the food wasn't very good, they had a wonderful time.
3 He was wearing a dark coat, ______ Hannah didn't see him at first.

d ➤ **p.128 Grammar Bank 2C.** Learn more about time sequencers and connectors and practise them.

e Complete the sentences in your own words. Then compare with a partner.

1 They fell in love on their first date. Two months later…
2 I went to bed early last night because…
3 The weather was beautiful, so we decided…
4 It was really cold that night, and when I woke up next morning…
5 Although we didn't play well in the final…
6 I was driving along the motorway listening to the radio. Suddenly…

Hannah met Jamie in the summer of 2010. It was Hannah's 21st birthday and she and her friends went to a club. They wanted to dance, but they didn't like the music, so Hannah went to speak to the DJ. 'This music is awful,' she said. 'Could you play something else?' The DJ looked at her and said, 'Don't worry, I have the perfect song for you.'

[1] *Two minutes later* he said, 'The next song is by Scouting For Girls. It's called *Blue As Your Eyes* and it's for a beautiful girl who's dancing over there.' Hannah knew that the song was for her. [2] __________ Hannah and her friends left the club, the DJ was waiting for her at the door. 'Hi, I'm Jamie,' he said to Hannah. 'Can I see you again?' So Hannah gave him her phone number.

[3] __________ Jamie phoned Hannah and invited her to dinner. He took her to a very romantic French restaurant and they talked all evening. Although the food wasn't very good, they had a wonderful time. [4] __________ Jamie and Hannah saw each other every day. Every evening when Hannah finished work they met at 5.30 in a coffee bar in the high street. They were madly in love.

[5] __________, Hannah was at work. As usual she was going to meet Jamie at 5.30. It was dark and it was raining. She looked at her watch. It was 5.20! She was going to be late! She ran to her car and got in. At 5.25 she was driving along the high street.

She was going very fast because she was in a hurry. [6] __________, a man ran across the road. He was wearing a dark coat, so Hannah didn't see him at first. Quickly, she put her foot on the brake…

2 PRONUNCIATION word stress

Stress in two-syllable words

Approximately 80% of two-syllable words are stressed on the first syllable.

Most two-syllable nouns and adjectives are stressed on the first syllable, e.g. *mother*, *happy*. However, many two-syllable verbs and prepositions or connectors are stressed on the second syllable, e.g. *arrive*, *behind*, *before*.

a Underline the stressed syllable in these words from the story.

a|cross af|ter a|gain a|long
al|though aw|ful be|cause birth|day
eve|ning in|vite per|fect se|cond

b 1 49 Listen and check.

3 VOCABULARY verb phrases

a Make verb phrases with a verb from box 1 and a phrase from box 2. All the phrases are from the story.

invite somebody to dinner

1
~~invite~~
have
drive
meet
give
take
wait
be
play
leave
run

2
along the high street
somebody your email / phone number
a song
across the road
in a hurry
in a coffee bar
for somebody
the club very late
~~somebody to dinner~~
somebody to a restaurant
a wonderful time

b Cover box 1. Try to remember the verb for each phrase.

4 SPEAKING & LISTENING

a Read the story of Hannah and Jamie in **1** again.

b In pairs, use pictures 1–5 to re-tell the story. Try to use connectors and the verb phrases in **3**.

1

2

3

4

5

c There are two different endings to the story. Have a class vote. Do you want to listen to the **happy ending** or the **sad ending**?

d 1 50, 51 What do you think is going to happen in the ending you have chosen? Listen once and check.

e Listen again. If you chose the happy ending, answer the questions in ➤ **Communication** *Happy ending p.101*. If you chose the sad ending, answer the questions in ➤ **Communication** *Sad ending p.106*.

5 1 52 SONG *Blue As Your Eyes* ♫

1&2 Revise and Check

GRAMMAR

Circle a, b, or c.

1 ______ any brothers or sisters?
a Have you b Do you c Do you have

2 ______ last night?
a Where you went
b Where did you go
c Where you did go

3 My brother ______ football.
a doesn't like b don't like c doesn't likes

4 Her parents ______ a small business.
a has b haves c have

5 I ______ to music when I'm working.
a never listen b don't never listen c listen never

6 In the picture the woman ______ a blue dress.
a wears b wearing c is wearing

7 A What ______? B I'm looking for my keys.
a you are doing b do you do c are you doing

8 She's at university. She ______ history.
a 's studing b 's studying c studying

9 We ______ to Malta last August.
a were b went c did go

10 I saw the film, but I ______ it.
a didn't liked b don't liked c didn't like

11 When I got home my parents ______ on the sofa.
a were sitting b was sitting c were siting

12 What ______ at 11 p.m.? You didn't answer my call.
a you were doing b you was doing c were you doing

13 She couldn't see him because she ______ her glasses.
a wasn't wearing b didn't wear c didn't wearing

14 We went to the cinema. ______ we decided to go for a walk.
a After b Then c When

15 We had a great time, ______ the weather wasn't very good.
a so b because c although

VOCABULARY

a Complete the phrases with a verb from the list.

book do drive invite leave
look play stay take wear

1 A What do you ______? B I'm a doctor.
2 A What does she ______ like? B She's tall and slim.
3 She doesn't usually ______ jewellery, only her wedding ring.
4 A Did you ______ any photos? B No, I didn't.
5 A Where did you ______? B In a small hotel.
6 Did you ______ your flights online?
7 A Let's ______ your parent to dinner. B Good idea.
8 A Are you going to ______ there?
B No, we're going to get the train.
9 A Go on! Ask the DJ to ______ our song! B OK.
10 A What time do we need to ______ home tomorrow?
B About 7.00. Our flight is at 9.00.

b Complete with *at*, *in*, or *on*.

1 The meeting is ______ March 13th.
2 A Where's Mum? B She's ______ the kitchen.
3 He was born ______ 1989.
4 A Where's the dictionary?
B It's ______ the shelf in my room.
5 Mark's not back yet – he's still ______ school.
6 It's a very quiet town, especially ______ night.
7 We went ______ holiday to Malta last year.

c Circle the word that is different.

1	straight	long	blonde	beard
2	clever	lazy	generous	funny
3	friendly	mean	stupid	unkind
4	dress	skirt	tights	tie
5	socks	gloves	trainers	sandals
6	necklace	bracelet	ring	scarf
7	windy	foggy	dirty	sunny
8	basic	dirty	uncomfortable	luxurious

PRONUNCIATION

a Circle the word with a different sound.

1	(tree)	E	G	J	V
2	(bird)	shirt	shorts	work	curly
3	/ɪz/	chooses	languages	lives	glasses
4	(bike)	weight	height	kind	night
5	(computer)	painter	trainers	university	trousers

b Underline the stressed syllable.

1 tal|ka|tive 3 pre|fer 5 comfor|ta|ble
2 mou|stache 4 dis|gu|sting

CAN YOU UNDERSTAND THIS TEXT?

a Read the newspaper article once. Does the journalist think that taking photos in museums is a good thing or a bad thing?

b Read the article again. Mark the sentences **T** (true) or **F** (false).

1 The journalist saw tourists taking photographs of works of art in Rome and New York.
2 When he first saw people taking photos in the MOMA he didn't understand what they were really doing.
3 Then he realised that the photographers were not looking at the paintings.
4 They were taking photos because they wanted to look at the paintings later.
5 Later a couple asked him to take a photo of them in front of a painting.
6 He suggests two possible ways of solving the problem.

c Look at the highlighted words in the text. Guess their meaning from the context. Check with your teacher or with a dictionary.

We were there!

The first time I noticed this phenomenon was a few years ago, in St Peter's Basilica in Rome – a crowd of people standing round Michelangelo's Pietà, taking photos with their cameras and mobile phones. Then last week I saw it again at the Museum of Modern Art (the MOMA) in New York. At first, I wasn't too worried when I saw people photographing the paintings. It was a bit irritating, but that was all. It didn't make me angry. Then the sad truth hit me. Most of the people were taking photos without looking at the paintings themselves. People were pushing me, not because they were trying to get a better view of the art, but because they wanted to make sure that no one blocked their photo. Was it possible that perhaps they were taking the photos so that they could admire the paintings better when they got home? This was very improbable. They were not there to see the paintings, but to take photos to prove that they had been there.

Then it got worse. Now people were taking photos of their partners or friends who were posing next to, or in front of some of the most famous paintings. Neither the photographers nor the person they were photographing had looked at the art itself, although I saw that sometimes they read the label, to make sure that the artist really was famous. At least nobody asked me to take a picture of them together, smiling in front of a Picasso!

I think that photography in museums should be banned, but I also have a less drastic solution. I think that people who want to take a photo of an exhibit should be forced to look at it first, for at least one minute.

Adapted from Marcel Berlin's article in The Guardian

CAN YOU UNDERSTAND THESE PEOPLE?

1 53))) **In the street** Watch or listen to five people and answer the questions.

Justin

Joanna

Sarah Jane

David

Andy

1 Justin ______.
  a looks like his mother
  b looks like his father
  c doesn't look like his father or his mother
2 Joanna's favourite painting is of ______.
  a a landscape b a person c an animal
3 Sarah Jane's last holiday was a ______ holiday.
  a beach b walking c sightseeing
4 David ______.
  a takes a lot of photos
  b is in a lot of photos
  c has a lot of photos on his phone
5 Andy says ______.
  a he enjoys crying at the end of a film
  b he thinks films with a sad ending are more realistic
  c most of his favourite films have a sad ending

CAN YOU SAY THIS IN ENGLISH?

Do the tasks with a partner. Tick (✓) the box if you can do them.

Can you...?

1 ☐ ask and answer six questions about work / studies, family, and free time activities
2 ☐ describe the appearance and personality of a person you know well
3 ☐ describe a picture in this book and say what is happening, what the people are wearing, etc.
4 ☐ ask and answer three questions about a recent holiday
5 ☐ describe a favourite photo and say what was happening when you took it
6 ☐ say three true sentences using the connectors *so*, *because*, and *although*

Short films A photographer
Watch and enjoy a film on iTutor.

G *be going to* (plans and predictions)
V airports
P sentence stress and fast speech

What are you going to do there?

I'm going to teach English

3A Plans and dreams

1 VOCABULARY airports

a When was the last time you were at an airport? Was it to travel somewhere (where?) or to meet someone (who?)?

b Look at the airport signs and match them to the words and phrases below.

1
2
3
4
5
6
7
8
9
10
G5-25
11
12

- [ ] Arrivals
- [ ] Baggage drop-off
- [ ] Baggage reclaim
- [ ] Check-in
- [ ] Customs
- [ ] Departures
- [ ] Gates
- [ ] Lifts
- [ ] Passport control
- [ ] Terminal
- [ ] Toilets
- [ ] Trolley

c 1 54 Listen and check. Then cover the words and look at the symbols. Remember the words and phrases.

2 LISTENING

a Look at the three travellers in the picture. Who do you think is…?

- going to work abroad for an NGO (= non-governmental organization)
- going to see an ex-partner
- going to do a photo shoot in an exotic place

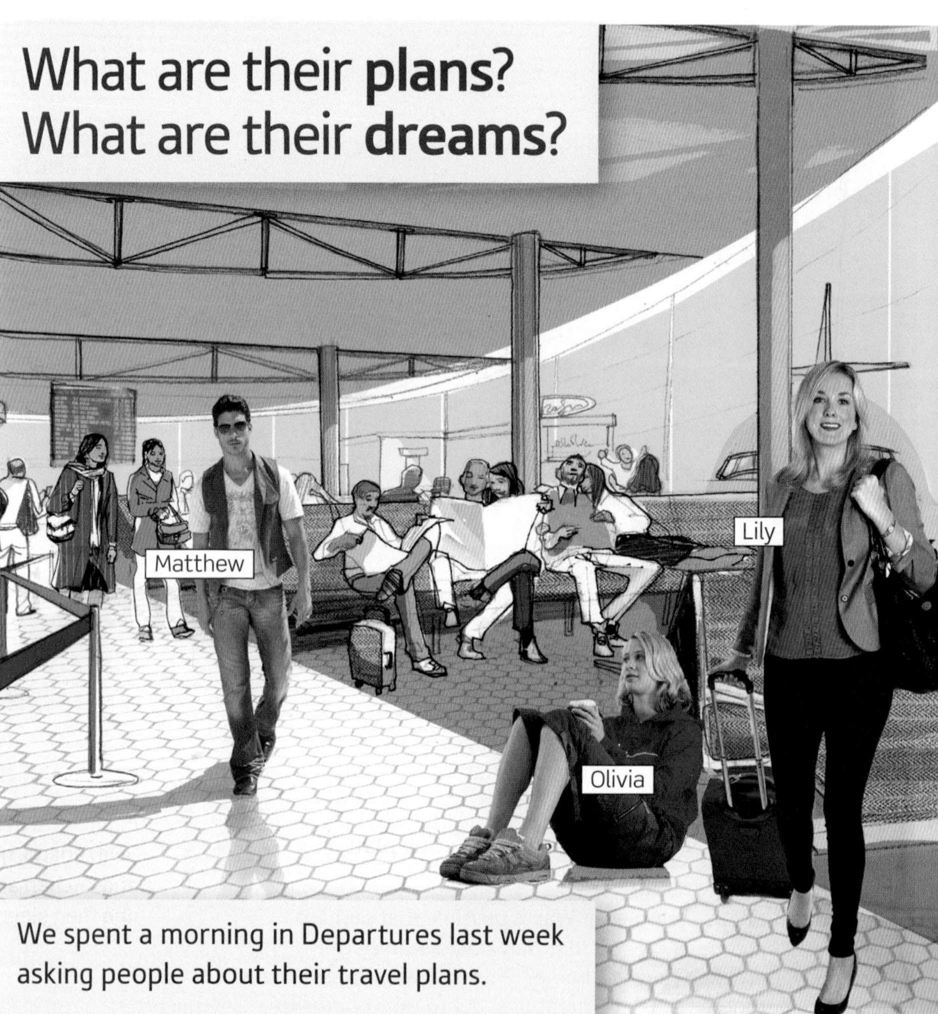

What are their **plans**?
What are their **dreams**?
Matthew
Lily
Olivia
We spent a morning in Departures last week asking people about their travel plans.

b 1 55 Listen and check your answers to **a**. Then listen again and complete the chart.

	Where to?	Why?	Other information
Olivia			
Matthew			
Lily			

3 GRAMMAR

be going to (plans and predictions)

a 1 56 Look at these sentences from the airport interviews and complete the gaps with a form of *be going to* + verb. Then listen and check.

1 ________________ English to young children.
2 How long ________________ there for?
3 It's winter in Australia now, so ________________ quite cold.
4 ________________ you at the airport?
5 I'm sure ________________ a great time.

b In pairs decide if sentences 1–5 are plans or predictions about the future. Write **PL** (plan) or **PR** (prediction).

c ➤ **p.130 Grammar Bank 3A.** Learn more about *be going to* and practise it.

4 PRONUNCIATION & SPEAKING

sentence stress and fast speech

a 1 58 Listen and repeat the sentences. Copy the rhythm.

1 **What** are you **going** to **do tonight**?
2 **Are** you **going** to **see** a **film**?
3 I'm **going** to **cook** a **meal** for you.
4 I **think** it's **going** to **rain**.
5 We **aren't going** to **have** a **holiday** this year.

> **Fast speech: *gonna***
> When people speak fast they often pronounce *going to* as *gonna* /ˈgɒnə/, e.g. *What are you going to do?* sounds like *What are you gonna do?*

b 1 59 Listen and write six sentences.

c ➤ **Communication** *What are your plans?* **A** *p.101* **B** *p.106*. Interview each other about your plans.

5 READING

a What is your nearest airport? What's it like? What can you do there while you're waiting for a flight?

b Read an article about the top airports in the world. Which is the best airport(s) if you...?

1 have a medical problem
2 would like to see a film
3 want to do some sport or exercise
4 need to leave your dog for the weekend
5 are worried about getting lost
6 want to sleep between flights
7 would like to see the city between flights

Singapore airport orchid garden

Top airports in the world

For many people airports are a nightmare – long queues when you check in and go through security and an even longer wait if your flight is delayed. But there are some airports where you can actually enjoy yourself. All good airports have excellent facilities for business people and children, free Wi-fi, restaurants, cafés, and shops. But the best airports have much more...

SINGAPORE AIRPORT is paradise for flower lovers, as it has an indoor orchid garden! It also has a rooftop swimming pool and a free sight-seeing tour for people who have at least five hours to wait for their connecting flight.

If you like computer games, you'll never be bored at HONG KONG INTERNATIONAL AIRPORT – there are dozens of free Playstations all over the terminals! It's also good for people with no sense of direction – there are 'Airport Ambassadors' in red coats, who help you to get from one place to another.

SEOUL AIRPORT is the place to relax. You can go to the hairdresser and have beauty treatments or a massage. Sports fans can also play golf at their 72-hole golf course!

MUNICH AIRPORT helps to keep passengers entertained with a 60-seat cinema and non-stop films. There is also free coffee and tea near all the seating areas, and lots of free magazines and newspapers.

If you worry about your health and like to be near medical services at all times, OSAKA AIRPORT in Japan is the perfect place to wait, as it has a dentist and doctor's surgery. And for people with animals, there is even a pet hotel!

If you have a long wait between flights at ZURICH AIRPORT in Switzerland, you can rent day rooms with their own bathroom and kitchen and wake-up call service. So you can have a shower and then sleep peacefully until you have to board your flight.

c Look at the highlighted words and phrases related to airports and guess their meaning.

d Roleplay with a partner.

A imagine you are at one of these airports and your flight is delayed for three hours. **B** calls you on your mobile. Tell **B** where you are and what you are going to do. Then swap roles. Do the same with other airports.

6 1 60 SONG *This is the Life* ♫

G present continuous (future arrangements)
V verbs + prepositions, e.g. *arrive in*
P sounding friendly

When are you leaving?

On Monday, and I'm coming back on Friday.

3B Let's meet again

1 READING & LISTENING

a 1 61 How do you say these dates? Listen and check.

3rd May 12th August 2012 31st December
22/6 5/2 20th July 1998

b Ben and Lily are old friends from university. Read their Facebook messages and number them in order.

Search | Home Profile

Lily Varnell
☐ Great. I'm going to book my tickets tomorrow, and then I can let you know my flight times.

Ben West
☐ OK. Why don't you phone me nearer the time, at the end of April? Then we can fix a day and a time to meet. I know a great restaurant...

Lily Varnell
1 Hi Ben! No news from you for ages. How are things? Are you still working at Budapest University? I have a conference there next month and I thought perhaps we could meet. I'd love to see you again! Lily.

Ben West
☐ It depends on the day. I'm going to Vienna one day that week, but it's not very far – I'm coming back the same day. I'm sure we can find a time that's good for both of us.

Lily Varnell
☐ It's from 3rd to 7th May, but I don't know my travel arrangements yet. What are you doing that week? Are you free any time?

Ben West
☐ Lily! Great to hear from you. Yes, I'm still at the university here and it's going very well – Budapest is a wonderful city to live in. When exactly is the conference?

Lily Varnell
☐ Fantastic. I can't wait!

c Read the messages again in the right order. Why does Lily get in touch with Ben? What are they planning to do?

d Match the highlighted words and phrases to their meaning.

1 ________ for a long time
2 ________ definite plans for the future
3 ________ I continue to be
4 ________ maybe
5 ________ the two
6 ________ to decide sth (e.g. a day / date)

e 1 62 Lily phones Ben and leaves him a message. Listen and complete her flight details.

Thank you for booking with easyJet

YOUR RESERVATION NUMBER IS: **I5CS2L**

Going out: Flight EZY4587 **Date:** ________
Depart London Gatwick at 11.10.
Arrive Budapest at ________.

Going back: Flight EZY4588 **Date:** ________
Depart Budapest at ________.
Arrive London Gatwick at 18.10.

Hotel reservations:
Six nights at Hotel ________.

2 GRAMMAR present continuous (future arrangements)

a In pairs, underline five present continuous verbs in the Facebook messages. Which two are about now? What time period do the other three refer to?

b 1 63))) Look at three extracts from the message Lily leaves Ben. Can you remember the missing verbs? Listen and check.

1 I'm ________ from Gatwick with Easyjet.
2 I'm ________ at Budapest airport at 14.40.
3 I'm ________ at a lovely old hotel.

c ➤ **p.130 Grammar Bank 3B.** Learn more about the present continuous for future arrangements and practise it.

d 1 65))) Lily phones Ben when she arrives at the hotel. Listen to the conversation. What day do they arrange to meet?

e Listen again. Complete Ben's diary for the week.

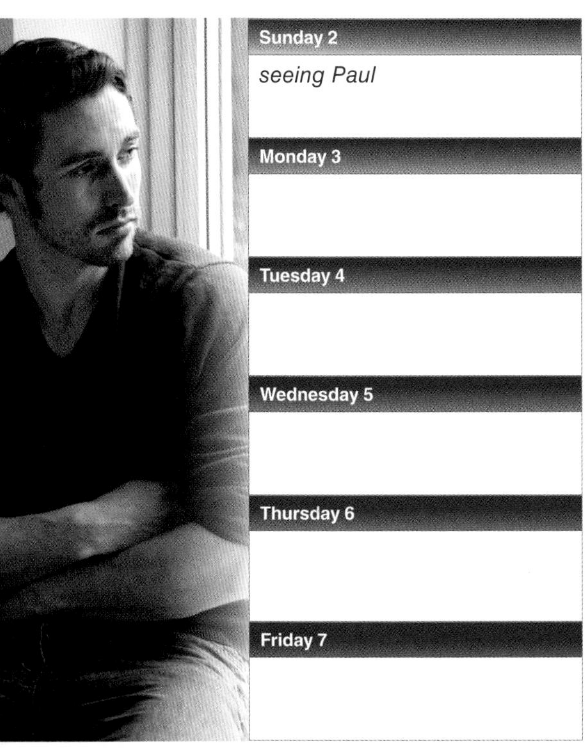

f Cover the diary. Work with a partner and test your memory.

What's Ben doing on Sunday?

He's seeing Paul. What's he doing on Monday?

g 1 66))) Listen. What happens when Ben and Lily meet?

3 PRONUNCIATION & SPEAKING sounding friendly

a 1 67))) Listen to another dialogue. Then listen again and repeat it sentence by sentence. Try to copy the speakers' intonation.

A Would you like to go out for dinner?
B I'd love to.
A Are you free on Thursday?
B Sorry, I'm going to the cinema.
A What about Friday? What are you doing then?
B Nothing. Friday's fine.
A OK. Let's go to the new Italian place.
B Great.

b Practise the dialogue with a partner. Try to sound friendly.

c Complete your diary with different activities for three evenings.

Monday	Wednesday	Friday	Sunday

Tuesday	Thursday	Saturday

d Talk to other students. Try to find days when you are both free and suggest doing something. Write it in your diary. Try to make an arrangement with a different person for every night.

Are you free on Friday evening? — *Yes, I am.*

Would you like to go to the cinema? — *Yes, I'd love to.*

4 VOCABULARY verbs + prepositions

a Look at things Lily and Ben say. What are the missing prepositions?

1 It depends ____ the day.
2 I'm arriving ____ Budapest at 14.40.
3 Paul invited me ____ dinner ages ago.

b ➤ **p.153 Vocabulary Bank** *Prepositions.* Do part 2 (Verbs + prepositions).

c Complete the questions with a preposition. Then ask and answer with a partner.

1 What do you usually ask ____ if you go to a café with friends?
2 Who do you think should pay ____ the meal on a first date?
3 Who do you normally speak ____ when you're worried ____ something?
4 Do you spend more money ____ clothes or ____ gadgets?
5 Do you think it's possible to fall ____ love ____ somebody without meeting them face-to-face?

5 WRITING

➤ **p.113 Writing** *An informal email.* Write an email about travel arrangements.

G defining relative clauses
V expressions for paraphrasing: *like*, *for example*, etc.
P pronunciation in a dictionary

What's a surgery?

It's a place where you can see a doctor or dentist.

3C What's the word?

1 LISTENING

a Do you like playing word games like *Scrabble* or doing crosswords? Look at the *Scrabble* letters on the page. How many words of four or more letters can you make in three minutes?

b 2 2 Listen to the introduction to a TV game show, *What's the word?* How do you play the game?

c 2 3 Now listen to the show. Write down the six words.

1 ________
2 ________
3 ________
4 ________
5 ________
6 ________

d 2 4 Listen and check your answers.

2 GRAMMAR defining relative clauses

a Look at three sentences from *What's the word?* and complete them with *who*, *which*, or *where*.

1 It's something ________ people use to speak to another person.
2 It's a place ________ people go when they want to go shopping.
3 It's somebody ________ works in a hospital.

b Read sentences 1–3 again. When do we use *who*, *which*, and *where*?

c ➤ **p.130 Grammar Bank 3C.** Learn more about defining relative clauses and practise them.

3 VOCABULARY paraphrasing

a What do you usually do if you're talking to someone in English and you don't know a word that you need?

a Look up the translation on your phone.
b Try to mime the word.
c Try to explain what you mean using other words you know.

b 2 6 Complete the useful expressions with these words. Then listen and check.

example kind like opposite similar somebody something somewhere

Useful expressions for explaining a word that you don't know:

1 It's ________ / a person who works in a hospital.
2 It's ________ / a thing which we use for everything nowadays.
3 It's ________ / a place where people go when they want to buy something.
4 It's a ________ of gadget.
5 It's the ________ of dark.
6 It's ________ light, but you use it to describe hair.
7 It's ________ to intelligent.
8 For ________, you do this to the TV.

c Complete the definitions for these words.

1 **a DJ** It's somebody…
2 **an art gallery** It's somewhere…
3 **a camera** It's something…
4 **a lift** It's a kind of…
5 **sunbathe** For example, you do this…
6 **curly** It's the opposite…

4 SPEAKING

➤ **Communication** *What's the word?* **A** *p.101* **B** *p.106*. Play a game and define words for your partner to guess.

5 READING

a Read the article. How many ways does it mention of creating new words? What are they?

b Look at the highlighted new words. What do you think they mean? Match them to the definitions below.

1 ________ *n* a young man who is going out with a much older woman
2 ________ *v* to send a message using a mobile phone
3 ________ *n* a person who works in a coffee bar
4 ________ *n* feeling angry because of the traffic or another person's driving
5 ________ *n* coffee with hot milk
6 ________ *n* a pub where you can also have very good food

c Can you explain the meaning of these other words from the text.

emoticon to tweet iPod to google Wi-fi ringtone smartphone

6 PRONUNCIATION

pronunciation in a dictionary

a Look at two dictionary extracts. What do the abbreviations mean?

search /sɜːtʃ/ *v* look carefully because you are trying to find sb or sth

busy /ˈbɪzi/ *adj* occupé

1 *v* ________ 3 *sb* ________
2 *adj* ________ 4 *sth* ________

b Look at the phonetic transcriptions in **a**. How do you pronounce the words?

> **Checking pronunciation in a dictionary**
> This symbol (ˈ) shows stress. The stressed syllable is the one after the symbol.
> The **Sound Bank** on *p.166* can help you to check the pronunciation of new words.

c 2 7 Look carefully at the pronunciation of the words below. Practise saying them correctly. Listen and check. Do you know what they mean?

1 YouTube /ˈjutjuːb/ 4 gadget /ˈgædʒɪt/
2 keyboard /ˈkiːbɔːd/ 5 message /ˈmesɪdʒ/
3 zoom /zuːm/ 6 hacker /ˈhækə/

900 new words in 3 months

Everyone knows the English language is changing. Every three months, the OED (Oxford English Dictionary) publishes updates to its online dictionary. One recent update contained 900 new words, new expressions, or new meanings for existing words. But where do they all come from?

New words are created in many different ways. We can make a new word by combining two words, like **gastropub** (gastronomy + pub) or **emoticon** (emotion + icon). Sometimes we put two words together in a new way, for example **road rage** or **toy boy**.

We also find that nouns can change into verbs. Take the word **text**. Text was always a noun (from about 1369, according to the OED), but it is now very common as a verb, **to text** somebody. Other new words already existed but with a different meaning. For example, **tweet** was the noise that a bird makes, but now we use it more often (as a verb or a noun) for a message that people put on the social networking site Twitter.

Another way in which we make new words is by 'adopting' words from foreign languages, like **barista** or **latte** (imported from Italian when coffee bars became really popular in the UK in the 1990s).

A lot of new words come from the names of brands or companies, for example we play music on an **iPod** and we **google** information. We also need more general words to describe new technology or new gadgets: **Wi-fi**, **ringtone**, and **smartphone** are some recent examples.

The invention of new words is not a new phenomenon. The word **brunch** (breakfast + lunch) first appeared in 1896, **newspaper** (news + paper) in 1667, and English speakers started to use the word **café** (from French) in the late 19th century. The difference now is how quickly new words and expressions enter the language and how quickly we start to use and understand them.

Practical English Restaurant problems EPISODE 2

1 IN THE NEW YORK OFFICE

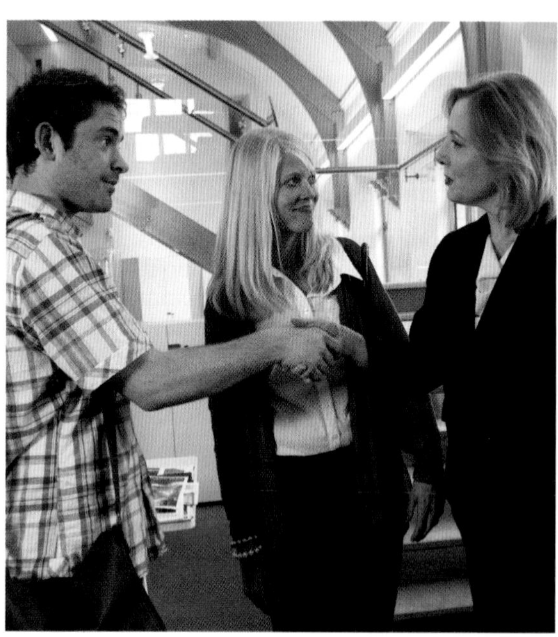

a 2.8 Watch or listen. Mark the sentences **T** (true) or **F** (false).

1 The New York office is smaller than the London office.
2 Barbara is the designer of the magazine.
3 Rob has never been to New York before.
4 Barbara is going to have lunch with Rob and Jenny.
5 Holly is going to work with Rob.
6 Holly wants to go to the restaurant because she's hungry.

b Watch or listen again. Say why the **F** sentences are false.

2 VOCABULARY restaurants

Do the restaurant quiz with a partner.

RESTAURANT QUIZ

What do you call...?
1 the book or list which tells you what food there is
2 the three parts of a meal
3 the person who serves you
4 the piece of paper with the price of the meal
5 extra money you leave if you are happy with your meal or with the service

What do you say...?
1 if you want a table for four people
2 when the waiter asks you what you want
3 when you are ready to pay

3 AT THE RESTAURANT

a 2.9 Cover the dialogue and watch or listen. Answer the questions.

1 What do they order?
2 What problems do they have?

b Watch or listen again. Complete the **You Hear** phrases.

You Hear	You Say
Are you ready to ________?	Yes, please.
Can I get you something to ________ with?	No, thank you. I'd like the tuna with a green salad.
And for you, sir?	I'll have the steak, please.
Would you like that with fries or a baked ________?	Fries, please.
How would you like your steak? Rare, ________, or well done?	Well done. Nothing for me.
OK. And to ________?	Water, please.
________ or sparkling?	Sparkling.
The tuna for you ma'am, and the steak for you, ________.	I'm sorry, but I asked for a green salad, not fries.
No problem. I'll ________ it.	Excuse me.
Yes, sir?	Sorry, I asked for my steak well done and this is rare.
I'm really sorry. I'll ________ it back to the kitchen.	

> **British and American English**
> *(French) fries* = American English
> *chips* = British English

c 2.10 Watch or listen and repeat the **You Say** phrases. Copy the rhythm.

d Practise the dialogue with a partner.

e In pairs, roleplay the dialogue.

A You are in the restaurant. Order a steak or tuna.

B You are the waiter/waitress. Offer **A** fries, a baked potato, or salad with the steak or tuna. You begin with *Are you ready to order?*

A There is a problem with your order. Explain it to the waiter/waitress.

B Apologize, and try to solve the problem.

f Swap roles.

4 HOLLY AND ROB MAKE FRIENDS

a 2.11 Watch or listen to Rob, Holly, and Jenny. Do they enjoy the lunch?

b Watch or listen again and answer the questions.

1. What's Rob going to write about?
2. How does Holly offer to help him with interviews?
3. What does she say they could do one evening?
4. What's the problem with the check?
5. Why does Jenny say it's time to go?
6. Do you think Jenny wanted Holly to come to lunch?

> **British and American English**
> *check* = American English
> *bill* = British English

c Look at the **Social English phrases**. Can you remember any of the missing words?

Social English phrases

Holly ________ tell me, Rob...
Rob Well, to ________ with...
Rob Do you have any ________?
Rob That would ________ great.
Jenny ________ we have the check (bill), please?
Jenny Excuse me, I think there's a ________.
Jenny OK, ________ to go.

d 2.12 Watch or listen and complete the phrases.

e Watch or listen again and repeat the phrases. How do you say them in your language?

Can you...?

- [ ] order food in a restaurant
- [ ] explain when there is a problem with your food, the bill, etc.
- [ ] ask what somebody is going to do today

iTutor

G present perfect + *yet, just, already*
V housework, *make* or *do*?
P /j/ and /dʒ/

Have you tidied your room yet?

Yes, I've just done it.

4A Parents and teenagers

1 READING

a Look at the definition of *teenager*. How do you pronounce it? Do you have a similar word in your language to describe a person of that age?

> **teenager** /ˈtiːneɪdʒə/ a person who is between 13 and 19 years old

b Read the article about some annoying habits. Write **P** if you think the comment is a parent talking about teenagers, or **T** if you think it is a teenager talking about his / her parents.

Teenagers have annoying habits – but so do their parents! Follow

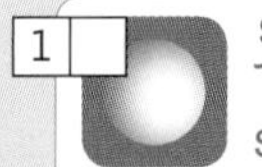

1 ☐ **Simon Fry** @simonfry 15m
They come into my room without knocking and then are surprised to see things they don't really want to know about.

2 ☐ **Rachel Black** @blackr 16m
They carry on texting when I'm telling them something really important and they say "Yeah, yeah I heard you". Of course they didn't.

3 ☐ **Anthony Smith** @tonysmith 20m
They always pick up the remote and change the channel when I'm watching something really interesting.

4 ☐ **Isla May** @ibmay 1h
They leave their room in a terrible mess and then roll their eyes when I ask them to tidy it.

5 ☐ **James Bright** @brightone 1h
They never pick up dirty clothes or wet towels from the floor. They think some elves come later and pick them up!

6 ☐ **Sarah Vine** @sarahvine 2h
They say no before I've even finished explaining what I want to do.

7 ☐ **Ed Scott** @edwardthescott 4h
They tell me to do the washing-up and then complain that I put things in the wrong place in the dishwasher.

8 ☐ **Sam James** @sujames 6h
Whenever I need to call them their mobile is either switched off or the battery is dead. #itreallyannoysme

c Compare with a partner. Do you agree?

d Look at the highlighted verbs and verb phrases. With a partner, say what you think they mean.

e Do any of the parents' or teenagers' habits annoy *you*? Which ones?

2 VOCABULARY
housework, *make* or *do*?

a Look again at the highlighted phrases from the text. Which three are connected with housework?

b ➤ **p.154 Vocabulary Bank** *Housework, make or do?*

3 GRAMMAR
present perfect + *yet, just, already*

a 2 15))) Look at the pictures. What do you think the people are arguing about? Listen and check.

1

2

3

b Listen again and complete the dialogues with a past participle from the list.

cleaned done dried
finished looked ~~seen~~

1 **A** Have you _seen_ my yellow jumper? I can't find it.
B No, I haven't. Have you __________ in your wardrobe?
A Of course I have. What's that under your bed?
B Oh, yes. I remember now. I borrowed it.

2 **A** Why aren't you doing your homework?
B I've already __________ it.
A Really? When?
B I did it on the bus this evening.

3 **A** Have you __________ yet?
B Nearly.
A I need the bathroom now.
B But I haven't __________ my hair yet.
A Well, hurry up then.

4 **A** Can you get a plate for that sandwich? I've just __________ the floor.
B OK. Oops – too late. Sorry!

c Look at the first two questions in dialogue 1. Are they about...?

a a specific time in the past
b a non-specific time (i.e. sometime between the past and now)

d Underline the sentences with *just*, *yet*, and *already* in dialogues 2–4. What do you think they mean?

e ➤ **p.132 Grammar Bank 4A.** Learn more about the present perfect and practise it.

f **2 18** Listen and make the ⊞ sentences negative and the ⊟ sentences positive.

I've finished. — *I haven't finished.*

It hasn't rained. — *It's rained.*

4 PRONUNCIATION & SPEAKING /j/ and /dʒ/

a **2 19** Listen and repeat the picture words and sounds.

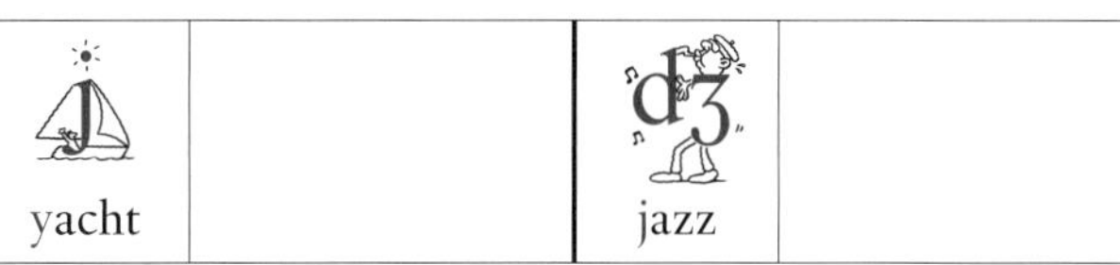

yacht		jazz	

b **2 20** Put the words in the right column. Listen and check. Then listen and repeat the words.

just yet jumper yellow change teenager
new uniform year student enjoy
beautiful jacket young bridge argue

c Practise saying these sentences.

I've just bought Jane a jumper and a jacket.
Have you worn your new uniform yet?

d ➤ **Communication** *Has he done it yet?* *p.101.*

e **2 21** Listen. Say what's just happened.

5 LISTENING

a **2 22** Listen to the first part of a radio programme about teenage carers. Answer the questions.

1 What reputation do teenagers have?
2 What do thousands of teenagers have to do?
3 How many hours do they have to help a week?

b **2 23** Now listen to the rest of the programme. In what way are the two teenagers unusual? Do they feel positive or negative about their lives?

c Listen again and answer with **A** (Alice), **D** (Daniel), or **B** (both of them).

Who...?

1 looks after their mother
2 looks after their brother and sister
3 does a lot of housework
4 can't cook
5 doesn't live with their father
6 gives their mother a massage
7 is sometimes angry with their friends
8 never goes out without their phone

d Do you know any teenagers like Alice and Daniel? What do they do?

G present perfect or past simple? (1)
V shopping
P *c* and *ch*

Have you ever been to that shop?

Yes. I bought this shirt there.

4B Fashion and shopping

1 READING

a With a partner, write down the names of three fashion designers. What nationality are they? Do they design more for men or for women? What kind of things does their company make?

b Read the introduction to an interview and look at the photos. Do you like the clothes?

c Read the interview. Complete the gaps with A–F.

A I absolutely hated dressing as a man.
B I really understand how women want to feel.
C My boyfriend at that time was very lucky.
D My feet were killing me!
E The only things I enjoyed there were art and sewing.
F They are so chic, and their sense of colour is so natural to them.

d Look at the highlighted words and phrases related to fashion and shopping, and guess their meaning.

THE STYLE INTERVIEW

LINDKA CIERACH is a fashion designer. She makes very exclusive clothes for women. She has made clothes for many celebrities including members of the British royal family, for example Kate Middleton and Sarah Ferguson, whose wedding dress she designed, and actresses like Helen Mirren.

DID YOU ALWAYS WANT TO BE A DESIGNER?
Not at all! When I was at school I had problems reading, and later I was diagnosed as dyslexic. ¹____ After school I did a secretarial course and then I got a job at Vogue magazine. I loved it, and there I realized that what I wanted to do was design clothes.

WHY DO YOU THINK PEOPLE LIKE YOUR CLOTHES?
Being a female designer has many advantages. ²____ My customers leave the studio feeling a million dollars!

WHAT NATIONALITY DO YOU THINK HAS THE BEST FASHION SENSE?
Probably the Italians. ³____

HAVE YOU EVER BEEN TO A FANCY DRESS PARTY?
I hate fancy dress parties. But I can remember one, when I was ten.

WHAT DID YOU GO AS?
My mother made me and my younger sister dress as a bride and bridegroom – I was the bridegroom! ⁴____

HAVE YOU EVER MET SOMEONE WHO WAS WEARING EXACTLY THE SAME AS YOU?
Never, thank goodness! I'm lucky because I can choose from a large selection of our Collection each season!

HAVE YOU EVER FALLEN OVER BECAUSE YOU WERE WEARING VERY HIGH HEELS?
I've never fallen over, but once I had to take off my shoes in the middle of a reception at the House of Lords! ⁵____

WHAT DID YOU DO?
I walked out into the street in bare feet and jumped into a taxi!

HAVE YOU EVER DESIGNED CLOTHES FOR A MAN?
Yes, I have.

WHEN WAS IT?
It was when I was studying at the London College of Fashion. I designed my first Men's Wear collection – shirts, trousers and leather jackets. ⁶____ He didn't need to buy any clothes that year!

Glossary
bride / bridegroom a woman / man on the day of her / his wedding
The House of Lords the second house of the British Parliament

2 GRAMMAR present perfect or past simple? (1)

a Look at the last four questions in the interview. Answer with a partner.

1 Which questions are about experiences sometime in Lindka's life?
2 Which questions are about a specific moment in Lindka's past?
3 What does *ever* mean in the questions that begin *Have you ever...?*

b ➤ **p.132 Grammar Bank 4B.** Learn more about the present perfect and past simple and practise them.

3 LISTENING

a 2 26))) Listen to four people answering the question *Have you ever bought something that you've never worn?* What did they buy? Write 1–4 in the boxes. (There is one item you don't need.)

☐ a coat ☐ some sports clothes ☐ a skirt
☐ some trousers ☐ a shirt

b Listen again. What was the problem with the clothes? Write 1–4 in the boxes.

This person...

☐ bought something online, but didn't like the clothes when they arrived.
☐ bought the clothes too quickly and later didn't like them.
☐ wanted to look like a famous singer, but looked like another.
☐ suddenly didn't need the new clothes any more.

c Have you ever bought something that you've never worn? What was it?

4 VOCABULARY shopping

a 2 27))) Listen to some sentences from the listening. Complete the gaps with one word. With a partner, say what the highlighted phrases mean.

1 I remember when I was in the _________ room I thought they looked fantastic.
2 I _________ it on eBay.
3 I hate clothes shopping and I never _________ things on.
4 I didn't have the receipt, so I couldn't _________ it back.
5 Well, I bought it _________ from a website that has cheap offers.

b ➤ **p.155 Vocabulary Bank** *Shopping*.

5 PRONUNCIATION *c* and *ch*

a How is *c* pronounced in these words? Put them in the right row.

account auction cinema city click
clothes credit card customer proceed
receipt shopping centre

k key	
s snake	

b 2 30))) Listen and check. When is *c* pronounced /s/?

c 2 31))) How is *ch* usually pronounced? Listen and (circle) the two words where *ch* is pronounced differently. How is it pronounced in these words?

changing rooms cheap checkout
chemist's chic choose

d Practise saying the words in **a** and **c**.

6 SPEAKING

a Complete the questions with the past participle of the verb.

1 **Have you ever** _____ (*buy*) or _____ (*sell*) anything on eBay? What? Did you pay or get a good price?
2 **Have you ever** _____ (*buy*) something online and had a problem with it? What was it? What did you do?
3 **Have you ever** _____ (*have*) an argument with a shop assistant? What was it about?
4 **Have you ever** _____ (*try*) to change something without the receipt? Were you successful?
5 **Have you ever** accidentally _____ (*take*) something from a shop without paying? What did you take? What happened?
6 **Have you ever** _____ (*buy*) shoes without trying them on? Did they fit?
7 **Have you ever** _____ (*get*) to the supermarket checkout and then found you didn't have enough money? What did you do?
8 **Have you ever** _____ (*lose*) your credit card? Where did you lose it? Did you get it back?

b Ask other students question **1**. Try to find somebody who says *Yes, I have.* Then ask them the past simple questions. Do the same for questions **2–8**.

G *something, anything, nothing, etc.*
V adjectives ending *-ed* and *-ing*
P /e/, /əʊ/, and /ʌ/

Did you do anything at the weekend?

No, nothing. I didn't do anything.

4C Lost weekend

1 LISTENING

a 2 32 Listen to a news story about Sven. How did he spend his weekend?

b Listen again and answer the questions.

1 What does Sven do?
2 What floor was his office on?
3 What happened when he first pressed the lift button?
4 How did he try to get help?
5 Where did Sven's wife think he was?
6 How did Sven get out of the lift on Monday morning? How did he feel?
7 What is Sven going to do every day now?

c Have you (or has anyone you know) ever had a similar experience? What happened?

2 GRAMMAR *something, anything, nothing, etc.*

a 2 33 Look at three sentences from the story. Can you remember the missing words? Listen and check.

1 I pressed the button again, but ______ happened.
2 The police couldn't find him ______.
3 They phoned the emergency number and ______ came and repaired the lift.

b Complete the rule with **people**, **places**, or **things**.

1 Use *something*, *anything*, and *nothing* for ______.
2 Use *somebody*, *anybody*, and *nobody* for ______.
3 Use *somewhere*, *anywhere*, and *nowhere* for ______.

c ➤ **p.132 Grammar Bank 4C.** Learn more about *something*, *anything*, *nothing*, etc. and practise them.

3 PRONUNCIATION /e/, /əʊ/, and /ʌ/

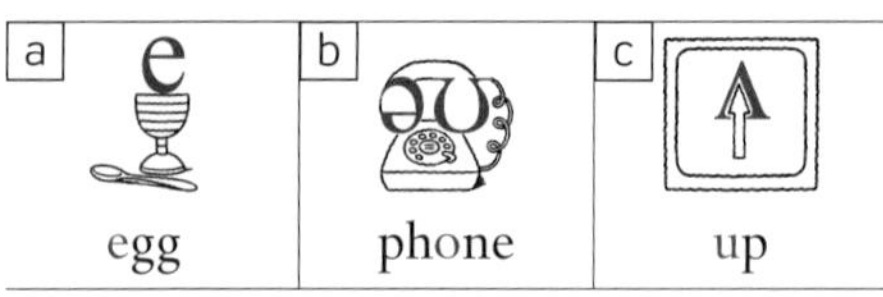

a What sound do the pink letters make? Write **a**, **b**, or **c**.

1 ☐ Nobody knows where he goes.
2 ☐ Somebody's coming to lunch.
3 ☐ I never said anything.
4 ☐ I've done nothing since Sunday.
5 ☐ Don't tell anybody about the message.
6 ☐ There's nowhere to go except home.

b 2 35 Listen and check. Practise saying the sentences.

c 2 36 Listen and answer the questions.

What did you buy? *Nothing. I didn't buy anything.*

4 READING

a Read the article once. What is the best summary?

a People in the UK have boring weekends.
b People who use Facebook have more exciting weekends.
c People sometimes don't tell the truth about their weekend.

b Read the article again. With a partner, choose a, b, or c.

1 The survey has shown that 25% of people…
 a have very exciting weekends.
 b lie about their weekend.
 c go out on a Saturday night.
2 30% of the people they interviewed…
 a needed to go to work at the weekend.
 b had a very tiring week.
 c didn't want to go out at the weekend.
3 Some people don't tell the truth about their weekend because…
 a their real weekend is very boring.
 b they don't want to make their friends jealous.
 c they forget what they have done.
4 Social networking sites make people…
 a spend more time on the computer.
 b try to make their lives seem more exciting.
 c be more truthful about their lives.

c Do you think a survey in your country would have similar results?

WHAT DID YOU REALLY DO AT THE WEEKEND?

The next time a friend or colleague tells you about their fantastic weekend, wait a moment before you start feeling jealous – maybe they are inventing it all!

A survey of 5,000 adults in the UK has shown that one person in four invents details about their weekend because they want to impress their friends. When they are asked, 'Did you have a good weekend?' they don't like to say that they just stayed at home and watched TV, because it sounds boring. So they invent the details. The most common lie that people told was 'I went out on Saturday night', when really they didn't go anywhere. Other common lies were 'I had a romantic meal', 'I went to a party', and 'I went away for the weekend'.

In fact, in the survey, 30% of people who answered the questions said that they spent their weekend sleeping or resting because they were so tired at the end of the week.

Another 30% said that they needed to work or study at the weekend. Psychologist Corinne Sweet says that people often don't tell the truth about their weekend 'because we don't want to feel that everyone else is having a better time than us, if we have had a boring weekend doing housework, paperwork, or just resting after a tiring week at work'. She also believes that networking sites such as Facebook and Twitter may be encouraging us to invent details about our social lives. 'People can create an illusion of who they want to be and the life they want to live,' says Corinne, 'and of course they want that life to seem exciting.'

5 SPEAKING

a Look at the questions in **b**. Plan your answers. Answer them truthfully, but **invent one answer** to make your weekend sound more exciting.

b Interview each other with the questions. Try to guess which answer your partner invented.

LAST WEEKEND

Friday
- Did you go anywhere exciting on Friday night?

Saturday
- Did you do anything in the house (cleaning, etc.) on Saturday morning?
- Did you work or study at all?
- What did you do on Saturday night?

Sunday
- Did you go anywhere nice on Sunday?
- What did you have for lunch?
- Did you do anything relaxing in the afternoon?

6 VOCABULARY
adjectives ending *-ed* and *-ing*

a Look at these two adjectives in the text: *tired* in line 13 and *tiring* in line 19. Which one describes how you feel? Which one describes things and situations?

b 2 37))) Circle the right adjective in questions 1–10. Listen and check. How do you say the adjectives?

1. Do you think Sundays are usually *bored* | *boring*?
2. Are you *bored* | *boring* with your job or studies?
3. What kind of weather makes you feel *depressed* | *depressing*?
4. Why do you think the news is often *depressed* | *depressing*?
5. What activity do you find most *relaxed* | *relaxing*?
6. Do you usually feel *relaxed* | *relaxing* at the end of the weekend? Why (not)?
7. What is the most *interested* | *interesting* book you've read recently?
8. What sports are you *interested* | *interesting* in?
9. Are you *excited* | *exciting* about your next holiday?
10. What's the most *excited* | *exciting* sports match you've ever watched?

c Ask and answer the questions with a partner. Give more information if you can.

7 2 38))) SONG
If You Love Somebody Set Them Free ♫

3&4 Revise and Check

GRAMMAR

Circle a, b, or c.

1 How long ______ to stay in Italy?
a do you go b are you going c you are going
2 I think ______ rain tonight.
a it's going b it goes to c it's going to
3 They ______ to get married until next year.
a aren't going b don't go c not going
4 I ______ to the cinema after class this evening.
a go b am going c going go
5 **A** What time ______ tomorrow? **B** At 8.00.
a you leave b do you leaving c are you leaving
6 He's the man ______ lives next door to Alice.
a who b which c where
7 Is that the shop ______ sells Italian food?
a who b which c where
8 **A** ______ your bed? **B** No, I'm going to do it now.
a Have you made
b Have you make
c Has you made
9 **A** Has Anne arrived ______?
B No, but she's on her way.
a yet b just c already
10 ______ already seen this film! Let's change channels.
a We're b We haven't c We've
11 **A** ______ been to Africa? **B** No, never.
a Have you ever b Did you ever c Were you ever
12 **A** When ______ those shoes? **B** Last week.
a do you buy b have you bought c did you buy
13 I've never ______ this coat. It's too small.
a wear b worn c wore
14 There's ______ at the door. Can you go and open it please?
a something b someone c somewhere
15 I don't want ______ to eat, thanks. I'm not hungry.
a nothing b anything c something

VOCABULARY

a Complete with a preposition.

1 We arrived ______ Prague at 7.15.
2 I'm coming! Wait ______ me.
3 What did you ask ______, meat or fish?
4 **A** Are you going to buy the flat?
B I don't know. It depends ______ the price.
5 How much did you pay ______ those shoes?

b Complete with *make* or *do*.

1 ______ the washing-up
2 ______ a mistake
3 ______ an exam
4 ______ exercise
5 ______ a noise

c Complete the missing words.

1 Dinner's ready. Please could you l______ the table.
2 I'll cook if you do the w______-up.
3 Where are the changing rooms? I want to tr______ o______ this sweater.
4 If you want to take something back to a shop, you need to have the r______.
5 These shoes don't f______ me. They're too small.
6 The flight to Berlin is now leaving from G______ 12.
7 If you have a lot of luggage, you can find a tr______ over there.
8 First you need to go to the ch______-i______ desk where you get your boarding pass.
9 International flights depart from T______ 2.
10 There are l______ to the first and second floors.

d Circle the right adjective.

1 This exercise is really *bored* / *boring*.
2 I never feel *relaxed* / *relaxing* the day before I go on holiday.
3 It was a very *excited* / *exciting* match.
4 Jack is a bit *depressed* / *depressing*. He lost his job.
5 Are you *interested* / *interesting* in art?

PRONUNCIATION

a Circle the word with a different sound.

1	just	Monday	something	trolley
2	nowhere	clothes	worry	go
3	search	chemist	cheap	choose
4	customer	centre	cinema	nice
5	jacket	change	enjoy	yet

b Underline the stressed syllable.

1 A|rri|vals 3 tee|na|ger 5 a|rrange|ment
2 o|ppo|site 4 de|li|ve|ry

CAN YOU UNDERSTAND THIS TEXT?

a Read the article. What were thieves stealing in a) Sweden b) Denmark? Answer the questions below.

1 Where did the first robbery take place?
2 Who were the thieves and what did they steal?
3 Who helped the police to solve the crime?
4 How long does it take to get from Malmö to Copenhagen?
5 Why were robberies taking place in both cities?
6 Did the police catch the thieves?
7 Why is it easier to steal from many stores these days?
8 Why is it not a solution to ask Danish shoe shops to display the left shoe?

b Look at the highlighted words or phrases in the text. Guess their meaning from the context. Check with your teacher or with a dictionary.

Shoe shops discover matching crimes

Swedish fictional detectives like Wallander and Lisbeth Salander are famous worldwide. But recently real-life Swedish police were completely puzzled by a mysterious crime. Somebody was stealing expensive designer shoes from shoe shops in Sweden – but not pairs of shoes, only the left shoes, the ones which were on display.

The first robbery took place in a shopping mall in Malmö, Sweden's third-largest city. Staff at a shoe shop saw two men stealing at their boutique. They escaped with seven left shoes which – if paired with the right shoes – were worth £900.

In the end it was shop assistants who pointed the police in the right direction – to Denmark, where shops traditionally display the right shoe in their shop windows. "We noticed that left shoes were disappearing in the past, but we never caught the thieves," said a shop assistant. "Since we know that Danish stores display the right shoes, we thought that the matching shoes were probably disappearing as well in stores in Denmark." Malmö, home to 125 shoe shops, is only a 30-minute train ride away from Copenhagen, which has several hundred shops, and many brands are sold in both cities.

Yesterday police finally announced that they had arrested the men responsible for the robberies. But Ms Johansson, a Swedish shoe shop owner, fears that shoe shop robberies will increase this year. "Shoes are attractive to steal – they are easy to move and easy to sell and they have become very expensive lately. Also many stores have cut the number of shop assistants they employ."

Police in Malmo have thought of asking Danish shoe shops to also display the left shoe. But this won't work. All the thieves will have to do is move to Germany – where they also display the right shoe...

Adapted from a British newspaper

CAN YOU UNDERSTAND THESE PEOPLE?

2 39 **In the street** Watch or listen to five people and answer the questions.

Paul

Gurjot

Ellie

Alise

Anya

1 Paul went to the airport ______.
   a to get a plane to London
   b to get a plane to Frankfurt
   c to meet a friend from Frankfurt
2 Tonight Gurjot is ______.
   a seeing a film
   b going to a Chinese restaurant
   c meeting an old friend
3 Ellie ______ ironing.
   a hates b doesn't mind c likes
4 The shoes Alise bought online ______.
   a were the wrong size
   b never arrived
   c were a beautiful colour
5 Last weekend Anya ______.
   a went to a friend's birthday party
   b had dinner with a friend
   c bought something for a friend's birthday

CAN YOU SAY THIS IN ENGLISH?

Do the tasks with a partner. Tick (✓) the box if you can do them.

Can you...?

1 ☐ talk about three plans you have for next month using *going to*, and make three predictions
2 ☐ say three arrangements you have for tomorrow using the present continuous
3 ☐ explain what the following three words mean, using expressions for paraphrasing:
   a a thief b a shopping mall c a shoe
4 ☐ say three things you have already done or haven't done yet today
5 ☐ ask a partner three questions about his/her experiences using *ever*. Answer your partner's questions
6 ☐ say three sentences using *something*, *anywhere*, and *nobody*

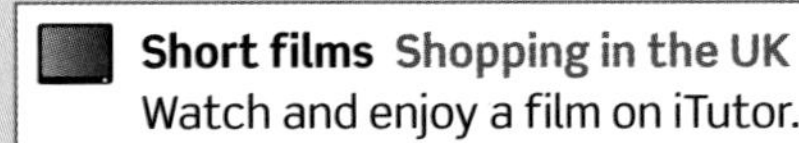
Short films Shopping in the UK
Watch and enjoy a film on iTutor.

G comparative adjectives and adverbs, *as...as*
V time expressions: *spend time*, etc.
P sentence stress

Are we living faster?

Yes, we need to slow down.

5A No time for anything

1 READING & VOCABULARY time expressions

a Read an article about living faster and match the headings to the paragraphs.

- ☐ No time for Snow White
- ☐ No time to write
- ☐ No time to wait
- ☐ More time on the road
- ☐ No time for Van Gogh
- ☐ No time to stop

b Read the article again. One paragraph contains an invented piece of information. Which one is it?

c Look at the highlighted time expressions and guess their meaning.

d In pairs, cover the text and look at the paragraph headings in **a.** Can you remember the information in the text? Have you noticed any of these things happening where you live?

e Look at a questionnaire about living faster. In pairs, ask and answer the questions. Answer with *often*, *sometimes*, or *never* and give more information.

We're living faster, but are we living better?

1

People in cities around the world walk 10% more quickly than they did twenty years ago. Singapore, a world business centre, is top of the list for fast walkers.

2

In the USA there is a book called One-Minute Bedtime Stories for children. These are shorter versions of traditional stories, especially written for busy parents who need to save time.

3

People aren't as patient as they were in the past. If the lift takes more than 15 seconds to arrive, people get very impatient because they think they're wasting time. It's exactly the same when an Internet page does not open immediately.

4

Written communication on the internet is getting shorter and shorter and using more and more abbreviations, like BFN (bye for now) or NP (no problem). Twitter only allows you to use 140 characters, and now a new social networking site has a limit of just ten words.

5

Even in our free time we do things in a hurry. Twenty years ago when people went to art galleries they spent ten seconds looking at each picture. Today they spend much less time – just three seconds!

6

Our cars are faster, but the traffic is worse, so we drive more slowly. The average speed of cars in New York City is 15 km/h. We spend more time than ever sitting in our cars, feeling stressed because we aren't going to arrive on time.

QUESTIONNAIRE

How fast is **your** life?

1. Do people tell you that you talk too quickly?
2. Do you get impatient when other people are talking?
3. Are you the first person to finish at mealtimes?
4. When you are walking along a street, do you feel frustrated when you are behind people who are walking more slowly?
5. Do you get irritable if you sit for an hour without doing anything, e.g. waiting for the doctor?
6. Do you walk out of shops and restaurants if there is a queue?

f ➤ **Communication** *How fast is your life? p.101.* Read the results. Do you agree?

2 GRAMMAR comparative adjectives and adverbs, *as...as*

a Look at the following words from the text. Are they adjectives, adverbs, or both?

quickly fast busy patient
bad slowly stressed

b Circle the right form. Tick (✓) if both are correct.

1 Life is *faster* | *more fast* than before.
2 Traffic in cities is *more bad* | *worse* than it was.
3 Everybody is *busyer* | *busier* than they were five years ago.
4 We are *more stressed* | *stresseder* than our grandparents were.
5 We do everything *more quickly* | *faster*.
6 People aren't *as patient as* | *as patient than* they were before.

c ➤ **p.134 Grammar Bank 5A.** Learn more about comparatives and *as...as* and practise them.

3 PRONUNCIATION sentence stress

> **The /ə/ sound**
> Remember! *-er*, and unstressed words like *a*, *as*, and *than* have the sound /ə/.

a 2 41))) Listen and repeat the sentences. Copy the rhythm and try to get the /ə/ sound right.

1 I'm **busier** than a **year** ago.
2 My **life** is **more stressful** than in the **past**.
3 I **work harder** than **before**.
4 I **walk** and **talk faster**.
5 I'm **not** as **relaxed** as I **was** a **few years ago**.

b Are any of the sentences true for you?

4 SPEAKING

a Think about how your life has changed over the last 3–5 years. Read the questions below and think about your answers.

1 Do you spend more or less time on these things? Say why.

working or studying | sleeping
getting to work / school | cooking
sitting in traffic | shopping
talking to friends | eating
meeting friends | using your phone
being online | using your computer

2 Do you have more or less free time? Why?
3 What *don't* you have time for nowadays? What would you like to have more time for?

b Answer the questions with a partner. Whose life has changed more?

5 LISTENING

a You're going to listen to an expert talking about how to live your life more slowly. Look at her five main tips (= good ideas). Guess what the missing words are.

1 Whatever you are doing, just try to ______ ______ and enjoy it.
Example: ______
2 Make a list of three things which are ______ ______ for you.
Example: ______
3 Don't try to do ______ ______ at the same time.
Example: ______
4 Sit down and do ______ for half an hour every day.
Example: ______
5 Be near ______.
Example: ______

b 2 42))) Listen and check. Then listen again and write one example for each tip.

c Are there any tips that you think you might use? Why (not)?

G superlatives (+ *ever* + present perfect)
V describing a town or city
P word and sentence stress

What did you think of Rio?

It's the most beautiful city I've ever been to.

5B Superlative cities

1 GRAMMAR superlatives (+ *ever* + present perfect)

a Match the photos and cities. Which European countries are the cities in? What do you know about them? Have you been to any of them?

☐ Barcelona ☐ Copenhagen ☐ Dublin ☐ Paris ☐ Venice

b Read the article and complete it with the cities in **a**.

Travel survey gives its verdict on European cities

London is **the dirtiest** city in Europe says a new survey by travel website TripAdvisor, but it has **the best** public parks and the best nightlife. According to the survey of almost 2,400 travellers…

1 ________ is **the most romantic** city.
2 ________ is **the cleanest** city.
3 ________ has **the best-dressed** people.
4 ________ has **the best** architecture.
5 ________ is **the friendliest** city.

'Europe's big cities all have their highs and lows, but they offer travellers a huge variety of culture and sights within very short distances,' said a TripAdvisor spokesman.

c Look at 1–5 in the survey in **b**. Think about your country or continent. Which cities would *you* choose?

d Look at the **bold** superlative adjectives in the survey. How do you make the superlative of…?

1 a one-syllable adjective
2 a two-syllable adjective that ends in *-y*
3 a three-syllable adjective
4 *good* and *bad*

e ➤ **p.134 Grammar Bank 5B.** Learn more about superlatives and practise them.

2 PRONUNCIATION word and sentence stress

a Underline the stressed syllable in the **bold** adjectives.

1 What's the most **beautiful** city you've ever been to?
2 What's the most **expensive** thing you've ever bought?
3 Who's the most **impatient** person you know?
4 Who's the most **generous** person in your family?
5 What's the most **frightening** film you've ever seen?
6 What's the most **exciting** sport you've ever done?
7 What's the most **interesting** book you've read recently?
8 What's the most **romantic** restaurant you've ever been to?

b 2 44 Listen and check. Listen again and repeat the questions. Copy the rhythm. Which words are stressed?

c Work with a partner. **A** answer question 1 with a sentence. **B** ask for more information. Swap roles for question 2, etc.

The most beautiful city I've ever been to is Rio de Janeiro.

When did you go there?

3 READING & SPEAKING

a Read the article. In pairs, answer the questions.

1 What are the three tests?
2 Do you think they are good ones?
3 Which city do you think will be the friendliest / most unfriendly?

All capital cities are unfriendly – or are they?

Big cities often have a reputation for being rude, unfriendly places for tourists. *Sunday Times* journalist Tim Moore went to four cities, *London*, *Rome*, *Paris*, and *New York*, to find out if this is true. He went dressed as a foreign tourist and did three (not very scientific!) tests to see which city had the friendliest and most polite inhabitants. The three tests were:

1 The photo test

Tim asked people in the street to take his photo (not just one photo, but several – with his hat, without his hat, etc.). Did he find someone to do it?

2 The shopping test

Tim bought something in a shop and gave the shop assistant too much money. Did the shop assistant give back the extra money?

3 The accident test

Tim pretended to fall over in the street. Did anybody come and help him?

b ➤ **Communication** *The friendliest city* **A** *p.102* **B** *p.107* **C** *p.110.* Read about what happened in New York, Paris, and Rome.

4 LISTENING

a 2 45))) Now listen to Tim Moore talking about what happened in London. How well does London do in each test?

b Listen again and answer the questions.

The photo test
1 Who did he ask first?
2 What did the person say?
3 Who did he ask next? What happened?

The shopping test
4 Where was the tourist shop?
5 How much did the bus and key ring cost?
6 How much did he give the man?
7 Did he get the right change?

The accident test
8 Where did he do the accident test?
9 Did anyone help him?
10 What did the man say?

c Think about the nearest big city to where you live. Imagine you did the three tests there. What do you think would happen? Is it a friendly city?

5 VOCABULARY describing a town or city

a Think about how to answer these questions about where you live. Compare with a partner.

- Do you live in a village, a town, or a city?
- Where is it?
- How big is it?
- What's the population?
- What's it like?

b ➤ **p.156 Vocabulary Bank** *Describing a town or city.*

6 WRITING

➤ **p.114 Writing** *Describing where you live.* Write a description of the place where you live.

7 2 49))) SONG *Nobody Does It Better* ♫

G quantifiers, *too, not enough*
V health and the body
P /ʌ/, /uː/, /aɪ/, and /e/

I watch too much TV.

I don't spend enough time in the sun.

5C How much is too much?

1 SPEAKING

a With a partner, answer the questions below.

DIET & LIFESTYLE QUESTIONNAIRE

1 Do you drink coffee? How many cups do you drink a day? What kind of coffee? What time do you drink your last cup of the day?

2 How much time do you spend a day in the sun...?
a in the winter
b in the summer
c when you're on holiday
Do you always wear sunscreen?

3 Do you play a lot of video or computer games? What are your favourite games? How much time do you spend a week playing them?

4 How often do you eat chocolate? What kind of chocolate do you prefer – milk, white, or dark?

5 How many hours a day do you watch TV...?
a during the week
b at weekends
What kind of programmes do you watch regularly?

b Do you think any of your habits are unhealthy?

2 READING & LISTENING

a Read the article once. Does it change what you think about your answers to the questionnaire?

b Read the article again. Look at the highlighted words related to health and the body. Match them to a picture or definition.

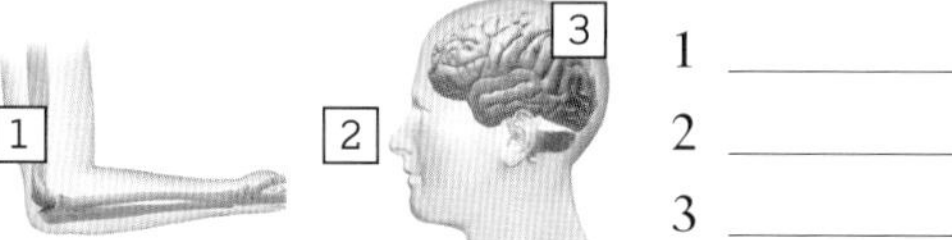

1 ____________
2 ____________
3 ____________
4 *noun* it covers the outside of a person's body
5 *verb* to stop sth from happening
6 *noun* sth which makes you unwell
7 *adj* feeling worried or nervous

Everything **BAD** is **GOOD** for you

COFFEE We all know that a cup of coffee helps to wake you up in the morning, but several studies show that drinking coffee helps to prevent some illnesses like diabetes and Parkinson's disease. Experts say that you can safely drink three cups of espresso during the day, but if you drink too much coffee it can make you feel anxious or keep you awake at night.

SUNLIGHT Spending a long time in the sun is dangerous and can give you skin cancer. But on the other hand, not spending enough time in the sun is also bad for you, as sunlight helps us to produce vitamin D. This vitamin is important for strong bones and a healthy immune system, and it also makes people feel happier. Nowadays many people don't get enough sunlight because they wear sunscreen all the time, especially on their faces. However, don't spend too long in the sun – 15 minutes a day without sunscreen is a healthy amount, and not at midday.

COMPUTER GAMES You probably worry about how much time you or your children waste playing computer games. But in fact some studies show that these games can help us learn important skills. It seems that computer games stimulate the brain and that people who often play them are probably better at solving problems and making quick decisions. But don't spend too many hours in front of the computer – not more than about two hours a day.

c (2.50) Listen and check. Practise saying the words.

d Now cover the text. Can you remember…?

1 what is good about coffee, sunlight, and computer games
2 what you need to be careful about

e (2.51) With a partner, decide in what ways you think chocolate and watching TV could be good for you. Listen to a radio programme and check your answers.

f Listen again. Answer the questions.

1 What does chocolate have in common with red wine?
2 What kind of chocolate is a) good for you b) not good for you?
3 How are TV series different from the ones 20 years ago? Why is this good for us?
4 What can we learn from reality TV shows?

g Do the article and the radio programme make you feel happier about your lifestyle?

3 GRAMMAR quantifiers, *too*, *not enough*

a Can you remember how to use *much, many*, etc? In pairs, choose the correct word or phrase for each sentence. Say why the other one is wrong.

1 How *much* | *many* cups of coffee do you drink a day?
2 I don't spend *much* | *many* time in the sun.
3 I eat *a lot of* | *many* chocolate.
4 Drinking *a few* | *a little* red wine can be good for you.
5 I only have *a few* | *a little* computer games.
6 My parents read *a lot* | *a lot of*.

b Look at some sentences from the reading and listening. Match the **bold** phrases in 1 and 2 to meanings **A** and **B**.

1 Don't eat **too much** chocolate or **too many** sweets if you don't want to put on weight.
Don't spend **too** long in the sun.
2 Nowadays many people **don't** get **enough** sunlight.
We are **not** active **enough**.

A less than you need or than is good for you
B more than you need or than is good for you

c Look again at the sentences with *enough*. What's the position of *enough* a) with a noun b) with an adjective?

d ➤ **p.134 Grammar Bank 5C.** Learn more about quantifiers, *too*, and *not enough* and practise them.

4 PRONUNCIATION & SPEAKING

/ʌ/, /uː/, /aɪ/, and /e/

a Cross out the word with a different pronunciation.

ʌ	up	enough much none busy
uː	boot	few cups too food
aɪ	bike	quite diet little like
e	egg	many any healthy water

b (2.54) Listen and check. Practise saying the words.

c Ask and answer the questions with a partner. Say why.

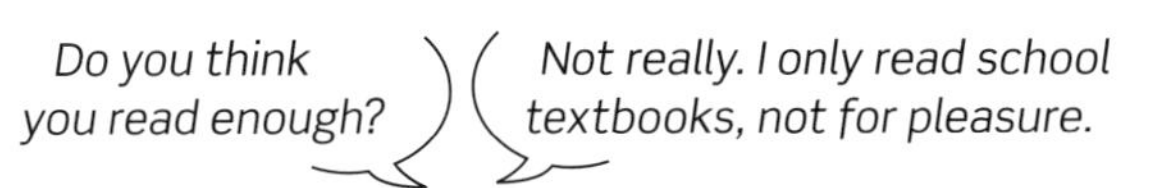

Do you think you read enough?
Not really. I only read school textbooks, not for pleasure.

Do you think you…?

- read enough
- eat enough fruit and vegetables
- do enough sport or exercise
- drink enough water
- have enough free time
- eat too much fast food
- spend too much time online
- spend too much money on things you don't need
- work or study too many hours
- have too many clothes
- do too much housework
- get too much homework

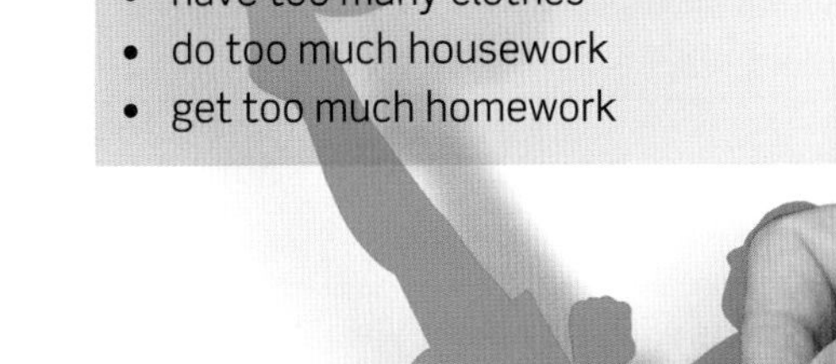

Practical English The wrong shoes

EPISODE 3

1 ROB HAS A PROBLEM

a 2.55 Watch or listen to Rob and Holly and answer the questions.

1. What reason does Rob give for why he isn't in shape?
2. Why does he find it difficult to eat less?
3. How does he keep fit in London?
4. Why doesn't he do the same in New York?
5. How does Jenny keep fit?
6. What does Holly think about this?
7. What does Holly suggest that Rob could do?
8. What does Rob need to do first?

British and American English
sneakers = American English; *trainers* = British English
store = American English; *shop* = British English

b 2.56 Look at the box on making suggestions. Listen and repeat the phrases.

Making suggestions with *Why don't you...?*
A Why don't you get a bike?
B That's a good idea, but I'm only here for a month.
A Why don't you come and play basketball?
B That's a great idea!

c Practise making suggestions with a partner.

A You have problems remembering English vocabulary. Tell **B**.
B Make two suggestions.
A Respond. If you don't think it's a good idea, say why.

d Swap roles.

B You are a foreigner in **A**'s country. You have problems meeting new people.

2 VOCABULARY shopping

Do the quiz with a partner.

SHOPPING QUIZ

1. What four letters do you often see in clothes which tell you the size?
2. What do the letters mean?
3. What's the name of the room where you can try on clothes?
4. What's the name of the piece of paper a shop assistant gives you when you buy something?
5. How do you say these prices?
   £25.99   75p $45   15c   €12.50

3 TAKING SOMETHING BACK TO A SHOP

a 2.57 Cover the dialogue and watch or listen. Answer the questions.

1. What's the problem with Rob's trainers?
2. What does he do in the end?

b Watch or listen again. Complete the **You Hear** phrases.

You Hear	You Say
Can I help you, sir?	Yes. Do you have these in an eight?
Just a ________, I'll go and check.	
Here you are, these are an eight. Do you want to ________ them on?	No, thanks. I'm sure they'll be fine. How much are they?
They're $83.91.	Oh, it says $72.99.
Yes, but there's an added sales tax of ________%.	Oh, OK. Do you take MasterCard?
Sure.	
Can I help you?	Yes, I bought these about half an hour ago.
Yes, I remember. Is there a ________?	Yes, I'm afraid they're too small.
What ________ are they?	They're an eight. But I take a UK eight.
Oh right. Yes, a UK eight is a US nine.	Do you have a pair?
I'll go and check. Just a minute.	
I'm ________, but we don't have these in a nine. But we do have these and they're the ________ price. Or you can have a refund.	Erm...I'll take this pair then, please.
No problem. Do you have the ________?	Yes, here you are.
Brilliant.	

A pair
We often use *a pair* to talk about plural clothes, e.g. *a pair of shoes, trainers, boots, jeans, trousers*, etc.

c 2 58 Watch or listen and repeat the **You Say** phrases. Copy the rhythm.

d Practise the dialogue with a partner.

e In pairs, roleplay the dialogue.

A You're a customer. You bought some jeans yesterday. They're too big.

B You're a shop assistant. You don't have the same jeans in **A**'s size. Offer **A** a different pair or a refund. You begin with *Can I help you, sir / madam?*

f Swap roles.

B You're a customer. You bought some boots yesterday. They're too small.

A You're a shop assistant. You don't have the same boots in **B**'s size. Offer **B** a different pair or a refund. You begin with *Can I help you, sir / madam?*

4 ROB DECIDES TO DO SOME EXERCISE

a 2 59 Watch or listen and circle the right answer.

1. Rob went to *Boston / Brooklyn*.
2. He *shows / doesn't show* Jenny his new trainers.
3. Jenny goes running every *morning / evening* in Central Park.
4. She wants to go running with him at *6.45 / 7.45*.
5. Rob thinks it's too *early / late*.
6. They agree to meet at *6.45 / 7.15*.
7. Holly thinks Rob *has / doesn't have* a lot of energy.

b Look at the **Social English phrases**. Can you remember any of the missing words?

Social English phrases
Rob Have you ________ a good day?
Jenny Oh, you ________. Meetings!
Jenny Why ________ you come with me?
Rob Can we ________ it a bit later?
Rob ________, seven forty-five?
Jenny ________ make it seven fifteen.

c 2 60 Watch or listen and complete the phrases.

d Watch or listen again and repeat the phrases. How do you say them in your language?

Can you...?
- [ ] make suggestions to do something
- [ ] take something you have bought back to the shop
- [ ] arrange a time to meet somebody

G *will / won't* (predictions)
V opposite verbs
P *'ll, won't*

I'm doing my driving test today.

You'll fail.

6A Are you a pessimist?

1 VOCABULARY opposite verbs

a With a partner, write the opposites of these verbs.

win ________ buy ________ remember ________
turn on ________ start ________ / ________

b ➤ **p.157 Vocabulary Bank** *Opposite verbs.*

2 GRAMMAR *will / won't* (predictions)

a Look at the cartoon. Which fish is an optimist? Why? Are you an optimist or a pessimist?

optimist pessimist

WHOA! HALF EMPTY! DEFINITELY HALF EMPTY!!
CHOKE GASP
JUST LISTEN TO YOU! ALWAYS THE PESSIMIST!

b Look at the phrase book app. Read the **You Say** phrases, then write the **A Pessimist Says** responses.

He won't pay you back. They'll be late. You won't pass. ~~It'll rain.~~ They'll lose. You won't understand a word. You won't find a parking space. You'll break your leg.

c 3 3)) Listen and check. Repeat the responses.

d Practise in pairs. **A** (book open) read the **You Say** phrases. **B** (book closed) say the **A Pessimist Says** responses. Then swap roles.

e Look at the **A Pessimist Says** phrases again. Do they refer to the present or the future?

f ➤ **p.136 Grammar Bank 6A.** Learn more about *will / won't* and practise them.

g Imagine now that you are an optimist. With a partner make positive predictions to respond to the **You Say** sentences in the phrase book.

1 *It'll be a great evening.*

3 PRONUNCIATION *'ll, won't*

a 3 5)) Listen and repeat the contractions. Copy the rhythm.

I'll	I'll be late	I'll be late for work.
You'll	You'll break	You'll break your leg.
She'll	She'll miss	She'll miss the train.
It'll	It'll rain	It'll rain tomorrow.
They'll	They'll fail	They'll fail the exam.

b 3 6)) Listen. Can you hear the difference?

clock	want	I want to pass.
phone	won't	I won't pass.

c 3 7)) Listen and write six sentences.

vodafone UK 3G 11:17
You Say
A Pessimist Says
1 We're having the party in the garden. = It'll rain.
2 I'm doing my driving test this afternoon. =
3 I'm having my first skiing lesson today. =
4 I've lent James some money. =
5 I'm going to see a film tonight in English. =
6 Our team are playing in the cup tonight. =
7 We're meeting Anna and Daniel at 7.00. =
8 We're going to drive to the city centre. =
The Pessimist's Phrase Book

4 READING

a Read an article about the actor Hugh Laurie. What two things do Hugh Laurie and Dr House have in common?

DR GREGORY HOUSE, the main character in the hit TV series *House M.D.*, is famous for being a pessimist. But it is not only Dr House who is a pessimist. Hugh Laurie, the actor who plays him, is a pessimist too.

Laurie never thought that *House M.D.* was going to be a success. Even after seven series he still feels pessimistic about it. He said in a recent interview, "If we do a bad show next week, they'll say, 'That's it. No more.' It'll just stop. I am of course someone who is constantly expecting a plane to drop on my head, if not today then tomorrow."

Like Dr House, Laurie is also a talented musician and is passionate about the blues. He recently went to New Orleans to record an album in which he plays 15 of his favourite songs. But of course he doesn't think that people will like it.

When he was asked on a TV show why he was so pessimistic about life, Laurie said it was because he is Scottish. 'I definitely think that's where it comes from.'

Because of his reputation as a pessimist, people always talk to him about positive thinking. He says that complete strangers come up to him in the street and say 'Cheer up, mate, it'll never happen!'

b Read the article again. Mark the sentences **T** (true) or **F** (false). Say why.

1 Hugh Laurie always thinks the worst will happen.
2 He thinks they will make many more series of *House M.D.*
3 He doesn't think his album will be successful.
4 He thinks that Scottish people are optimistic.
5 People often try to make him feel happier.

c Have you seen any episodes of *House M.D.*? Do you like...?
a the character   b the actor

5 LISTENING & SPEAKING

a 3 8))) Listen to the introduction to a radio programme. Why is positive thinking good for you?

b Try to guess the missing words in these callers' tips.

Caller 1 Live in the ________, not in the ________.
Caller 2 Think ________ thoughts, not negative ones.
Caller 3 Don't spend a lot of time reading the ________ or watching the ________ on TV.
Caller 4 Every week make a list of all the ________ ________ that happened to you.
Caller 5 Try to use ________ ________ when you speak to other people.

c 3 9))) Listen and check.

d Listen again. Write down any extra information you hear. Which tips do you think are useful? Do you have any tips of your own?

e Ask and answer with a partner. Use a phrase from the box and say why. Which of you is more optimistic?

ARE YOU A **POSITIVE** THINKER?

Do you think...

+ you'll have a nice weekend?
+ you'll pass your next English exam?
+ you'll get a good (or better) job in the future?
+ you'll get an interesting email or message from someone tonight?
+ you'll meet some new friends on your next holiday?
+ you'll live to be 100?
+ you'll get to the end of this book?

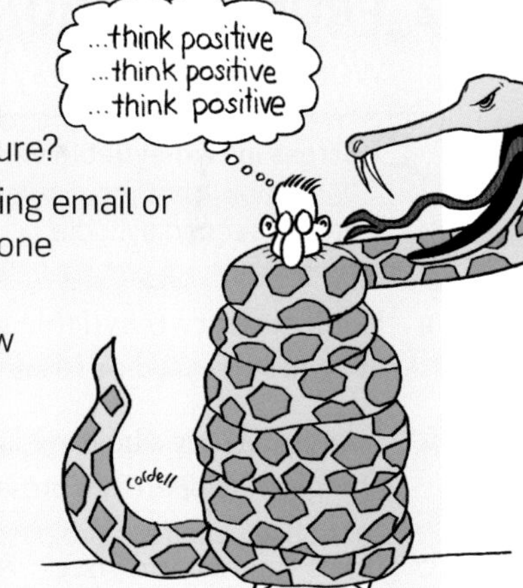

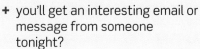

Responding to predictions
I hope so. / I hope not.
I think so. / I don't think so.
I doubt it.
Maybe. / Perhaps.
Probably (not).
Definitely (not).

Do you think you'll have a nice weekend?

I hope so. I think the weather will be good and...

G *will / won't* (decisions, offers, promises)
V verb + *back*
P word stress: two-syllable verbs

It's a secret.

OK, I won't tell anyone.

6B I'll never forget you

1 GRAMMAR

will / won't (decisions, offers, promises)

a Look at the cartoons. What do you think the missing phrases are?

b 3 10 Listen and complete the gaps.

c Look at the cartoons again. In which one does somebody...?

- ☐ promise to do something
- ☐ decide to have something
- ☐ offer to do something

d ➤ **p.136 Grammar Bank 6B.** Learn more about making offers, promises, and decisions and practise them.

e ➤ **Communication** *I'll / Shall I? game p.102.* Play the game.

2 PRONUNCIATION

word stress: two-syllable verbs

Stress in two-syllable verbs
Remember that most two-syllable verbs are stressed on the second syllable.

a Look at the two-syllable verbs below. Which syllable are they stressed on? Put them in the right column.

a|gree a|rrive bo|rrow com|plain de|cide de|pend for|get ha|ppen im|press in|vent in|vite o|ffer prac|tise pre|fer pro|mise re|ceive re|pair sun|bathe

1st syllable	2nd syllable

b 3 12 Listen and check.

1 **A** That's two burgers, a double portion of chips, and two ice cream sundaes. Anything else?
B Yes, _______________, please.

2 **A** Do I want to go back to the previous version? Do I press Yes or No?
B I need to do my homework now. _______________ when I finish.

3 **A** _______________! I promise!
B Well, hurry up. I can't wait much longer.
A Just one more kiss...

3 SPEAKING & LISTENING

a Look at the sentences. Talk to a partner.

1 When do you think people say them?
2 What do you think they all have in common?

I won't tell anyone.

I'll do it later.

I'll pay you back.

I'll come back and finish the job tomorrow.

I'll text you when I get there.

We'll build new schools and hospitals.

This won't hurt.

b Look at the title of a newspaper article. Do you think it's another promise that people often break?

I'll never forget you

Steve Smith from Devon in the UK met Carmen Ruiz-Perez from Spain 17 years ago when they were both in their 20s. Carmen was studying English at a language school in Steve's town, Torbay.

They fell in love and got engaged. But a year later Carmen moved to France to work, and the long-distance relationship first cooled and then ended.

A few years later Steve tried to get in touch with Carmen again, but she had changed her address in Paris. So he sent her a letter to her mother's address in Spain. In the letter he asked her if she was married and if she ever thought of him. He gave her his telephone number and asked her to get in touch. But Carmen's mother didn't send the letter to her daughter and it fell down behind the fireplace, where it stayed for ten years...

Adapted from a British newspaper

c Read the article and answer the questions.

1 What were Carmen and Steve doing in Torbay?
2 Why didn't they get married?
3 Why didn't Steve's letter get to Carmen?

d 3 13))) Now listen to part of a news programme and answer the questions.

What happened...?

1 when the builders found the letter
2 when Carmen got the letter
3 when Carmen called Steve
4 when they met in Paris
5 last week

4 VOCABULARY verb + *back*

a Look at the sentences. What's the difference between *go* and *go back*?

I'm **going** to work. I'm **going back** to work.

b Complete the dialogues with a phrase from the list.

call you back come back give it back
pay me back send it back take it back

1 **A** The shirt you bought me is too small.
B Don't worry. I'll _________ to the shop and change it. I still have the receipt.

2 **A** Hi, Jack. It's me, Karen.
B I can't talk now, I'm driving – I'll _________ in 15 minutes.

3 **A** Could I see the manager?
B She's at lunch now. Could you _________ in about half an hour?

4 **A** That's my pen you're using! _________!
B No, it's not. It's mine.

5 **A** Can you lend me 50 euros, Nick?
B It depends. When can you _________?

6 **A** I bought this jacket on the internet, but it's too big.
B Can't you _________?

c 3 14))) Listen and check. In pairs, practise the dialogues.

d Ask and answer in groups. Ask for more information.

1 When someone leaves you a message on your phone do you usually **call** them **back** immediately?
2 If you buy something online that is not exactly what you wanted, do you always **send** it **back**?
3 Have you ever lent somebody money and they didn't **pay** you **back**?
4 When you **come back** after a holiday do you usually feel better or worse than before?
5 When you borrow a book or a DVD from a friend do you usually remember to **give** it **back**? What about if you lend something to your friends?
6 If you buy something to wear from a shop and then decide you don't like it, do you usually **take** it **back**?

5 3 15))) SONG

Reach Out I'll Be There ♫

G review of verb forms: present, past, and future
V adjectives + prepositions
P the letters *ow*

I dreamt about a road.

That means you're going to travel.

6C The meaning of dreaming

1 READING & LISTENING

a Do you often remember your dreams? Do you think dreams can tell us anything about the future?

b 3 16 Listen to a psychoanalyst talking to a patient about his dreams. Number the pictures 1–6 in the correct order.

c Listen again and complete the gaps with a verb in the right form.

Dr Allen So, tell me, what did you dream about?
Patient I was at a party. There were a lot of people.
Dr What were they [1]_______?
P They were drinking and [2]_______.
Dr Were you drinking?
P Yes, I was [3]_______ champagne.
Dr And then what happened?
P Then, suddenly I was in a garden. There [4]_______ a lot of flowers...
Dr Flowers, yes... what kind of flowers?
P I [5]_______ really see – it was dark. And I could hear music – somebody was [6]_______ the violin.
Dr The violin? Go on.
P And then I [7]_______ an owl, a big owl in a tree...
Dr How did you [8]_______? Were you frightened of it?
P No, not frightened really, no, but I [9]_______ I felt very cold. Especially my feet – they were freezing. And then I [10]_______.
Dr Your feet? Mmm, very interesting, very interesting indeed. Were you [11]_______ any shoes?
P No, no, I wasn't.
Dr Tell me. Have you ever [12]_______ this dream before?
P No, never. So what does it [13]_______, Doctor?

d What do you think the patient's dream means? Match five of the things in his dream with interpretations 1–5.

Understanding your dreams

You dream...	This means...
☐ that you are at a party.	1 you are going to be very busy.
☐ that you are drinking champagne.	2 you're feeling positive about the future.
☐ about flowers.	3 you want some romance in your life.
☐ that somebody is playing the violin.	4 you need to ask an older person for help.
☐ about an owl.	5 you'll be successful in the future.

e 3 17 Listen to Dr Allen interpreting the patient's dream. Check your answers to **d**.

f 3 18 Dr Allen is now going to explain what picture 6 means. What do you think the meaning could be? Listen and find out.

2 GRAMMAR review of verb forms

a Look at the sentences below. Which one is the present perfect? Mark it **PP**. Then look at the other sentences. What time do they refer to? Mark them **P** (the past), **PR** (the present) or **F** (the future).

1 ☐ I was drinking champagne.
2 ☐ Maybe you'll have a meeting with your boss.
3 ☐ I saw an owl.
4 ☐ You are feeling positive.
5 ☐ You're going to meet a lot of people.
6 ☐ You work in an office.
7 ☐ I'm meeting her tonight.
8 ☐ Have you ever had this dream before?

b ➤ **p.136 Grammar bank 6C.** Revise all the verb forms you've studied in Files 1–6 and practise them.

3 SPEAKING

a ➤ **Communication** *Dreams* **A** *p.103* **B** *p.107.* Roleplay interpreting your partner's dream.

b Interview a partner with the questionnaire. Choose two questions from each group. Ask for more information.

REVISION QUESTIONNAIRE

- Where do you usually buy your clothes?
- What do you like doing at the weekend?
- Are you watching any TV series at the moment?
- Are you studying for an exam at the moment?

- Where did you go on holiday last year?
- Did you do anything exciting last Saturday night?
- Where were you at 10 o'clock last night? What were you doing?
- Were you sleeping when the alarm clock rang this morning?

- Have you ever had the same dream again and again?
- Have you ever dreamed about something that then happened?

- Are you going to learn a new foreign language next year?
- Are you going to do anything exciting next weekend?
- Do you think it will be sunny tomorrow?
- Do you think your country will win the next football World Cup?
- What are you doing tonight?

4 PRONUNCIATION the letters *ow*

Pronunciation of *ow*
Be careful: *ow* can be pronounced /aʊ/, e.g. *flower* or /əʊ/, e.g. *window.*

a 3 20 Listen and repeat the two words and sounds.

 owl		 phone	

b Write the words in the list in the right columns.

blow borrow brown crowded
down how know low
now show shower snow
throw towel town

c 3 21 Listen and check.

d Practise saying the sentences.

Show me the flowers.
The town is very crowded now.
Don't throw snow at the windows.
How do you know?
Can I borrow a towel for the shower?

5 VOCABULARY adjectives + prepositions

Adjectives + prepositions
Some adjectives are usually followed by certain prepositions, e.g. *Were you* ***frightened of*** *the owl?* It's useful to learn the prepositions with the adjectives.

a Complete the gaps with a preposition.

1 Are you afraid ___ the dark?
2 Do you think chocolate is good ___ you?
3 Is your town full ___ tourists in the summer?
4 What is your country famous ___?
5 At school, what subjects were you bad ___?
6 Are you good ___ dancing?
7 Do you often get angry ___ your family? What ___?
8 Are people in your country very different ___ the English?
9 Are people in your country nice ___ tourists?
10 Are you interested ___ politics?

b Ask and answer the questions with a partner. Say why.

5&6 Revise and Check

GRAMMAR

Circle a, b, or c.

1 She drives ______ than her brother.
a faster b more fast c more fastly

2 His new book isn't as good ______ his last one.
a than b that c as

3 Women spend ______ time cooking than in the past.
a less b little c fewer

4 Friday is ______ day of the week.
a the busier b the busiest c the most busy

5 It's the ______ road in the world.
a more dangerous
b dangerousest
c most dangerous

6 It's the hottest country I've ______ been to.
a never b always c ever

7 My sister drinks ______ coffee.
a too b too much c too many

8 These jeans are ______ small. Do you have them one size bigger?
a too b too much c too many

9 You haven't spent ______ on your homework.
a time enough
b enough time
c many time

10 They're playing really badly. They ______ the match.
a want win b won't win c won't to win

11 **A** My exam is today.
B Don't worry. ______.
a You'll pass b You pass c You're passing

12 **A** It's cold in here. **B** ______ the window.
a I close b I'm closing c I'll close

13 They met for the first time when they ______ in Madrid.
a were living b are living c was living

14 **A** Have you been to the USA?
B Yes, I ______ to New York last year.
a 've been b went c was going

15 **A** ______ today? **B** No, she's on holiday.
a Does she work
b Is she working
c Will she work

VOCABULARY

a Circle the right verb or phrase.

1 I *waste* / *lose* a lot of time playing games on my phone.
2 We *spend* / *take* a lot of time sitting in our cars every day.
3 Can you *borrow* / *lend* me 50 euros?
4 I'm leaving tonight and I'm *coming* / *coming back* on Friday.
5 This is Ben. He's *teaching* / *learning* me to play the piano.

b Write the opposite verb.

1 buy ______ 3 remember ______ 5 teach ______
2 push ______ 4 pass ______

c Write words for the definitions.

1 **cr**______ (adj) full of people or things
2 **s**______ (adj) opposite of *dangerous*
3 **n**______ (adj) opposite of *quiet* (for a place)
4 **s**______ (adj, noun) opposite of *north*
5 **m**______ (noun) a building where you can see old things
6 **p**______ (noun) the place where a king or queen lives
7 **m**______ (noun) a religious building for Muslims
8 **b**______ (noun) you have 206 of these in your body
9 **br**______ (noun) the organ we use to think
10 **sk**______ (noun) it covers the outside of your body

d Complete the sentences with a preposition.

1 My husband's always late. He's never ______ time for anything.
2 Are you interested ______ this TV programme?
3 When I was a child I was afraid ______ dogs.
4 I'd really like to be good ______ dancing.
5 Eating too many sweets and biscuits is bad ______ you.

PRONUNCIATION

a Circle the word with a different sound.

1 uː	too	lose	polluted	much
2 e	eat	many	healthy	mend
3 ɒ	lot	won't	borrow	offer
4 aʊ	shower	now	snow	towel
5 k	receive	castle	mosque	active

b Underline the stressed syllable.

1 im|pa|tient 2 in|teres|ting 3 in|vent 4 prac|tise 5 de|cide

CAN YOU UNDERSTAND THIS TEXT?

a Read the text once. Does the journalist think music made him run faster?

b Read the text again and mark the sentences **T** (true) or **F** (false).

1 The psychologist says that all kinds of music can help us exercise better.
2 He says that exercise is more fun with music.
3 Men and women prefer different music when they exercise.
4 Music helped Haile Gebreselassie break a record.
5 Most top athletes use music when they run.
6 Music can help amateur runners to run faster.
7 The journalist chose his music for the marathon.
8 All the songs helped him run faster.

c Look at the highlighted words or phrases in the text. Guess their meaning from the context. Check with your teacher or with a dictionary.

Can music really make you run faster?

Costas Karageorghis, a sports psychologist at Brunel University in the UK, calls music 'sport's legal drug'. He says that exercising with music can improve athletic performance by 15%. The music must be carefully chosen so that the tempo or 'beat' is synchronised with the exercise you are doing. According to Professor Karageorghis, music also makes you feel less pain and makes an exercise session less boring and more enjoyable.

The UK's biggest gym chain, *Fitness First*, recognizes the importance of music to workouts, and plays music in all its clubs. The most popular song for male gym members is Survivor's *Eye of the Tiger*, while women love Abba's *Dancing Queen*.

Music works well with weightlifting, and other repetitive actions, but it can also help with running. The best example of this is Haile Gebreselassie, perhaps the world's greatest distance runner, who used the techno-pop song *Scatman* as a metronome when he broke the world 2,000m record. But if music was so important to Gebreselassie, why do other top runners never race with headphones?

Karageorghis says 'Research has shown that for most top athletes music is less effective. Elite athletes focus more on their bodies, and less on outside stimuli like music.' So although music can help amateur runners run faster and further, most top athletes prefer silence.

I decided to try running with music myself. I was going to run a half marathon, and a sports doctor gave me the perfect playlist of songs for running. When I did the race, I found that some of the tracks, like Von Kleet's *Walking on Me*, made running easier. Others made me want to throw away the mp3 player. When I crossed the line, I had beaten my previous personal best by one minute, but was it because of the music? To be honest, I felt it was probably because of the extra training.

Warren Pole in The Times

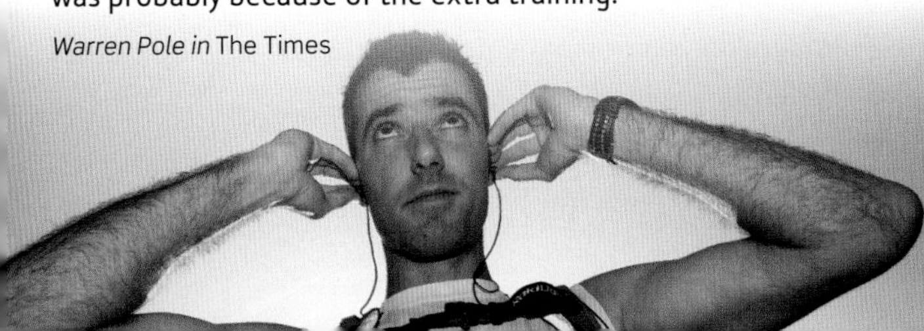

CAN YOU UNDERSTAND THESE PEOPLE?

3 22 **In the street** Watch or listen to five people and answer the questions.

Ian

Yvonne

Ben

Joanna

Anya

1 Three years ago Ian ______.
  a retired
  b had more free time
  c was working part time
2 When Yvonne talks about why she loves Rome, she *doesn't* mention ______.
  a the scenery b the food c the buildings
3 Ben eats ______ sugar.
  a too much b a lot of c a little
4 Joanna says her friends ______.
  a are mostly pessimists
  b think she is a pessimist
  c think she is an optimist
5 Anya often has bad dreams ______.
  a when she's having problems at work
  b after she's had a big meal
  c when she's having problems with her partner

CAN YOU SAY THIS IN ENGLISH?

Do the tasks with a partner. Tick (✓) the box if you can do them.

Can you...?

1 ☐ compare two members of your family using adjectives and adverbs
2 ☐ talk about your town using four superlatives (*the biggest, the best*, etc.)
3 ☐ talk about your diet using (*not*) *enough* and *too much* | *too many*
4 ☐ make three predictions about the future using *will* | *won't*
5 ☐ make a promise, an offer, and a decision using *will* | *won't*

Short films Chicago
Watch and enjoy a film on iTutor.

Communication

1A WHAT'S HIS NAME? HOW DO YOU SPELL IT? Student A

a Ask **B** questions to complete the missing information.

Photo 1 – What's her surname? How do you spell it?

b Answer **B**'s questions.

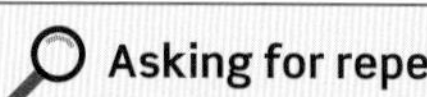

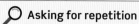

Asking for repetition
If you don't hear or understand somebody, you can say:
Sorry? Can you say that again? Can you repeat that?

1B ALEXANDER AND OLIVER Student A

a Ask **B** questions and complete the chart for Oliver.

Name	Alexander	Oliver
How old / ?	32	
Where / from?	London	
Where / live?	Brighton	
What / do?	journalist	
What / like?	modern art, classical music	
What / not like?	sport	

b Answer **B**'s questions about Alexander.

1C DESCRIBE AND DRAW Student A

a Look at your painting for a minute.

b Describe your painting for **B** to draw.

c Listen to **B** describing his / her painting. Try to draw it. Don't look at it. Ask **B** questions to help you.

d Now compare your drawings with the original paintings. Are they similar?

2B *AT, IN, ON* Student A

a Ask **B** your questions.

1 When were you born?
2 Where do you usually have breakfast?
3 What time do you usually have lunch?
4 What days of the week do you usually go out in the evening?
5 What time of day do you usually do your English homework?
6 When do you usually have a holiday?
7 Where do you normally listen to music?
8 When's your birthday?

b Answer **B**'s questions using *at*, *in*, or *on*. Ask *What about you?* for each question.

2C HAPPY ENDING

1 Why didn't Hannah see the man who was crossing the road?
2 Who was the man?
3 Why did he cross without looking?
4 Where did they go after that?
5 What did they order?
6 Why was Jamie in the High Street?
7 What and when was the concert?
8 What was special about the day?

3A WHAT ARE YOUR PLANS? Student A

a Ask **B** your questions using *going to*. Ask for more information.

- What / you / do after class?
- What time / you / get up tomorrow?
- Where / you / have lunch tomorrow?
- What / you / do on Saturday night?
- Where / you / go for your next holiday?
- / you / study English next year?

b Answer **B**'s questions. Give more information.

3C WHAT'S THE WORD? Student A

a Look at the six words or phrases on your card. Think for a minute how you are going to define them.

b You have two minutes to communicate your words to **B**. Remember you can't use any part or form of the words on the card.

c Now listen to **B**'s definitions. Try to guess the words.

4A HAS HE DONE IT YET? Students A+B

Look at the picture for one minute and try to remember what's in it. Then go to p.102.

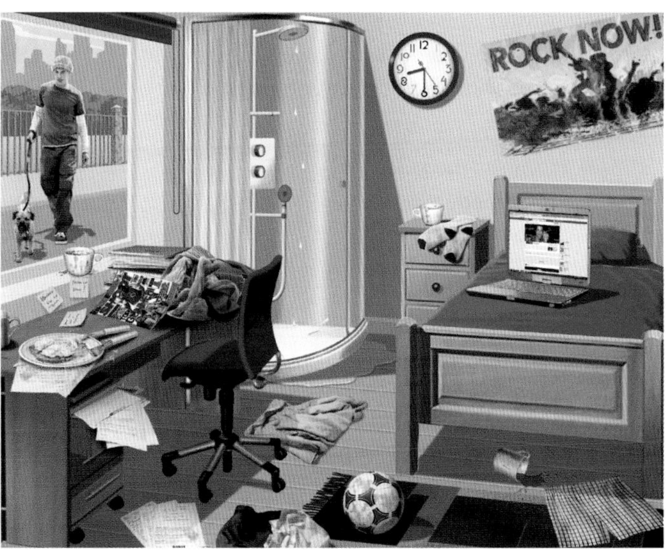

5A HOW FAST IS YOUR LIFE? Students A+B

Check your partner's score and tell him or her. Then read to see what it means.

How to score:
1 point for never
2 points for sometimes
3 points for often

Is your score between 6 and 9? You are living life in the slow lane. Compared to most people you take things easy and don't get stressed by modern-day living. You are patient, relaxed, and easy-going. Most of the time this is good news, but sometimes it can be a problem. For example, are you sometimes late for appointments?

Is your score between 10 and 14? You have a medium pace of life. You are probably somebody who can change the speed at which you live depending on the situation.

Is your score between 15 and 18? You are living life in the fast lane, rushing around and trying to do many different activities and projects at the same time. You are impatient and you find it difficult to relax. You are probably very productive, but your relationships and health could suffer as a result.

Adapted from Richard Wiseman's Quirkology website

Communication

4A HAS HE DONE IT YET? Students A+B

a Work individually. Look at the list of things Max always does every morning. Has he already done them? Try to remember what was in the picture. Write sentences.

He's already made the bed.
OR *He hasn't made the bed yet.*

- make the bed
- wash up his coffee cups
- tidy his desk
- pick up his towel
- take the dog for a walk
- turn off his computer
- put his clothes in the cupboard
- have a shower
- have breakfast

b Work in pairs. Compare your sentences with your partner. Are they the same? Then go back to p.101 and compare your sentences with the picture. Were you right?

5B THE FRIENDLIEST CITY Student A

a Read about what happened when Tim did the three tests in New York. Try to remember the information.

New York

The photo test
I asked an office worker who was eating his sandwiches to take a photo of me. He was really friendly and said 'Of course I'll take your picture.' When I asked him to take more photos he said 'Sure! No problem.' When he gave me back my camera he said 'Have a nice day!'

The shopping test
I went shopping near Times Square and I bought an 'I love New York' T-shirt and some drinks from two different people. I gave them too much money, but they both gave me the exact change back.

The accident test
I went to Central Park and I fell over. I only had to wait about thirty seconds before a man came to help me. 'Is this your camera?' he said, 'I think it's broken.'

b In your own words tell **B** and **C** what happened in New York.

First he did the photo test...

c Listen to **B** and **C** tell you what happened in Paris and Rome.

d Together decide which of the cities is the friendliest so far.

6B *I'LL / SHALL I?* GAME Students A+B

Play the game.

6C DREAMS Student A

a Last night you dreamt about these things. Prepare to tell **B** about your dream.

b **B** is a psychoanalyst. Tell him / her about your dream. He / she will tell you what it means.

Last night I dreamt about a river...

c Swap roles. Now you are a psychoanalyst. Listen to **B**'s dream. Number the things below in the order he / she talks about them.

- ☐ **Ice cream** – you will get some money (from the lottery or from a relative).
- ☐ **Long hair** – you want to be free. Perhaps you have problems with your family or a partner.
- ☐ **A key** – you have a problem and you are looking for a solution.
- ☐ **People speaking other languages** – you think your life is boring and you would like to have a more exciting life.
- ☐ **Travelling by bus** – you are worried about a person who is controlling your life.

d Now use the information in **c** to interpret **B**'s dream.

Useful language
First you dreamt about...
This tells me that...
This means you are going to...
This represents...

1A WHAT'S HIS NAME? HOW DO YOU SPELL IT? Student B

1 _____ Dylan	2 Kieran _____	3 _____ Webb
4 Cally _____	5 _____ Scott	6 Michael _____

a Answer **A**'s questions.

b Ask **A** questions to complete the missing information.

Photo 1 – What's her first name? How do you spell it?

Asking for repetition
If you don't hear or understand somebody, you can say:
Sorry? Can you say that again? Can you repeat that?

1B ALEXANDER AND OLIVER Student B

a Answer **A**'s questions about Oliver.

Name	Alexander	Oliver
How old / ?		25
Where / from?		Scotland
Where / live?		London
What / do?		doctor
What / like?		sport, music, good books and films
What / not like?		clubs and discos

b Ask **A** questions and complete the chart for Alexander.

Communication

1C DESCRIBE AND DRAW Student B

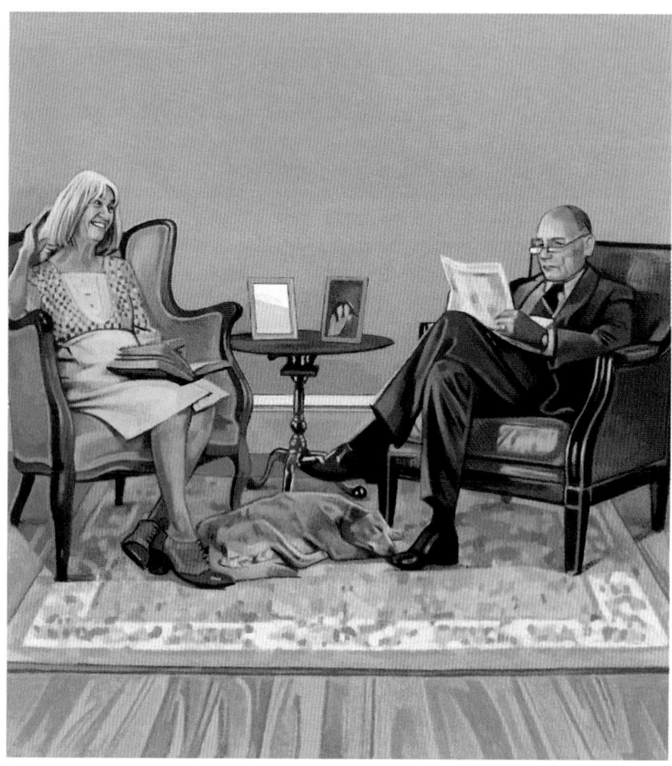

a Look at your painting for a minute.

b Listen to **A** describing his / her painting. Try to draw it. Don't look at it. Ask **A** questions to help you.

c Now describe your painting for **A** to draw.

d Compare your drawings with the original paintings. Are they similar?

2B *AT, IN, ON* Student B

a Answer **A**'s questions using *at*, *in*, or *on*. Ask *What about you?* for each question.

b Ask **A** your questions.

1. Where were you born?
2. What time do you usually get up during the week?
3. Where do you usually have lunch?
4. What time of day do you usually meet friends?
5. When do you usually go shopping?
6. Where do you usually do your English homework?
7. When do you do housework?
8. Where can you have a nice walk near where you live?

2C SAD ENDING

1. Why didn't Hannah see the man who was crossing the road?
2. What happened?
3. Where did she go then and what did she do?
4. Who arrived at her house two hours later?
5. What news did she have for Hannah?
6. How was Jamie?
7. What did she tell Hannah about the car and the driver?
8. What happened in the end?

3A WHAT ARE YOUR PLANS? Student B

a Answer **A**'s questions. Give more information.

b Ask **A** your questions using *going to*. Ask for more information.

- / you / go out this evening?
- What / you / have for dinner tonight?
- What / you / wear tomorrow?
- / you / go anywhere next weekend?
- What / you / do next summer?
- When / you / do your English homework?

3C WHAT'S THE WORD? Student B

a Look at the six words or phrases on your card. Think for a minute how you are going to define them.

b Listen to **A**'s definitions. Try to guess the words.

c You have two minutes to communicate your words to **A**. Remember you can't use any part or form of the words on the card.

5B THE FRIENDLIEST CITY Student B

a Read about what happened when Tim did the three tests in Paris. Try to remember the information.

> **Paris**
>
> The photo test
> I was standing in front of the Eiffel Tower and I asked some gardeners to take some photos of me. They couldn't stop laughing when they saw my hat, but they took the photos.
>
> The shopping test
> I went to a greengrocer's and I bought some fruit. I gave the man a lot of euro coins and he carefully took the exact amount.
>
> The accident test
> I fell over in the Champs Elysées. The street was very busy, but after a minute someone stopped and said to me, 'Are you OK?' He was Scottish!

b Listen to **A** tell you what happened in New York.

c In your own words tell **A** and **C** what happened in Paris.

First he did the photo test...

d Listen to **C** tell you what happened in Rome.

e Together decide which of the cities is the friendliest so far.

6C DREAMS Student B

a Last night you dreamt about these things. Prepare to tell **A** about your dream.

b You are a psychoanalyst. Listen to **A**'s dream. Number the things below in the order he / she talks about them.

- ☐ **Having a bath** – you have a secret which nobody knows about.
- ☐ **Dogs** – you are looking for friends.
- ☐ **Losing hair** – you are going to lose some money.
- ☐ **Lost luggage** – a problem you have will soon get better.
- ☐ **A river** – you are going to be very lucky.

c Now use the information in **b** to interpret **A**'s dream.

> **Useful language**
> First you dreamt about...
> This tells me that...
> This means you are going to...
> This represents...

d Swap roles. Now **A** is a psychoanalyst. Tell him / her about your dream. **A** will tell you what it means.

Last night I dreamt about ice-cream...

5B THE FRIENDLIEST CITY Student C

a Read about what happened when Tim did the three tests in Rome. Try to remember the information.

Rome

The photo test

I asked a very chic woman who was wearing sunglasses to take some photos. She took a photo of me with my hat on, then without my hat. Then another photo with my sunglasses. Then she asked me to take a photo of her!

The shopping test

I bought a copy of *The Times* newspaper from a newspaper seller near the railway station. It was three euros. I gave the man four euros and he didn't give me any change.

The accident test

I went to a busy street near the station. When I fell over about eight people immediately hurried to help me.

b Listen to **A** and **B** tell you what happened in New York and Paris.

c In your own words tell **A** and **B** what happened in Rome.

First he did the photo test...

d Together decide which of the cities is the friendliest so far.

1 DESCRIBING A PERSON

a Read Charlie's email. The computer has found ten mistakes. They are grammar, punctuation, or spelling mistakes. Can you correct them?

From: Charlie [barcacarlos@hotmail.com]
To: Lucy [lucyathome1989@yahoo.com]
Subject: Hi from Spain

Hi Lucy

My name's Charlie. Well, it's really Carlos but everyone calls me Charlie. I'm from Barcelona and I live at home with my parents and my dog. I have 21 years old, and I'm at university. I'm studing physics. I'm in my last year and I really like it.

I'm going to tell you about myself. As you can see from the foto, I have black hair and browns eyes. My father always says I have a big nose, but I don't think so, I think it's a Roman nose!

I think I'm a positive person. My freinds say I'm funny and it's true, I like making people laugh. But I can to be serious too when I need to be!

I dont have many free time becuase when I'm not in class I have to do projects or write reports. But when I can, I like watching TV series, especially science fiction series and comedies. I watch them in english with subtitles. I also like playing computer games like *World of Warcraft* and *Starcraft*.

Please write soon and tell me about you and your life.

Best wishes

Charlie

b Read the email again from the beginning. Then cover it and answer the questions from memory.

1 Where's Charlie from?
2 What's his real name?
3 Who does he live with?
4 What does he do?
5 What does he look like?
6 What's he like?
7 What are his favourite free time activities?

c Write a similar email about you or a person you know. Write four paragraphs.

Paragraph 1	name, nationality, age, family, work / study
Paragraph 2	physical appearance
Paragraph 3	personality
Paragraph 4	hobbies and interests

d Check your email for mistakes (grammar, punctuation, and spelling).

◀ *p.7*

2 MY FAVOURITE PHOTO

MY FAVOURITE PHOTO BLOG

POST YOUR FAVOURITE PHOTO ON THE WEBSITE, TOGETHER WITH A SHORT DESCRIPTION OF WHY THE PHOTO IS IMPORTANT TO YOU.

This week's winner is Ellie, a student from Cardiff.

1 One of my favourite photos is this one of my friend Anna.

2 I took the photo ________ the summer of 2011 when I was ________ holiday with some friends ________ Ireland.

3 We were at a place called Tara. It's a hill which is famous because there's a big stone ________ top of it, and people say that the old kings of Ireland were crowned there. Anna was telling us all about the history of the stone, and she put her arms ________ it. When I took the photo we thought she was meditating, but in fact we later realised she was sleeping! She woke up after a few minutes and she said the magic of the place made her sleepy!

4 I love this photo because it's mysterious, like the place, and it reminds me of a lovely holiday.

5 I have the photo ________ my phone and ________ my computer with other photos ________ Ireland.

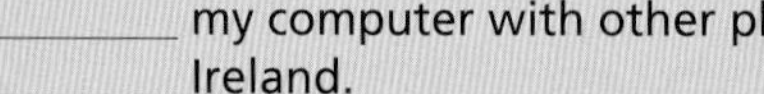

a Match the questions with paragraphs 1–5.

- ☐ **What was happening when you took the photo?**
- ☐ **Where do you keep it?**
- ☐ **Why do you like it?**
- ☐ **What's your favourite photo?**
- ☐ **Who took it? When? Where?**

b Complete the text with *in*, *of*, *on*, or *round*.

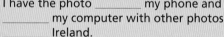

You can keep a photo...

in	an album.	**on**	the wall.	**by**	your bed.
	your wallet.		a table.		
	your bedroom.		your phone.		
	a frame.		your computer.		

c Write about your favourite photo. Answer the questions in **a** in the right order.

d Check your description for mistakes (grammar, punctuation, and spelling). Attach a copy of the photo if you can. Show your description to another student. Is the photo similar in any way to yours?

◄ p.15

3 AN INFORMAL EMAIL

a Goran is a student from Croatia who's going to study English in the UK. He's going to stay with a family. Read the email from Mrs Barnes and complete it with expressions from the list.

Best wishes   Dear Goran
PS   Looking forward to hearing from you

b Read the email again and answer the questions.

1 When is Goran coming to the UK?
2 How is he travelling?
3 Who is going to meet him at the airport?
4 Does Goran have to share a room?
5 Does *Looking forward to hearing from you* mean...?
   a I hope you write again soon.
   b I'm going to write to you again soon.
6 Does *PS* mean...?
   a This isn't very important information.
   b I forgot to say this before.
7 Why does Mrs Barnes send Goran a photo?

c Imagine you are going to stay with Mrs Barnes. Answer her email using your own information. Write three paragraphs. End the email with *Best wishes* and your name.

Paragraph 1	Thank her for her email.
Paragraph 2	Say when you are arriving, etc.
Paragraph 3	Answer her other questions.

d Check your email for mistakes (grammar, punctuation, and spelling).

◄ p.23

From: Sally Barnes [Barnes@hotmail.com]
To: Goran [gorangrec@yahoo.com]
Subject: Your trip

1 ____________

Thank you for your email. We're very happy that you're coming to stay with us this summer, and we're sure you're going to enjoy your stay with us.

What time are you arriving at Stansted airport? If you send us your flight number and arrival time, we can all meet you in Arrivals. Can you send us your mobile number too?

Could you also give us some other information? What day are you going back to Croatia? Is there anything you can't eat or drink? Do you want your own room, or do you prefer to share a room with another student? Is there anything special you would like to do or see in the UK?

2 ____________ .

3 ____________

Sally Barnes

4 ____________ I'm attaching a photo of the family, so you can recognize us at the airport!

4 DESCRIBING WHERE YOU LIVE

a Read the text and complete it with these words.

area ~~city~~ food historic modern
nature population rivers weather

b Match the questions with paragraphs 1–5.

- ☐ What's it famous for?
- ☐ What's the weather like?
- ☐ What's the best thing about it? Do you like living there?
- ☐ What's your home town like? What is there to see there?
- ☐ Where do you live? Where is it? How big is it?

c Write a description of the place where you live. Write five paragraphs. Answer the questions in **b** in the right order. First, make notes on the questions in **b**.

d Check your email for mistakes (grammar, punctuation, and spelling). Show your description to other students in your class. Which place that you read about would you most like to visit?

◀ p.39

THE PLACE WHERE I LIVE

1 I live in Kayseri, which is an important [1]*city* in Central Anatolia in Turkey. It has a [2]__________ of over 1,000,000 people. It's near the famous Cappadocia [3]__________, so there are a lot of tourists in the summer.

2 Kayseri is one of the richest cities in Turkey because it has a lot of industry. It is a university town, and there are also many [4]__________ buildings, for example Kayseri Castle, Hunat Hatun Mosque, and the Grand Bazaar around Cumhuriyet Square, with its famous statue of Ataturk. But Kayseri also has [5]__________ residential areas full of luxury blocks of flats, shopping centres, and stylish restaurants.

3 The [6]__________ in Kayseri is typical of the Middle Anatolia Region. Winters are cold and snowy – great for skiing – and summers are hot and dry. It sometimes rains in the spring and autumn.

4 Kayseri is famous for its mountains. Mount Erciyes is the symbol of the city and it has a well-known ski resort, and on Mount Ali there are national and international paragliding championships. It's also famous for its [7]__________ and has many local specialities like *pastirma*, which is dried beef with spices, and *manti*, which is a kind of Turkish ravioli. They're delicious!

5 What I like best about Kayseri is that we are so close to [8]__________. When I'm tired of city life, I can easily get out and enjoy the mountains, [9]__________, waterfalls, and thermal spas, which are only a short distance away.

Listening

1 14

My first impression of Alexander was that he was much older than me. In fact he was 32, but I thought he was older. But when we started talking I really liked him. He was extrovert and funny and he had a very good sense of humour. He works for a TV company and he told me a lot of good stories about his work. He was also interested in the same things as me – art and music, and we talked a lot about that. Physically he wasn't really my type. It's difficult to say why. He was tall and dark and quite good-looking and he had a nice smile but there just wasn't any chemistry between us. I could imagine going to a concert or theatre with him, but as a friend. Sorry Mum, but no.

1 15

When I first saw Oliver I thought he looked warm and friendly, and more attractive than Alexander. He was quite tall with short blond hair and he had lovely blue eyes, a bit like the actor Jude Law. He was a bit shy and quiet at first but when we started chatting he relaxed and we found we had a lot of things in common – we both like books, and the cinema. He was generous too – he wanted to pay for everything. I really enjoyed the evening. When it was time to go he asked for my phone number and said he wanted to meet again. We walked out of the restaurant and went to look for a taxi. And then something happened, and I knew that it was impossible for me to go out with him. He said 'At last!' and took out a packet of cigarettes. That was it, I'm afraid. I could never have a boyfriend who was a smoker. I think perhaps for my next date I'm going to choose the man myself. I don't think another person can really choose a partner for you.

1 24

Mr and Mrs Clark and Percy is by the British artist David Hockney, and it's considered to be one of the greatest British paintings of the 20th century. It was painted in 1971 and it's a portrait of two of his friends, Ossie Clark and his wife Celia, and their cat Percy. Ossie Clark and Celia were fashion designers and they had a very successful clothes shop in London. In the 1960s they dressed a lot of the famous pop stars of the time, including The Rolling Stones and Eric Clapton. Hockney painted Ossie and Celia a few months after they got married in their flat at Notting Hill in London. He painted them in their bedroom, because he liked the light there, and on the wall on the left of the window you can see one of his own paintings.

Mr and Mrs Clark and Percy is a very big painting, approximately 3 metres wide and 2 metres high. The couple are wearing typical clothes of the late 1960s. Celia is wearing a long dress, and in fact she was expecting a baby at that time. Her husband isn't wearing any shoes, and he's putting his feet into the carpet. This was because Hockney had a lot of problems painting his feet. He just couldn't get them right.

Hockney said that his aim with this painting was to paint the relationship between the two people. Traditionally, when a painter paints a married couple the woman is sitting down and the man is standing up. In this painting the man is sitting and the woman is standing. Usually in a painting the married couple are close together, but in this painting they are separated by a big open window which symbolizes the distance between them. The white cat, sitting on Mr Clark, is a symbol of infidelity. It seems that Hockney didn't think that their marriage was going to be very happy, and in fact the couple got divorced four years later.

Celia often posed as a model for Hockney, but she says that this painting, his most famous picture of her, is not her favourite. She said "It's a wonderful painting, but it makes me look too heavy." In 1996, twenty five years after this picture was painted, Ossie Clark died. He was murdered by his lover in his Kensington flat.

1 26

My name's Jenny Zielinski. I live and work in New York. I'm the assistant editor of a magazine called *NewYork24seven*. A few months ago, I visited our office in London to learn more about the company. I met the manager, Daniel O'Connor. I had lots of meetings with him, of course. And a working dinner on my birthday... But I spent more time with Rob Walker. He's one of the writers on the London magazine. We had coffees together. We went sightseeing. I even helped Rob buy a shirt! He was fun to be with. I liked him a lot. I think he liked me too. Rob isn't the most punctual person in the world, but he is a great writer. We invited him to work for the New York magazine for a month... and he agreed! So now Rob's coming to New York. I know he's really excited about it. It's going to be great to see him again.

1 29

Jenny So, here you are in New York at last.
Rob Yeah, it's great to be here. It's really exciting.
Jenny And how's your hotel?
Rob It's fine. My room is really...nice.
Jenny Do you have a good view from your room?
Rob I can see lots of other buildings.
Jenny Tomorrow I'm going to show you around the office and introduce you to the team. Barbara's looking forward to meeting you. You remember, Barbara, my boss?
Rob Oh...yeah, sorry.
Jenny And then you can start thinking about your blog and the column. Have you got any ideas yet, Rob? ... Rob?
Rob What? Sorry, Jenny.
Jenny You must be really tired.
Rob Yes, I am a bit. What time is it now?
Jenny It's nine o'clock.
Rob Nine o'clock? That's two o'clock in the morning for me.
Jenny Let's finish our drinks. You need to go to bed.
Rob I guess you're right.
Jenny So, I'll see you in the office at eleven in the morning.
Rob At eleven?
Jenny Is that OK?
Rob It's perfect. Thanks, Jenny.
Jenny There's just one thing.
Rob What's that?
Jenny Don't be late.
Rob By the way. It's great to see you again.
Jenny Yeah. It's great to see you, too.

1 34

Mia It was a really terrible holiday. It was my fault, I mean I wanted to go to Thailand, but I knew before I went that I didn't really want to have a serious relationship with Joe. And the holiday just showed how different we are. He irritated me all the time. He wanted to stay in some really cheap hostels, because he thought the hotels were too expensive. I didn't want 5-star luxury, but when I go on holiday I want to be comfortable. The places where Joe wanted to stay were very basic and had very small rooms. There's nothing worse than being in a very small room with someone when you're not getting on very well. Another thing I didn't like was that Joe got very jealous. When you're travelling, part of the fun is talking to other travellers, but he hated it if I talked to other people, especially other men. And then he kept taking photos! Hundreds of them. Every time we saw a monument he said 'Go and stand over there so I can take a photo.' I hate being in photos. I just wanted to enjoy the sights. The holiday was all a big mistake. Never go on holiday with a boyfriend if you're not sure about the relationship. It's sure to be a disaster!

1 35

Linda Oh, it was a wonderful holiday. I loved every moment! Venice is just a paradise. We did everything – we went on a gondola, we saw all the museums, and we had some fantastic meals. And you know, everyone says that Venice is expensive, but I didn't think it was – it wasn't an expensive holiday at all. I thought it was quite reasonable. We all got on very well. I think I'm going to suggest to Isabelle and Laura that we go on holiday together again next year...

1 44

In May 1968, I came back to Paris. It was a very exciting time. There were a lot of demonstrations, and fighting between students and the police. I wasn't really interested in politics – I wasn't a communist or an anarchist. But I loved the atmosphere. All the students were fighting for freedom, for revolution, and the French police were everywhere. On May the 15th I was with thousands of other young people. We were walking towards the Place de la Bastille. I was tired, so a friend picked me up and I sat on his shoulders. Another boy who was walking next to us was carrying a Vietnamese flag (it was the time of the Vietnam war) and he said to me 'Hey, could you carry the flag for me?' and I said OK. There was so much happening that I didn't notice all the photographers. The next day the photo was on the cover of magazines all over the world. When my grandfather saw it, he immediately ordered me to come to his house. He was furious – really really angry. He said 'That's it! You're a communist! I'm not going to leave you anything. Not a penny!' I walked out of the room and I never saw him again. Six months later he died, and I didn't get any money from him. Nothing.

1 50

Happy ending

Narrator Suddenly, a man ran across the road. He was wearing a dark coat so Hannah didn't see him at first. Quickly she put her foot on the brake. She stopped just in time. She got out of her car and shouted at the man.
Hannah Don't you usually look before you cross the road? I nearly hit you. I didn't see you until the last moment.
Jamie Sorry! Hey, Hannah it's me. It's Jamie.
Hannah Jamie! What are you doing here? I nearly killed you!
Jamie I was buying something. I was in a hurry and I crossed the road without looking.
Hannah Come on. Get in!
Narrator Hannah and Jamie drove to the coffee bar. They sat down in their usual seats and ordered two cups of coffee.

Waiter Here you are. Two cappuccinos.
Hannah / Jamie Thanks.
Hannah What an evening! I nearly killed you.
Jamie Well, you didn't kill me, so what's the problem?
Hannah But what were you doing in the high street? I thought you were here, in the café, waiting for me.
Jamie I went to the theatre to buy these tickets for the Scouting For Girls concert. I know you wanted to go. And it's on the 15th of October – next Saturday. Our anniversary.
Hannah Our anniversary?
Jamie Yes. Three months since we first met. We met on Saturday the 15th of July. Remember?
Hannah Gosh, Jamie. I can't believe you remember the exact day! What a romantic! It's lucky I didn't hit you in the street...

1 51

Sad ending
Narrator Suddenly, a man ran across the road. He was wearing a dark coat so Hannah didn't see him at first. Quickly she put her foot on the brake. Although Hannah tried to stop she couldn't. She hit the man. Hannah panicked. She drove away as fast as she could. When she arrived at the coffee bar Jamie wasn't there. She called him but his mobile phone was turned off. She waited for ten minutes and then she went home. Two hours later a car arrived at Hannah's house. A policewoman knocked at the door.
Policewoman Good evening, Madam. Are you Hannah Davis?
Hannah Yes, I am.
Policewoman I'd like to speak to you. Can I come in?
Narrator The policewoman came in and sat down on the sofa.
Policewoman Are you a friend of Jamie Dixon?
Hannah Yes,
Narrator said Hannah.
Policewoman Well, I'm afraid I have some bad news for you.
Hannah What? What's happened?
Policewoman Jamie had an accident this evening.
Hannah Oh no! What kind of accident?
Policewoman He was crossing the road and a car hit him.
Hannah When...When did this happen? And where?
Policewoman This evening at 5.25. He was crossing the road in the high street by the theatre.
Hannah Oh no! How is he?
Policewoman He's in hospital. He's got a bad injury to his head and two broken legs.
Hannah But is he going to be OK?
Policewoman We don't know. He's in intensive care.
Hannah Oh no. And the driver of the car?
Policewoman She didn't stop.
Hannah She?
Policewoman Yes, it was a woman in a white car. Somebody saw the number of the car. You have a white car outside don't you, Madam? Is your number plate XYZ 348S?
Hannah Yes...yes, it is.
Policewoman Can you tell me where you were at 5.25 this evening?

1 55

Olivia
Interviewer Excuse me, do you have a moment?
Olivia Yes, sure.
Interviewer Where are you going?
Olivia To Nicaragua.
Interviewer For a holiday?
Olivia No, I'm going to do voluntary work. I'm going to teach English to young children.
Interviewer Where exactly in Nicaragua are you going?
Olivia To a town called Estelí. It's about 150 kilometres from Managua.
Interviewer How long are you going to be there for?
Olivia I'm going to be in Estelí for six weeks and after that I'm going to travel round Nicaragua for a month.
Interviewer That sounds amazing.
Olivia Yes, I'm really looking forward to it.
Interviewer Are you feeling nervous at all?
Olivia A bit, because I don't speak much Spanish. But they're going to give us a 40-hour language course when we arrive, so I hope that's enough to start with.
Interviewer Well, good luck and have a great time.
Olivia Thanks. I'm sure it's going to be a fantastic experience.

Matthew
Interviewer Excuse me, do you have a moment?
Matthew Yeah, OK.
Interviewer Where are you going?
Matthew To Australia.
Interviewer That's a long flight. Are you going to stop on the way?
Matthew No, I'm going direct to Melbourne.
Interviewer Why Melbourne?
Matthew I'm going to work there. I'm a model and we're going to do a photo shoot for a magazine.
Interviewer That sounds exciting. What kind of clothes are you going to model?
Matthew Winter clothes, for next season. It's winter in Australia now so it's going to be quite cold. That's why we're going there.
Interviewer Of course, it's their winter. How cold do you think it's going to be?
Matthew I'm not quite sure. About eight or nine degrees during the day and colder at night, I suppose.
Interviewer Well, have a good trip, and I hope the photos are fabulous!
Matthew Thanks.

Lily
Interviewer Excuse me, do you have a moment?
Lily OK, sure.
Interviewer Where are you going?
Lily To Budapest.
Interviewer Why are you going there?
Lily I'm going to a conference.
Interviewer So it's a work trip.
Lily Yes. But I'm also going to see an old friend there. Actually, an old boyfriend. Someone I went out with a long time ago.
Interviewer When did you decide to meet up again?
Lily Well, I knew he was working at Budapest University, so when the conference came up about a month ago I got in touch with him on Facebook.
Interviewer Is he going to meet you at the airport?
Lily I don't think so! But who knows?
Interviewer How do you feel about it?
Lily Quite excited. It's going to be strange meeting again after all these years.
Interviewer Well, good luck. I'm sure you're going to have a great time. And enjoy the conference, too.
Lily Thanks very much.

1 62

Ben Hi. This is Ben West. Sorry I can't take your call. Please leave a message.
Lily Hi Ben. It's me, Lily. Hope you're OK. I've booked my flight and hotel. I'm coming on Sunday the 2nd of May – I couldn't get a flight on the first. I'm flying from Gatwick with Easyjet and I'm arriving at Budapest airport at 14.40. I'm going back on Saturday the 8th leaving at 16.35. I'm staying at a lovely old hotel, quite a famous one I think. It's called the Hotel Gellert or Jellert – I'm not sure how you pronounce it, but it's G-E-double L-E-R-T. I'm sure you know it. I'll call you on Sunday night when I get there. See you soon – I'm really looking forward to seeing you again.

2 2

Presenter Good evening, ladies and gentlemen and welcome to *What's the word?* And our first contestants tonight are Martin and Lola. Hello to you both. Are you nervous?
Lola Just a bit.
Presenter Well, just try and relax and play *What's the word?* with us. If you're watching the show for the first time, here's how we play the game. As you can see Martin has a TV screen in front of him and six words are going to appear on the screen. Martin has two minutes to describe the words to Lola so that she can guess what they are. But he can't use any part of the words on the screen. So, for example, if the word is taxi driver, he can't use the word taxi or driver or drive.
Presenter Martin, Lola, are you ready?

2 3

Presenter Martin, Lola, are you ready?
Martin/Lola Yes.
Presenter OK, Martin you have two minutes to describe your six words starting now!
Martin OK, word number 1. It's a person. It's somebody who works in a hospital.
Lola A doctor.
Martin No, no, no it's the person who helps the doctor and looks after the patients.
Lola Oh, a [*bleep*].
Martin That's right. Word number 2. It's a place. It's somewhere where people go when they want to buy things.
Lola A shop.
Martin Not exactly. It's bigger and you can buy all kinds of different things there, especially food.
Lola A [*bleep*]?
Martin Yes, well done. OK, word number 3. It's a thing. It's something which we use for everything nowadays. For the internet, for talking to people, for taking photos...It's a kind of gadget. Everyone has one.
Lola A [*bleep*]?
Martin That's it! Word number 4. It's an adjective. It's the opposite of dark.
Lola Light?
Martin It's like light, but you only use it to describe hair.
Lola [*bleep*]?
Martin Yes! Word number 5. It's an adjective again. Er...You use it to describe a person who's ... er, who's quick at learning things.
Lola Intelligent?
Martin No, but it's similar to intelligent. It's the opposite of stupid.
Lola [*bleep*]!
Martin Yes, brilliant. And word number six, the last one. OK. It's a verb. For example, you do this to the TV.
Lola Watch?
Martin No... It's what you do when you finish watching TV at night.
Lola Er...go to bed?
Martin No! Come on! You do it to the TV before you go to bed.
Lola Oh, [*bleep*]?
Martin Yes!

2 8

Jenny Well, I think that's everything. What do you think of the office?
Rob It's brilliant. And much bigger than our place in London.
Jenny Oh, here's Barbara. Rob, this is Barbara, the editor of the magazine.
Barbara It's good to finally meet you, Rob.
Rob It's great to be here.
Barbara Is this your first time in New York?
Rob No, I came here when I was eighteen. But only for a few days.
Barbara Well, I hope you get to know New York much better this time!
Jenny Barbara, I'm going to take Rob out for lunch. Would you like to come with us?
Barbara I'd love to, but unfortunately I have a meeting at one. So, I'll see you later. We're meeting at three, I think.
Jenny That's right.
Barbara Have a nice lunch.
Holly Hey, are you Rob Walker?

Rob Yes.
Holly Hi, I'm Holly. Holly Tyler.
Rob Hello, Holly.
Holly We're going to be working together.
Jenny Really?
Holly Didn't Barbara tell you? I'm going to be Rob's photographer!
Jenny Oh, well...We're just going for lunch.
Holly Cool! I can come with you. I mean, I had a sandwich earlier, so I don't need to eat. But Rob and I can talk. Is that OK?
Jenny Sure.
Holly So let's go.

2 11

Holly So tell me, Rob. What are you going to write about?
Rob Well, to start with, my first impressions of New York. You know, the nightlife, the music, things like that.
Holly Are you planning to do any interviews?
Rob I'd like to. Do you have any suggestions?
Holly Well, I know some great musicians.
Rob Musicians?
Holly You know, guys in bands. And I also have some contacts in the theatre and dance.
Rob That would be great.
Holly Maybe we could go to a show, and after you could talk to the actors.
Rob I really like that idea.
Waitress Can I bring you anything else?
Jenny Could we have the check, please?
Waitress Yes, ma'am. Here's your check.
Jenny Thanks. Excuse me. I think there's a mistake. We had two bottles of water, not three.
Waitress You're right. I'm really sorry. It's not my day today! I'll get you a new check.
Jenny Thank you.
Holly We're going to have a fun month, Rob.
Rob Yeah, I think it's going to be fantastic.
Jenny OK, time to go. You have your meeting with Barbara at three.
Rob Oh yeah, right.

2 22

Presenter Teenagers today have a bad reputation. People say that they are lazy and untidy and that they do very little to help their parents in the house. But there are some teenagers for whom this description is just not true at all.
It is estimated that there are more than 200,000 teenagers in the UK who have to look after a member of their family, their mother or father or brother or sister. In many cases these young helpers, or 'carers' as they are called, have to do between 25 and 50 hours work helping in their house, as well as doing their school work.

2 23

Presenter I'd like to welcome to the programme two of these teenagers, Alice and Daniel, who are 17 years old, and who both look after members of their family. Hello, Alice, hello Daniel.
Alice / Daniel Hi.
Presenter Who do you look after?
Alice I look after my mum. She has ME – it's an illness which means that she feels tired all the time and she can't walk very well. And I also look after my younger brother and sister. He's six and she's four.
Daniel I look after my mum too. She had a bad car accident seven years ago and she can't walk. I also look after my little sister.
Presenter You both do a lot of housework. What exactly do you do?
Alice On a normal day I get up early and I clean the house and I do the ironing. After school I sometimes take my mum to the shops in her wheelchair. In the evening my dad makes the dinner – I'm not very good at cooking! But I make sure my brother and sister eat their dinner and then I put them to bed.
Daniel My day's quite similar. I clean the house and iron but I also do the cooking and the shopping. My dad left home four years ago so we're on our own. I take my sister to school and make sure that my mum is OK. I need to give her massages every evening.
Presenter How do you feel about the way you live?
Alice I don't really mind looking after my mum. She's ill and she needs my help. But sometimes I feel a bit sad when I can't go out because there are things to do in the house. And I sometimes get angry with my school friends. They don't really understand the problems I have at home. All they think about are clothes, boys, and going out.
Daniel I enjoy what I do because I'm helping my mum and I'm helping my sister at the same time. Of course it's true that I can't go out much, because I need to spend most of my time at home. I sometimes go out with my friends but I don't like leaving my mum on her own. I always make sure that I have my mobile. If my mum needs anything, she calls me and I go back home. It's not a problem for me. It's just part of my life.
Presenter You're both doing a great job, thanks very much for coming on the programme.

2 26

1 **Interviewer** Have you ever bought something that you've never worn?
A Yes – hasn't everyone? I remember some trousers I bought that I never wore.
Interviewer What was the problem with them?
A They were very tight, black leather trousers that I bought from a second-hand shop near Portobello Road, when I was about 20 years old. I remember when I was in the changing room I thought they looked fantastic. I thought I looked like Jim Morrison from the Doors. But when I got home, in the cold light of day, I realised that I looked more like one of the women from Abba! That's why I never wore them.
2 **Interviewer** Have you ever bought something that you've never worn?
A Yes, a karate suit. I decided that I wanted to do karate, and I signed up for a course and bought the suit and the orange belt but then I changed my mind and decided not to do the course.
Interviewer Why not?
A I was worried that someone would knock my teeth out.
Interviewer Do you still have the suit?
A No, I sold it on eBay.
3 **Interviewer** Have you ever bought something that you've never worn?
A Sadly it happens to me quite often, because I hate clothes shopping, and I never try things on. For example, I have a shirt in my wardrobe now that I've never worn.
Interviewer Why not?
A Well, I bought it in a hurry a few months ago and then I put it away in my wardrobe. A few weeks later I took it out and looked at it and I thought 'Why did I buy this?' It's horrible – pink and purple stripes. And of course I didn't have the receipt, so I couldn't take it back.
4 **Interviewer** Have you ever bought something that you've never worn?
A Lots of things, I'm afraid. The last one was a brown leather coat.
Interviewer What was wrong with it?
A Well, I bought it online, from a website that has cheap offers, but when it arrived it looked completely different from what it looked like on screen and I decided I didn't like it. So it's in my wardrobe. I'm sure I'm never going to wear it, but perhaps I'll give it to someone as a present.

2 32

Presenter Last Friday Sven, a lawyer from Stockholm, was looking forward to a relaxing two days in the mountains. He and his wife had a reservation in a luxury hotel at a skiing resort, so they could spend the weekend skiing. But the weekend didn't work out exactly as they were expecting. Sven worked until late on Friday evening. His office was on the 12th floor. When he finished, at 8 o'clock, he locked his office and got into the lift ... and he didn't get out again until Monday morning!
Sven I pressed the button for the ground floor and the lift started going down but then it stopped. I pressed the button again but nothing happened. I pressed the alarm and shouted but nobody heard me. Most people had already gone home. I tried to phone my wife but my mobile didn't work in the lift. I couldn't do anything. I just sat on the floor and hoped maybe somebody would realize what had happened. But on Saturday and Sunday I knew nobody would be there. I slept most of the time to forget how hungry I was.
Presenter Meanwhile Sven's wife, Silvia, was waiting for her husband to come home.
Silvia I was very worried when he didn't come home on Friday evening and I couldn't understand why his mobile wasn't working. I phoned the police and they looked for him but they couldn't find him anywhere. I thought maybe he was with another woman.
Presenter So Sven was in the lift the whole weekend from Friday evening until Monday morning. At eight o'clock, when the office workers arrived, they phoned the emergency number and somebody came and repaired the lift.
Sven I was very happy to get out. I hadn't eaten since Friday afternoon and I was very hungry. It's lucky that I am not claustrophobic because the lift was very small. The first thing I did was to phone my wife to say that I was OK.
Presenter Sven will soon be the fittest man in his office – from now on he's going to take the stairs every day – even though it's 12 floors.

2 42

Interviewer Today we talk to Laurel Reece, who's writing a book about how to live more slowly. She's going to give us five useful tips.
Laurel My first tip is something which is very simple to say, but more difficult to do in practice. Whatever you're doing, just try to slow down and enjoy it. If you're walking somewhere, try to walk more slowly; if you are driving, make yourself drive more slowly. It doesn't matter what you are doing, cooking, having a shower, exercising in the gym, just slow down and really enjoy the moment. We all try to do too many things that we just don't have time for. So my second tip is make a list of the three things which are most important for you, your priorities in life. Then when you've made your list make sure that you spend time doing those things. Imagine for example that your three things are your family, reading, and playing sports. Then make sure that you spend enough time with your family, that you have space in your life for reading, and that you have time to do sports. And forget about trying to do other things that you haven't got time for.
Tip number three is don't try to do two things at the same time. The worst thing you can do is to multitask. So for example, don't read your emails while you are talking to a friend on the phone. If you do that, you aren't really focusing on your emails or your friend and you aren't going to feel very relaxed either.
Tip number four is very simple: once a day, every day, sit down and do nothing for half an hour. For example, go to a café and sit outside, or go to a park and sit on a bench. Turn off your phone so that nobody can contact you, and then just sit and watch the world go by. This will really help you to slow down.
OK. My fifth and final tip. One of the most relaxing things you can do is to be near water or even better, to be on water. So if you live near a lake or river, go and sit by the river, or go boating. If you live near the sea, go and sit on the beach.

Relax and listen to the sound of the wind and the water. You will feel your body and mind slowing down as the minutes go past.

2 45

First I did the photo test. I was near Charing Cross station. I stopped a man who was walking quite slowly down the road and I said, 'Excuse me, could you take my photo?' The man said, 'No, no, no time for that,' and just continued walking. Then I asked a businessman in a grey suit who was walking towards the station. He took one photo, but when I asked him to take another one he walked away quickly.

Next, it was the shopping test. I went to a tourist shop in Oxford Street and I bought a key ring and a red bus. The red bus was very expensive. The total price was forty pounds. I gave the man a hundred pounds. He gave me sixty pounds back.

Finally, it was time for the accident test. For this test I went down into the Tube – the London Underground. As I went down the stairs I fell over and sat on the floor. A man immediately stopped and looked down at me. I thought he was going to help me but he didn't – he just said 'Why don't you look where you're going?'

2 51

Presenter Next in our list of things which you thought were bad for you is chocolate. Jane, our food expert, is going to tell us why actually it can be good for us.

Jane Well, there have been a lot of studies recently about chocolate. Remember, chocolate is something that we've been eating for hundreds of years, it's not a modern invention. And the studies show that chocolate, like red wine, contains antioxidants. In fact chocolate has more antioxidants than wine. These antioxidants can protect us against illnesses like heart disease.

Presenter Really?

Jane Yes, but, and this is very important, all the good antioxidants are only in dark chocolate. So don't eat milk chocolate or white chocolate – they aren't healthy at all. And of course you also need to remember that although dark chocolate is good for you, it contains quite a lot of calories, so if you're worried about your weight, don't eat too much. One or two pieces a day is enough.

Presenter Great news for me because I love chocolate! And now to Tony, our TV journalist. Tony, newspaper articles are always telling us about studies which say that we watch too much TV, that we spend too much time sitting in front of the TV and that as a result we don't do enough exercise. They also say that watching TV makes us stupid. Is this all true Tony?

Tony Well, it's almost certainly true that we watch too much television, but it probably isn't true that watching TV makes us stupid. I've just finished reading a book by a science writer, Steven Johnson, called *Everything bad is good for you*. One thing he says in his book is that modern TV series like *The Sopranos* or *House* or *Mad Men* are more intellectually stimulating than TV series were 20 years ago. He says that these shows are complicated and very clever and that they help to make us more intelligent.

Presenter Well, I can believe that, but what about reality shows that are so popular on TV. I can't believe that these are good for us.

Tony Well, Steven Johnson says that we can even learn something from reality shows – he says this kind of programme can teach us about group psychology, about how people behave when they're in a group.

Presenter Well, thank you, Tony and Jane. So now you know what to do this evening. You can sit down in front of the TV with a box of dark chocolates…

2 55

Holly Hey, Rob, come on. Keep up.

Rob Sorry. I'm a bit tired this morning.

Holly You aren't exactly in good shape, are you?

Rob I know, I know. I think I'm eating too much.

Holly Then eat less!

Rob It isn't easy. I eat out all the time. And the portions in American restaurants are enormous.

Holly You don't do enough exercise.

Rob I walk a lot.

Holly Walking isn't enough, Rob. Do you do anything to keep fit?

Rob I cycle when I'm in London…

Holly So why don't you get a bike here?

Rob I'm only here for another three weeks. Anyway, my hotel's near the office. I don't need a bike.

Holly You know, Jennifer goes running all the time. Before and after work. But I just think that running is just so boring. I mean, where's the fun?

Rob Yeah, I'm not very keen on running.

Holly So why don't you play basketball with me and my friends?

Rob OK. That's a great idea! But I don't have any trainers.

Holly Trainers? Sneakers! You can buy some.

Rob Is there a sports shop near here?

Holly Sure, there's one across the street.

2 59

Rob Hi Jenny.

Jenny Oh, hi.

Rob Have you had a good day?

Jenny Oh, you know. Meetings! What about you?

Rob It was great. I went to Brooklyn and met some really interesting people.

Jenny And you had time to go shopping, too.

Rob What? Oh yeah. I've just bought these.

Jenny What are they?

Rob A pair of trainers – er, sneakers.

Jenny Nice. Why did you buy sneakers?

Rob I think I need to get a bit fitter.

Jenny Oh, I'm impressed. You know, I go running every morning in Central Park.

Rob Do you?

Jenny It's so beautiful early in the morning. Why don't you come with me?

Rob Er… sure. Why not?

Jenny Great! I'll come by your hotel tomorrow morning.

Rob OK. What time?

Jenny Six forty-five?

Rob Six…?

Jenny Forty-five.

Rob Can we make it a bit later? Say, seven forty-five?

Jenny That's too late, Rob. Let's make it seven fifteen.

Rob OK.

Jenny Excellent. See you later.

Rob Great.

Holly Basketball and running, Rob. You must have a lot of energy.

Rob Er… yeah.

3 8

Presenter Today's topic is 'positive thinking'. We all know that people who are positive enjoy life more than people who are negative and pessimistic. But scientific studies show that positive people are also healthier. They get better more quickly when they are ill, and they live longer. A recent study has shown that people who are optimistic and think positively live, on average, nine years longer than pessimistic people. So, let's hear what you the listeners think. Do you have any ideas to help us be more positive in our lives?

3 9

Presenter Our first caller this evening is Andy. Hi Andy. What's your tip for being positive?

Andy Hello. Well, I think it's very important to live in the present and not in the past. Don't think about mistakes you made in the past. You can't change the past. The important thing is to think about how you can do things better now and in the future.

Presenter Thank you, Andy. And now we have another caller. What's your name, please?

Julie Hi, My name's Julie. My tip is think positive thoughts, not negative ones. We all have negative thoughts sometimes, but when we start having them we need to stop and try to change them into positive ones. Like, if you have an exam tomorrow and you start thinking 'I'm sure I'll fail', then you'll fail the exam. So you need to change that negative thought to a positive thought. Just think to yourself 'I'll pass'. I do this and it usually works.

Presenter Thank you, Julie. And our next caller is Martin. Hi Martin.

Martin Hi. My tip is don't spend a lot of time reading the papers or watching the news on TV. It's always bad news and it just makes you feel depressed. Read a book or listen to your favourite music instead.

Presenter Thanks, Martin. And our next caller is Miriam. Miriam?

Miriam Hi.

Presenter Hi Miriam. What's your tip?

Miriam My tip is every week make a list of all the good things that happened to you. Then keep the list with you, in your bag or in a pocket, and if you're feeling a bit sad or depressed, just take it out and read it. It'll make you feel better.

Presenter Thanks, Miriam. And our last call is from Michael. Hi Michael. We're listening.

Michael Hi. My tip is to try to use positive language when you speak to other people. You know, if your friend has a problem, don't say 'I'm sorry' or 'Oh, poor you', say something positive like 'Don't worry! Everything will be OK'. That way you'll make the other person think more positively about their problem.

Presenter Thank you, Michael. Well, that's all we've got time for. A big thank you to all our callers. Until next week then, goodbye.

3 13

Presenter Earlier this year, ten years after Steve sent the letter, some builders were renovating the living room in Carmen's mother's house. When they took out the fireplace they found Steve's letter, and gave it to Carmen's sister, and she sent the letter to Carmen in Paris. Carmen was now 42, and she was still single.

Carmen When I got the letter I didn't call Steve straight away because I was so nervous. I kept picking up the phone and putting it down again. I nearly didn't phone him at all. But I knew that I had to make the call.

Presenter Carmen finally made the call and Steve answered the phone. He was also now 42 and also single.

Steve I couldn't believe it when she phoned. I've just moved house, but luckily I kept my old phone number.

Presenter Steve and Carmen arranged to meet in Paris a few days later.

Steve When we met it was like a film. We ran across the airport and into each other's arms. Within 30 seconds of seeing each other again we were kissing. We fell in love all over again.

Presenter Last week the couple got married, 17 years after they first met.

Carmen I never got married in all those years, but now I have married the man I always loved.

Presenter So Steve and Carmen are together at last. But will they keep their promises?

3 17

Patient So what does it mean, doctor?

Dr Well, first the party. A party is a group of people. This means that you're going to meet a lot of people. I think you're going to be very busy.

Patient At work?

Dr Yes, at work… you work in an office, I think?

Patient Yes, that's right.
Dr I think the party means you are going to have a lot of meetings.
Patient What about the champagne?
Dr Let me look at my notes again. Ah yes, you were drinking champagne. Champagne means a celebration. It's a symbol of success. So we have a meeting or meetings and then a celebration. Maybe in the future you'll have a meeting with your boss, about a possible promotion?
Patient Well, it's possible. I hope so. What about the garden and the flowers? Do they mean anything?
Dr Yes, yes. Flowers are a positive symbol. So the flowers mean that you are feeling positive about the future. So perhaps you already knew about this possible promotion?
Patient No, I didn't. But it's true, I am very happy at work and I feel very positive about my future. That's not where my problems are. My problems are with my love life. Does my dream tell you anything about that?
Dr Mm, yes it does. You're single, aren't you?
Patient Yes, well, divorced.
Dr Because the violin music tells me you want some romance in your life – you're looking for a partner perhaps?
Patient Yes, yes, I am. In fact I met a woman last month – I really like her… I think I'm in love with her. I'm meeting her tonight.
Dr In your dream you saw an owl in a tree.
Patient Yes, an owl... a big owl.
Dr The owl represents an older person. I think you'll need to ask this older person for help. Maybe this 'older person' is me? Maybe you need my help?
Patient Well, yes, what I really want to know is does this person, this woman… love me?

3 18

Patient Well, yes, what I really want to know is does this person, this woman… love me?
Dr You remember the end of your dream? You were feeling cold?
Patient Yes, my feet were very cold.
Dr Well, I think perhaps you already know the answer to your question.
Patient You mean she doesn't love me.
Dr No, I don't think so. I think you will need to find another woman. I'm sorry. Perhaps you can find someone on the internet? I have heard of a very good website…

1

1A word order in questions

questions with *do / does / did* in present simple and past simple

question word	auxiliary	subject	infinitive (= verb) 1 3
	Do	you	**live** with your parents?
	Did	you	**have** a holiday last year?
Where	**does**	your sister	**work**?
When	**did**	you	**start** studying English?
What	**did**	they	**talk** about?

- Use **ASI** (**A**uxiliary, **S**ubject, **I**nfinitive) and **QUASI** (**Qu**estion word, **A**uxiliary, **S**ubject, **I**nfinitive) to remember word order in questions.

questions with *be*

question word	*be*	subject	adjective, noun, etc. 1 4
	Are	you	hungry?
	Is	there	a bank near here?
What	**was**	that	noise?
Where	**are**	you	from?
	were	you	born?

- Make questions with the verb *be* by inverting the verb and the subject.
  She is a teacher. ***Is she*** a teacher?

1B present simple

	I / you / we / they	*he / she / it* 1 12
+	I usually **work** at home.	Holly **knows** me very well.
-	They **don't live** near here.	It **doesn't** often **rain** here.
?	**Do** you **speak** French?	**Does** Alice **like** jazz?
✓ ✗	Yes, I **do**. / No, I **don't**.	Yes, she **does**. / No, she **doesn't**.

- Use the present simple for things you do every day / week / year, or for things which are generally true or always happen.
- Use *don't/doesn't* to make negative sentences, and *do/does* to make questions.

spelling rules for the 3rd person -s (*he, she, it*)

infinitive	3rd person	spelling
work	works	add -s
study	studies	consonant + *y* > *ies*
finish	finishes	add -*es* after *ch, ce, ge, sh,*
go / do	goes / does	add -*es*
have	has	change to -s

adverbs and expressions of frequency

1 We **often** go out on Friday night. 1 13
She doesn't **usually** study at weekends.
I'm **never** ill.
He's **always** late for work.
2 She gets up early **every day**.
We have English classes **twice a week**.

1 We often use the present simple with adverbs of frequency (*always, usually, often, sometimes, hardly ever, never*).
- Adverbs of frequency go before the main verb.
- Adverbs of frequency go after *be*.
  *She's **never** ill.* **NOT** ~~*She's ill never.*~~
- Remember to use a + verb with *never*.
  It never rains. **NOT** ~~*It doesn't never rain.*~~

2 Expressions of frequency (*every day, once a week,* etc.) usually go at the end of a sentence.

1C present continuous: *be* + verb + *-ing*

1 **A** What **are you doing**? 1 22
B **I'm sending** a message to Sarah.
2 My brother **is doing** a two-month course in the UK.
3 In this picture the woman **is standing** near the window.

- Use the present continuous:
  1 for things that are happening now, at this moment.
  2 for temporary things that are happening now, this week, etc.
  3 to describe a picture.

	I	you / we / they		he / she / it	
+ -	**I'm working** **I'm not working**	You We They	**'re working** **aren't working**	He She It	**'s working** **isn't working**

? ✓ ✗		
	Are you **working**?	**Yes**, I **am**. / **No**, I'm **not**.
	Is he **working**?	**Yes**, he **is**. / **No**, he **isn't**.

spelling rules for the *-ing* form

infinitive	*-ing* form	spelling
cook study	cook**ing** study**ing**	add *-ing*
live	liv**ing**	cut the final *e* and add *-ing*
run	runn**ing**	double the final consonant and add *-ing*

present simple or present continuous?

A What **do you do**? **B** **I work** for Microsoft. 1 23
A What **are you doing**? **B** **I'm checking** my emails.

- Use the present simple for things that are generally true or always happen.
- Use the present continuous for an action happening now or at this moment.
- We normally use verbs which describe states or feelings (non-action verbs), e.g. *want, need, like,* in the present simple, not continuous.

1A

a Put the word or phrase in the right place in the question.

How *old* are you? (old)

1 Where do you from? (come)
2 Where the train station? (is)
3 How often you read magazines? (do)
4 Where your friends from? (are)
5 Why you write to me? (didn't)
6 Do you often to the cinema? (go)
7 What this word mean? (does)
8 What time did arrive? (your friends)
9 Does finish at 8.00? (the class)
10 Where were born? (you)

b Put the words in the right order to make questions.

you live where do ? *Where do you live?*

1 you a do have car ?
2 older is brother your you than ?
3 often he how to write does you ?
4 this time start does what class ?
5 Brazil from is friend your ?
6 languages how you many do speak ?
7 she born where was ?
8 last go where you summer did ?
9 father doctor your is a ?
10 come bus to you by school did ?

◄ p.5

1B

a Write sentences and questions with the present simple.

he / usually get up late [+] *He usually gets up late.*

1 Anna / like music [?]
2 my sister / have a lot of hobbies [+]
3 I / get on very well with my parents [-]
4 my brother / study at university [+]
5 my neighbours / have any children [-]
6 when / the film start [?]
7 he / go out twice a week [+]
8 we / often talk about politics [-]
9 how often / you email your brother [?]
10 I / go on Facebook very often [-]

b Put the words in the right order.

go cinema we often the to *We often go to the cinema.*

1 always before go I bed 11.00 to
2 ever her Kate sees family hardly
3 Saturdays never shopping on go we
4 a to I dentist's year go twice the
5 in they breakfast the sometimes garden have
6 usually morning the we the listen in radio to
7 in day park every Alan the runs
8 after drink I coffee 4.00 never
9 often John to go doesn't cinema the
10 visit I once my month a mum

◄ p.7

1C

a Write sentences with the present continuous.

It / rain [-] *It isn't raining.*

1 John / wear a shirt today! [+]
2 It's hot. Why / wear a coat [?]
3 Anna / sit next to Jane today [-]
4 Hey! You / stand on my foot! [+]
5 what book / you read [?]
6 we / think of you at the moment [+]
7 she / wear make-up [?]
8 they / make a big mistake [+]
9 your mother / shop in town [?]
10 she / live with her parents at the moment [-]

b Complete the sentences with the present simple or present continuous.

The girl in the painting <u>*is playing*</u> the guitar. (play)

1 My dog's not dangerous. He ________. (not bite)
2 Why ________ you ________ sunglasses? It ________! (wear, rain)
3 You can turn off the radio. I ________ to it. (not listen)
4 I ________ to go to the bank. I ________ any money. (need, not have)
5 Be careful! The baby ________ that pen in her mouth! (put)
6 **A** ________ you usually ________ at weekends? (cook)
B No, we normally ________ out. (eat)
7 **A** What ________ you ________ here? (do)
B I ________ for Emma. She's late, as usual. (wait)
8 I usually drink tea, but I ________ a coffee today. (want)
9 My sister ________ from 9.00 to 5.00. She's a secretary. (work)
10 We ________ in Paris, but we ________ in Nice at the moment. (live, stay)

◄ p.8

2

2A past simple: regular and irregular verbs

	regular	**irregular** 1 36
+ - ?	I **stayed** with friends. I **didn't stay** in a hotel. **Did** you **stay** for the weekend?	We **went** to Brazil on holiday. We **didn't go** to São Paolo. **Did** you **go** to Rio?
✓ ✗	Yes, I **did**.	No, we **didn't**.
Wh ?	Where **did** you **stay**?	Why **did** you **go** there?

- Use the past simple to talk about finished actions in the past.
- The form of the past simple is the same for all persons.
- To make the past simple + of regular verbs add *-ed*. See the spelling rules in the chart.
- Many common verbs are irregular in the + past simple, e.g. *go* > ***went***, *see* > ***saw***. See **Irregular verbs** *p.164*.

- Use the infinitive after *didn't* for negatives and *Did...?* for questions.
- Use **ASI** and **QUASI** to remember word order in questions.

spelling rules for regular verbs		
infinitive	**past**	**spelling**
work stay	work**ed** stay**ed**	add *-ed*
like	like**d**	add *-d* if verb finishes in *e*
study	stud**ied**	*y* > *ied* after a consonant
stop	stop**ped**	if verb finishes in consonant–vowel–consonant, double the final consonant

2B past continuous: *was / were* + verb + *-ing*

At 8.45 last Saturday I **was working** in my office. 1 39
I **wasn't doing** anything important.
My friends **were having** breakfast. They **weren't working**.
A **Was** it **raining** when you got up? **B** No, **it wasn't**.
A What **were** you **doing** at 11 o'clock last night? **B** **I was watching** TV.

+	I / He / She / It	**was working**	You / We / They	**were working**
-	I / He / She / It	**wasn't working**	You / We / They	**weren't working**

? ✓ ✗	**Was** he **working**?	**Yes**, he **was**. / **No**, he **wasn't**.
	Were they **working**?	**Yes**, they **were**. / **No**, they **weren't**.

- Use the past continuous to describe an action in progress at a specific moment in the past.
- We often use the past continuous to describe the situation at the beginning of a story or narrative.

past simple or past continuous?

I **was working** in my office when the boss **walked in**. 1 40
I **was having** lunch when my sister **arrived**.

- Use the past simple for a completed action in the past.
- Use the past continuous for an action in progress before or at the time of the past simple action.

2C time sequencers

On our first date we went to the cinema. **After that** we started meeting every day. 1 46
On Thursday I had an argument with my boss. **Next day** I decided to look for a new job.
We sat down to eat. **Two minutes later** the phone rang.
When I came out of the club he was waiting for me.
The accident happened **when** I was crossing the road.

- We use time sequencers to say when or in what order things happen.
- We use *when* as a time sequencer and also to join two actions.
  I ***was watching*** TV ***when*** the phone ***rang***. (two verbs joined by *when*)

then, after that
The most common way of linking consecutive actions is with *then* or *after that*, but **NOT** with *after*, e.g. *I got up and got dressed.* ***Then / After that*** *I made a cup of coffee.* **NOT** ~~*After I made a cup of coffee.*~~

connectors: *because, so, but, although*

because and *so*

She was driving fast **because** she was in a hurry. (reason) 1 47
She was in a hurry, **so** she was driving fast. (result)

- Use *because* to express a reason.
- Use *so* to express a result.

but and *although*

She tried to stop the car, **but** she hit the man. 1 48
Although she tried to stop the car, she hit the man.
She was very tired, **but** she couldn't sleep.
She couldn't sleep, **although** she was very tired.

- Use *but* and *although* to show a contrast.
- *Although* can go at the beginning or in the middle of a sentence.

2A

a Put the verbs in brackets in the past simple.

Two summers ago we *had* (have) a holiday in Scotland. We [1]________ (drive) there from London, but our car [2]________ (break) down on the motorway and we [3]________ (spend) the first night in Birmingham. When we [4]________ (get) to Edinburgh we [5]________ (not can) find a good hotel – they [6]________ (be) all full. We [7]________ (not know) what to do, but in the end we [8]________ (find) a Bed and Breakfast and we [9]________ (stay) there for the week. We [10]________ (see) the castle, [11]________ (go) to the Arts Festival, and we [12]________ (buy) a lot of souvenirs. We [13]________ (want) to go to Loch Ness, but we [14]________ (not have) much time and it [15]________ (be) quite far away. The weather [16]________ (not be) very good, and it [17]________ (start) raining the day we [18]________ (leave).

b Complete the questions in the past simple.

Where did you go on holiday last year?
We went to Vancouver.

1 ________________________ a good time?
Yes, we had a great time.

2 ________________________ with?
I went with my family.

3 ________________________?
We stayed in a hotel.

4 ________ the plane ticket ________?
It cost £500.

5 ________________________ the weather like?
It was hot and sunny.

6 ________________________ at night?
We went to bars and restaurants. ◄ p.13

2B

a Complete the sentences with a verb in the past continuous.

I *was eating* dinner, so I didn't answer the phone. (eat)

1 I took this photo when my wife ________ in the garden. (work)
2 He met his wife when he ________ in Japan. (live)
3 They ________ for us when we arrived. (not wait)
4 ________ she ________ a coat when she went out? (wear)
5 The sun ________ when I left for work. (shine)
6 What ________ you ________ at 7.30 last night? (do)
7 I ________ when you gave the instructions. (not listen)
8 We ________ TV when you phoned. (not watch)

b Put the verbs into the past simple or past continuous.

She *arrived* when we *were having* dinner. (arrive, have)

1 I ________ my arm when I ________ football. (break, play)
2 ________ you ________ fast when the police ________ you? (drive, stop)
3 It ________ when we ________ the pub. (snow, leave)
4 I ________ the match because I ________. (not see, work)
5 When you ________ me, I ________ to my boss. (call, talk)
6 We ________ in Cambridge when we ________. (study, meet)
7 ________ they ________ in Rome when they ________ their first baby? (live, have)

◄ p.14

2C

a Put the sentences in the right order.

a ☐ He told me he was a policeman and that they were looking for a thief.
b ☐ Then another man tried to do the same.
c [1] One day in 2011 I was standing in the queue for a bus.
d ☐ Next day I read the story in a newspaper.
e ☐ When the second man went in front of me, I told him to go and stand in the queue.
f ☐ A few seconds later, the first policeman got off the bus with a man.
g ☐ Suddenly a man ran in front of me and got on the bus.
h ☐ After that, a police car came and took the men away.

b Complete the sentences with *so*, *because*, *but*, or *although*.

We couldn't find a taxi, *so* we walked home.

1 ________ it was very cold, she wasn't wearing a coat.
2 I woke up in the night ________ there was a noise.
3 I called him, ________ his mobile was turned off.
4 ________ she's very nice, she doesn't have many friends.
5 There was nothing on TV, ________ I went to bed.
6 All the cafés were full ________ it was a public holiday.
7 She wanted to be a doctor, ________ she failed her exams.
8 The garden looked very beautiful, ________ I took a photograph.
9 ________ the team played well, they didn't win.

◄ p.16

3

3A *be going to*

1 I'm **going to** work for an NGO. 1 57
He's **going to** meet me at the airport.
2 I'm sure England **are going to lose** tomorrow.
It's **going to** rain tonight.

	I	you / we / they		he / she / it		
+	**I'm going to**	You We They	**'re going to**	He She It	**'s going to**	work for an NGO.
−	**I'm not going to**	You We They	**aren't going to**	He She It	**isn't going to**	work for an NGO.

?	✓ ✗
Are you **going to** work for an NGO? **Is** he **going to** work for an NGO?	**Yes**, I **am**. / **No**, I'm **not**. Yes, he **is**. / **No**, he **isn't**.

1 Use *be going to* + infinitive to talk about future plans or intentions.
2 We use *be going to* + infinitive to make a prediction when we know or can see that something is going to happen.
It's winter there so it's ***going to be*** *cold.*
Look at that car! It's ***going to crash****.*

3B present continuous (future arrangements)

+ I'm **seeing** a friend tonight. 1 64
She's **arriving** at lunchtime.
− She **isn't leaving** until Friday.
They **aren't coming** to the party.
? What **are** you **doing** this evening?
Is she **meeting** us at the restaurant?

- We often use the present continuous with a future meaning, especially for future arrangements, i.e. for plans we have made at a fixed time or place in the future. Don't use the present simple for this. **NOT** ~~*I see some friends tonight.*~~

be going to **or present continuous?**
We can often use either with no difference in meaning, e.g. ***I'm going to see*** *Anna on Tuesday.* **OR** ***I'm seeing*** *Anna on Tuesday.*
It's very common to use the present continuous with the expressions *tonight, tomorrow, this weekend*, etc. and with verbs describing travel arrangements, e.g. *go, come, leave, arrive.*
I'm leaving *on Monday* is more common than ***I'm going to leave*** *on Monday.*

3C defining relative clauses with *who, which, where*

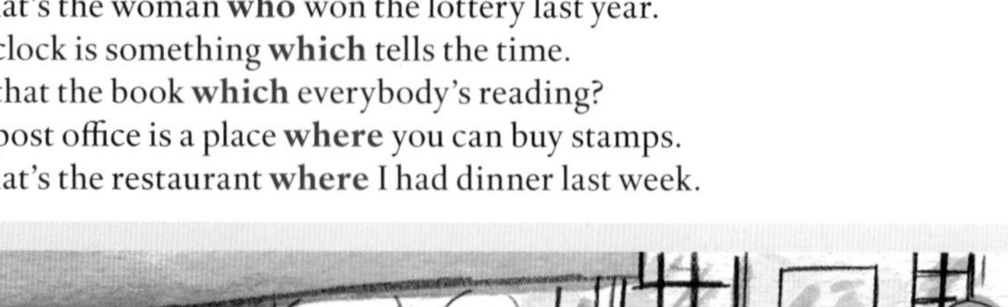
A cook is a person **who** makes food. 2 5
That's the woman **who** won the lottery last year.
A clock is something **which** tells the time.
Is that the book **which** everybody's reading?
A post office is a place **where** you can buy stamps.
That's the restaurant **where** I had dinner last week.

- Use defining relative clauses to explain what a person, thing or place is or does.
- Use *who* for a person, *which* for a thing and *where* for a place.

that
You can use *that* instead of *who* or *which*.
She's the girl ***who*** */* ***that*** *works with my brother.*
It's a thing ***which*** */* ***that*** *connects two computers.*

3A

a Complete with *going to* + a verb.

be cook do get not go learn not listen ~~see~~ stay

What film *are* you *going to see* tonight?

1 __________ your sister __________ Chinese?

2 You __________ in class 3 next year.

3 We __________ camping next summer. We __________ in a hotel.

4 We __________ a taxi to the airport.

5 I __________ a wonderful meal tonight.

6 You can talk, but I __________ to you.

7 What __________ you __________ when you leave school?

b Look at the pictures. Make sentences with *going to* + a verb.

be (x2) love ~~rain~~

It'*s going to rain*.

2 Not that one. It __________ too expensive.

1 We __________ late for work!

3 You __________ this book!

◀ p.21

3B

a Read the sentences. Write **N** for now, **F** for future.

[*F*] I'm meeting Joe at two o'clock.

1 [ ] I'm living in a flat with two Swedish boys.

2 [ ] We're coming back on Monday.

3 [ ] She's moving to Canada soon.

4 [ ] I'm waiting for the postman.

5 [ ] I'm reading a really good book about science.

6 [ ] We're meeting Sally and James for lunch on Sunday.

7 [ ] Karl is arriving at 6 o'clock.

8 [ ] I'm studying for my maths exam.

b Complete the dialogue between two flatmates.

A What *are you doing* (do)?

B I [1] __________ (pack) my suitcase.

A Why?

B Because I [2] __________ (fly) to Vienna at 8 o'clock tonight.

A Oh, I didn't know. Why [3] __________ (go) to Vienna?

B I [4] __________ (see) the boss of *VTech Solutions* tomorrow.

A Why [5] __________ (meet) him?

B I [6] __________ (work) on a project for him at the moment and I need to discuss it with him.

A Oh, well have a good trip!

◀ p.23

3C

a Complete the definitions with *who*, *which*, or *where*.

A postman is the person *who* brings you your letters.

1 An octopus is an animal __________ lives in the sea and has eight legs.

2 A lawnmower is a machine __________ cuts the grass.

3 A waiter is the person __________ serves you in a café.

4 A changing room is a room __________ people try on clothes.

5 A porter is the person __________ helps you with your luggage.

6 Garlic is a kind of food __________ keeps vampires away.

7 A garage is a place __________ people fix cars.

b Write sentences with *who*, *which*, or *where*.

She / the woman / catch the same bus as me
She's the woman who catches the same bus as me.

1 That / the dog / always barks at night

2 That / the shop / I bought my wedding dress

3 That / the actor / was in *Glee*

4 They / the children / live next door to me

5 This / the restaurant / they make great pizza

6 That / the switch / controls the air conditioning

7 He / the teacher / teaches my sister

8 That / the room / we have our meetings

9 This / the light / is broken

◀ p.24

4

4A present perfect

I've **finished** my homework. 2 16
She's **cleaned** the kitchen.
He **hasn't done** the washing up.
A **Has she turned off** her phone? B No, **she hasn't**.

- We often use the present perfect to talk about the recent past, not saying exactly when things happened.
- We often use the present perfect to give news.
  *Mary's **had** her baby! A parcel **has arrived** for you.*

full form	contraction	negative	past participle
I **have** You **have** He / She / It **has** We **have** They **have**	I**'ve** You**'ve** He / She / It**'s** We**'ve** They**'ve**	I **haven't** You **haven't** He / She / It **hasn't** We **haven't** They **haven't**	**finished** the exercise.
Have you **finished** the exercise? Yes, I **have**. / No, I **haven't**. **Has** he **done** the homework? Yes, he **has**. / No, he **hasn't**.			

- For regular verbs the past participle is the same as the past simple (+ *-ed*). For irregular verbs the past participle is sometimes the same as the past simple (e.g. *buy, bought, bought*) and sometimes different (e.g. *do, did, done*). See **Irregular verbs** *p.164*.

yet, just, already

1 A Have you done your homework **yet**? 2 17
  B No, not **yet**. I haven't finished **yet**.
2 My sister's **just** started a new job.
3 A Do you want to see this film?
  B No, I've **already** seen it three times.

- We often use *yet, just* and *already* with the present perfect.
  1 Use *yet* in [?] and [-] sentences to ask if something has happened or to say if it hasn't happened. Put *yet* at the end of the sentence.
  2 Use *just* in [+] sentences to say that something happened very recently. Put *just* before the main verb.
  3 Use *already* in [+] sentences to say that something happened before now or earlier than expected. Put *already* before the main verb.

4B present perfect or past simple? (1)

Have you ever been to a fancy dress party? 2 24
She's seen that film twice.
I've never met Nina's husband.

- We often use the present perfect to talk about past experiences in our lives when we don't specify a time.

been and gone
Compare the present perfect of *be* and *go*.
*Mike has **been** to Paris.* = He went to Paris and came back.
*Mike has **gone** to Paris.* = He's in Paris now.

present perfect or past simple?

A **Have you ever been** to Mexico? 2 25
B Yes, I **have**.
A When **did you go** there?
B I **went** last year.

A **Have you seen** his new film?
B Yes, I **have**.
A What **did you think** of it?
B I **loved** it.

- Conversations often begin in the present perfect (with a general question) and then change to the past simple to ask for or give specific details, e.g. *when, what, where, who with*, etc.

4C *something, anything, nothing*, etc.

people 2 34

[+] **Somebody** / **Someone** has taken my pen!
[-] I didn't speak to **anybody** / **anyone**.
[?] Did **anybody** / **anyone** phone?
[✗] No, **nobody** / **no one. Nobody** / **No one** phoned.

things

[+] I bought **something** for dinner.
[-] I didn't do **anything** at the weekend.
[?] Is there **anything** in the fridge?
[✗] No, **nothing**. There's **nothing** in the fridge.

places

[+] Let's go **somewhere** this weekend.
[-] We didn't go **anywhere** this summer.
[?] Is there **anywhere** to park?
[✗] No, **nowhere**. There's **nowhere** to park.

- Use *somebody / someone, something, somewhere* with a [+] verb when you don't say exactly who, what, or where.
- Use *anybody / anyone, anything, anywhere* in questions or with a [-] verb.
  *I **didn't** do **anything** last night.* **NOT** ~~*I didn't do nothing.*~~
- Use *nobody / no one, nothing, nowhere* in short answers or in sentences with a [+] verb.

4A

a Write sentences in the present perfect.

He / clean the car [+] *He's cleaned the car.*

1 She / buy a new jacket [+]
2 He / find a job yet [-]
3 / you speak to Mr Jackson [?]
4 We / find a fantastic hotel [+]
5 They / finish eating [-]
6 / you see Peter this morning [?]
7 / you do your homework this week [?]
8 We / reply to Mr Jones's email yet [-]

b Write sentences or questions with *already*, *just*, or *yet*.

He / arrive. (already) *He's already arrived.*

1 I / have / breakfast. (just)
2 / you / finish / your homework? (yet)
3 The film / start. (already)
4 I / not meet / his girlfriend. (yet)
5 They / get married. (just)
6 You're too late. He / go / home. (already)
7 / you speak / to him? (yet)
8 I / not read / his new book. (yet)

◀ p.29

4B

a Complete with the verb in the present perfect.

Have you *done* the shopping today? (do)

1 ________ you ever ________ clothes from that shop? (buy)
2 I ________ always ________ a pair of designer shoes. (want)
3 I ________ the newspaper today. (not read)
4 We ________ to the new shopping centre yet. (not be)
5 ________ your brother ________ abroad all his life? (live)
6 They ________ to live in South America. (go)
7 She ________ before. (not fly)
8 James ________ his girlfriend's family yet. (not meet)
9 ________ you ________ in this restaurant before? (eat)
10 Jane ________ to the gym – she'll be back in an hour. (go)

b Complete the dialogue with the present perfect or past simple.

A Oh no! *I've seen* this film before! (see)
B Really? When [1] ________ it? (see)
A I [2] ________ to the cinema in March and it was on then. (go)
B Oh, never mind. I [3] ________ to the cinema in ages. The last film I [4] ________ was *Mamma Mia!* (not be, see)
A [5] ________ it? (enjoy)
B Of course! I [6] ________ it! (love)

c Complete with *been* or *gone*.

'Where's Rob?' 'He's *gone* to the football match.'

1 The kids aren't here. They've all ________ out.
2 Have you ever ________ to the swimming pool in town?
3 I haven't ________ to Sue's new flat yet.
4 My sister has ________ to teach in France.
5 Oh good. Dad's ________ to the shop – the fridge is full.

◀ p.31

4C

a Complete with *something*, *anything*, *nothing*, etc.

Are you doing *anything* tonight?

1 Did you meet ________ last night?
2 ________ phoned when you were out. They're going to call back later.
3 I've seen your wallet ________, but I can't remember where.
4 There's ________ interesting on TV tonight. Let's go out.
5 Did ________ call while I was out?
6 Did you go ________ exciting at the weekend?
7 I've bought you ________ really nice for Christmas!
8 I rang the doorbell, but ________ answered.
9 We went shopping, but we didn't buy ________.
10 There's ________ more expensive than London!

b Answer with *Nobody*, *Nowhere*, or *Nothing*.

1 What did you do last night? ________
2 Where did you go yesterday? ________
3 Who did you see? ________

c Answer the questions in **b** with a full sentence.

1 I didn't do ________.
2 ________.
3 ________.

◀ p.32

5

5A comparatives

1 My brother's **older than** me. 2 40
It's **more dangerous** to cycle **than** to drive.
2 People walk **more quickly than** in the past.
3 I'm **less relaxed** this year **than** I was last year.
4 The service in this restaurant isn't **as good as** it was.
She doesn't drive **as fast as** her brother.

- To compare two people, places, things or actions use:
  1 comparative adjectives.
  2 comparative adverbs (for actions).
  3 *less* + adjective or adverb.
  4 (*not*) *as* + adjective / adverb + *as*.

comparative adjectives: regular

adjective	comparative	
short	short**er**	one syllable: add *-er*
big	big**ger**	one vowel + one consonant: double final consonant
busy	bus**ier**	consonant + *y*: *y* + *-ier*
relaxed	**more** relaxed	two or more syllables: *more* + adjective

comparative adjectives: irregular

adjective	comparative
good	**better**
bad	**worse**
far	**further**

comparative adverbs: regular

quickly	**more** quickly
slowly	**more** slowly

irregular

hard	**harder**
well	**better**
badly	**worse**

Comparatives with pronouns
After comparative + *than* or *as...as* we use an object pronoun (*me, her*, etc.) or a subject pronoun + auxiliary verb, e.g.
My brother's taller than ***me****. My brother's taller than* ***I am****.*
He's not as intelligent as ***her****. He's not as intelligent as* ***she is****.*

5B superlatives

1 It's **the dirtiest** city in Europe. 2 43
It's **the most popular** holiday destination in the world.
2 It's **the most beautiful** city **I've ever been to**.
It's **the best** film **I've seen** this year.

adjective	comparative	superlative
cold	cold**er**	**the** cold**est**
hot	hot**ter**	**the** hot**test**
pretty	pret**tier**	**the** pret**tiest**
beautiful	**more** beautiful	**the most** beautiful
good	**better**	**the best**
bad	**worse**	**the worst**
far	**further**	**the furthest**

1 Use *the* + superlative adjective to say which is the biggest, etc. in a group.
- After superlatives we use *in* + names of places or singular words for groups of people, e.g.
  It's ***the noisiest*** *city* ***in*** *the world.*

2 We often use *the* + superlative adjective with the present perfect + *ever*.

5C quantifiers

too much, too many, too

1 I'm stressed. I have **too much** work. 2 52
He talks **too much**.
2 My diet is unhealthy. I eat **too many** cakes and sweets.
3 I don't want to go out. I'm **too** tired.

- Use *too much, too many, too* to say 'more than is good'.
  1 Use *too much* + uncountable noun (e.g. *coffee, time*) or after a verb.
  2 Use *too many* + countable noun (e.g. *cakes, people*).
  3 Use *too* + adjective **NOT** ~~*I'm too much tired.*~~

enough

1 Do you eat **enough** vegetables? 2 53
I don't drink **enough** water.
2 She doesn't sleep **enough**.
3 My fridge isn't big **enough**.
I don't go to bed early **enough**.

1 Use *enough* before a noun to mean 'all that is necessary'.
2 Use *enough* after a verb with no object.
3 Use *enough* after an adjective or adverb.

5A

a Write sentences with a comparative adjective or adverb + *than*.

New York is *more expensive than* Miami. (expensive)

1 Modern computers are much ______ the early ones. (fast)
2 My sister is ______ me. (tall)
3 I'm ______ this week ______ last week. (busy)
4 Newcastle is ______ from London ______ Leeds. (far)
5 I thought the third *Men in Black* film was ______ the first two. (bad)
6 Manchester United played ______ Arsenal. (good)
7 The French exam was ______ the German. (hard)
8 My new job is ______ my old one. (boring)
9 My new apartment is ______ my old one. (big)
10 I'm not lazy – I just work ______ you! (slowly)

b Rewrite the sentences so they mean the same. Use *as… as*.

James is stronger than Clive.
Clive isn't *as strong as James*.

1 Adam is shorter than Jerry.
Jerry isn't ______.
2 Your bag is nicer than mine.
My bag isn't ______.
3 Tokyo is bigger than London.
London isn't ______.
4 Tennis is more popular than cricket.
Cricket isn't ______.
5 Children learn languages faster than adults.
Adults don't ______.
6 I work harder than you.
You don't ______.
7 England played better than France.
France didn't ______.

p.37

5B

a Complete the sentences with the superlative.

Is this *the biggest* city in the world? (big)

1 Thais are ______ people I've ever met. (polite)
2 Yesterday was ______ day of the year. (hot)
3 This is ______ time to drive to the city. (bad)
4 She's ______ girl at school. (friendly)
5 This is ______ part of the exam. (important)
6 ______ time to visit New England is autumn. (good)
7 Ulan Bator is one of ______ cities in the world. (polluted)
8 ______ I've ever flown is to Bali. (far)
9 That's definitely ______ film I've ever seen. (funny)
10 Rob's daughters are all pretty, but I think Emily is ______. (pretty)

b Write sentences with a superlative + *ever* + the present perfect.

It / good film / I / see
It's the best film I've ever seen.

1 It / hot country / I be to
2 She / unfriendly person / I / meet
3 It / easy exam / he / do
4 They / expensive trousers / I / buy
5 It / long film / I / watch
6 He / attractive man / I / see
7 It / bad meal / I / eat
8 He / interesting teacher / I / have
9 It / exciting job / we / do

◄ p.38

5C

a Circle the correct form.

How *much* / *many* milk do you drink?

1 I eat *too* / *too much* chocolate.
2 I eat *too much* / *too many* crisps.
3 I don't drink *enough water* / *water enough*.
4 I can't come. I am *too busy* / *too much busy*.
5 You work *too much* / *too many*.
6 I don't have *enough time* / *time enough*.
7 I don't *go out enough* / *enough go out*.
8 She's *too lazy* / *too much lazy*.

b Complete the sentences with *too*, *too much*, *too many*, or *enough*.

You eat *too much* red meat. It isn't good for you.

1 I'm not very fit. I don't do ______ exercise.
2 I can't walk to school. It's ______ far.
3 There are ______ cars on the roads today.
4 I spend ______ time on the computer – it gives me headaches.
5 I don't sleep ______ – only five or six hours, but I really need eight.
6 I was ______ ill to go to work yesterday.
7 There were ______ people at the party, so it was impossible to dance.
8 I always have ______ work and not ______ free time.

◄ p.41

6

6A *will / won't* (predictions)

A I'm seeing Jane at six. **B** **She'll be** late. 3 4

The film's in French. **We won't understand** anything.
It's a great book. I'm sure **you'll like** it.
I don't think **it'll rain** tomorrow.

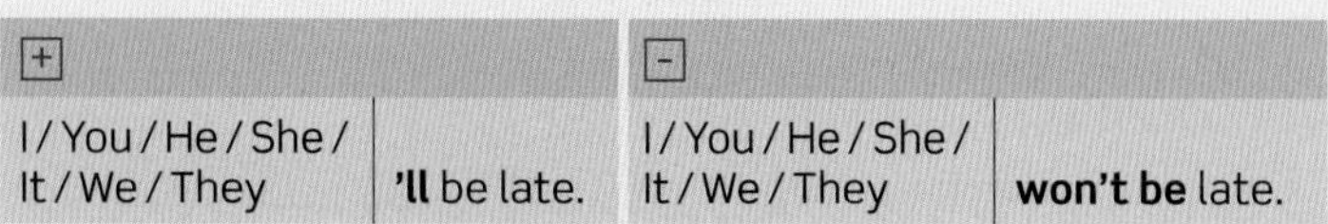

+		−	
I / You / He / She / It / We / They	**'ll** be late.	I / You / He / She / It / We / They	**won't be** late.

Contractions: *'ll* = *will*; *won't* = *will not*

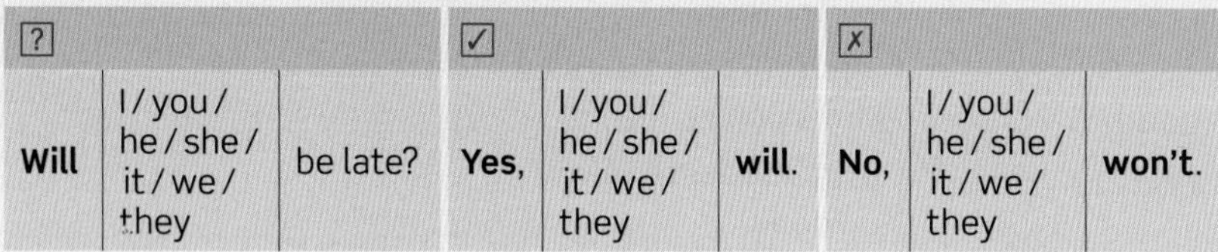

?			✓			✗		
Will	I / you / he / she / it / we / they	be late?	**Yes,**	I / you / he / she / it / we / they	**will.**	**No,**	I / you / he / she / it / we / they	**won't.**

- We often use *will* / *won't* + infinitive for future predictions, i.e. to say things we think, guess or know about the future.
- We often use *I think* / *I don't think* + *will.*
  ***I think** he'**ll fail** the exam. **I don't think** he'**ll pass** the exam.* **NOT** *~~I think he won't pass.~~*

be going to for predictions
We can also use *be going to* to predict something you know or can see is going to happen (see **3A**), e.g.
*Look at the clouds. It'**s going to** rain.*
*They're playing very well. I'm sure they'**re going to** win.*

6B *will / won't* (decisions, offers, promises)

3 11

decisions
I **won't stay** for dinner. I think I'**ll go** home early.

offers
I'**ll help** you with your homework. **Shall I open** the window?

promises
I'll always **love** you. I **won't tell** anybody.

- Use *will* / *won't* + infinitive for making decisions, offering and promising.
  *I'**ll help** you with those bags.* **NOT** *~~I help you.~~*
- When an offer is a question, we use *Shall I…?* or *Shall we…?*
  ***Shall I** pay? **Shall we** do the washing-up?*

6C review of tenses: present, past and future

tense	example	use 3 19
present simple	I **live** in the city centre. She **doesn't smoke**.	things that happen always or usually
present continuous	He'**s looking** for a new job.	things that are happening now or in the near future
	I'**m leaving** tomorrow.	things that we have arranged for the future
past simple	We **saw** a good film last night. We **didn't do** anything yesterday.	finished actions in the past
past continuous	He **was working** in Paris. What **were** you **doing** at 7.00?	actions that were in progress at a past time
be going to + infinitive	I'**m going to see** Tom tonight.	future plans
	Look! It'**s going to rain**.	predictions when we know / can see what's going to happen
will / *won't* + infinitive	You'**ll love** New York.	predictions
	I'**ll phone** her later.	instant decisions
	I'**ll help** you.	offers
	I'**ll pay** you back tomorrow.	promises
present perfect	I'**ve finished** the book.	recently finished actions (we don't say when)
	Have you **ever been** to Iran?	past experiences

6A

a Write sentences and questions with *will* / *won't*. Use contractions where you can.

[-] it / be easy to pass *It won't be easy to pass.*
1 [+] I think they / lose the match
2 [?] the meeting / be long
3 [-] she / get the job – she's not qualified
4 [?] you / see him at work later
5 [+] I don't want to go. it / be impossible to park
6 [-] you / like that book
7 [+] I think she / love the present I bought her
8 [-] there / be a lot of traffic in the morning
9 [+] you / find a good job, I'm sure
10 [+] everything / be OK, so there's no need to worry

b Complete with *will* + a verb from the list.

~~be~~ (2) get like pass snow

A Do you think the traffic *will be* bad?
B No, because it's a holiday today.
1 **A** Do you like this band?
B Yes, I think they ________ famous one day.
2 **A** Is this a good film.
B Yes, I'm sure you ________ it.
3 **A** Do you think it ________?
B No, it's not cold enough.
4 **A** What do you think I ________ for Christmas?
B I don't know. What did you ask for?
5 **A** I'm so worried about the exam!
B Don't worry. I'm sure you ________.

◄ p.44

6B

a Match the sentences.

It's hot in here. [G]
1 I'm thirsty. [ ]
2 I have a headache. [ ]
3 This exercise is hard. [ ]
4 I'm hungry. [ ]
5 These bags are heavy. [ ]
6 I left my wallet at home. [ ]
7 I need that photo urgently. [ ]
8 We haven't got any milk. [ ]

A I'll help you to do it.
B Shall I make you a sandwich?
C Shall I carry one for you?
D I'll lend you some money.
E I'll buy some on my way home.
F I'll send it by email now.
G Shall I open the window?
H Shall I turn off the music?
I I'll get you a glass of water.

b Complete the sentences with *will* / *won't* (or *shall*) + a verb.

buy call forget get ~~have~~ help pay take tell

A What would you like? **B** *I'll have* the fish.

1 **A** I can't do this crossword.
B ________ you?
2 **A** It's a secret.
B I ________ anyone, I promise.
3 **A** When will I hear from you again?
B I ________ you tonight.
4 **A** Can I borrow €50?
B When ________ you ________ me back?
5 **A** It's my birthday next week.
B Don't worry. I ________.
6 **A** I feel ill.
B ________ I ________ you home?
7 **A** This chocolate you bought isn't very nice.
B Yes, I know. I ________ it again.
8 **A** These shoes are too small.
B I ________ a bigger pair for you, madam.

◄ p.46

6C

a Complete the questions with one word.

Where *do* you usually have lunch?
I didn't see you at work last week. *Were* you ill?
1 ________ you often remember your dreams?
2 ________ you listen to the match on the radio last night?
3 Who do you think ________ win the election next year?
4 ________ your brother like rock music?
5 What ________ you going to watch on TV tonight?
6 ________ it snowing when you left?
7 Were you at the party last night? I ________ see you.
8 ________ you been to the supermarket?
9 ________ the film finished yet?

b Put the verb in the right form.

A What *are* we *doing* tonight? (do)
B We [1]________ dinner with Jack and Mary. (have)
A But we [2]________ dinner with them last week! (have)
B Yes, but they [3]________ to tell us some good news. (want)
A Oh, OK then. [4]________ I ________ some champagne? (buy)
B It's 8 o'clock! Where [5]________ you ________? (be)
A I'm sorry. When I [6]________ home I [7]________ to buy the champagne. And then I [8]________ Mark in the shop… (walk, stop, see)
B Well, hurry up. We [9]________ late! (be)
A It's OK. I [10]________ a taxi and I'll be ready in five minutes. (already order)

◄ p.49

Describing people

1 APPEARANCE

a Match the sentences and pictures.

What does he / she look like?

- [ ] She has curly red hair.
- [ ] She has long straight hair.
- *1* She has big blue eyes.
- [ ] She has dark wavy hair.
- [ ] He has a beard and a moustache.
- [ ] He's bald.
- [ ] He's very tall and thin.
- [ ] He's quite short and a bit overweight.
- [ ] He's medium height and quite slim.

b 1 10 Listen and check.

> ***thin* or *slim*? *fat* or *overweight*?**
>
> *Thin* and *slim* are both the opposite of *fat*, but *slim* = thin in an attractive way.
>
> *Fat* is not very polite. It is more polite to say someone is (*a bit*) *overweight*.
>
> **Using two adjectives together**
>
> We often use two adjectives together (without *and*) to describe hair or eyes, e.g. *She has long curly hair* or *He has big brown eyes*. Adjectives go in this order: **size>style>colour** noun.

2 PERSONALITY

a Match the adjectives with the definitions.

What's he like? What's she like?

clever /ˈklevə/ friendly /ˈfrendli/ funny /ˈfʌni/ generous /ˈdʒenərəs/ kind /kaɪnd/ lazy /ˈleɪzi/ shy /ʃaɪ/ talkative /ˈtɔːkətɪv/

		Adjective	Opposite
1	A person who is open and warm is	*friendly*	______
2	A person who talks a lot is	______	______
3	A person who likes giving people things is	______	______
4	A person who is friendly and good to other people is	______	______
5	A person who doesn't want to work is	______	______
6	A person who makes people laugh is	______	______
7	A person who is quick at learning and understanding things is (synonym *intelligent*)	______	______
8	A person who can't talk easily to people he / she doesn't know is	______	______

b Complete the **Opposite** column with an adjective from the list.

extrovert /ˈekstrəvɜːt/ hard-working /hɑːd ˈwɜːkɪŋ/ mean /miːn/ quiet /ˈkwaɪət/ serious /ˈsɪəriəs/ stupid /ˈstjuːpɪd/ unfriendly /ʌnˈfrendli/ unkind /ʌnˈkaɪnd/

c 1 11 Listen and check.

d In pairs, ask and answer about a member of your family or a good friend.

A *What does your sister look like?*

B *She's quite tall and she has short dark hair.*

A *What's she like?*

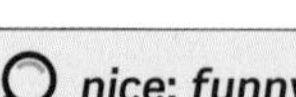

> ***nice*; *funny* or *fun*?**
>
> *Nice* is a very common + adjective of personality, e.g. *He's a very nice person. Nice* describes a person who is friendly and kind.
>
> A person who is *funny* makes you laugh. A person who is *fun* is a person who you have a good time with.

p.6

Things you wear

a Match the words and pictures.

Clothes

- cardigan /'kɑːdɪgən/
- coat /kəʊt/
- dress /dres/
- jacket /'dʒækɪt/
- jeans /dʒiːnz/
- shirt /ʃɜːt/
- *1* shorts /ʃɔːts/
- skirt /skɜːt/
- suit /suːt/
- sweater (synonym *jumper*) /'swetə/
- top /tɒp/
- tracksuit /'træksuːt/
- trousers /'traʊzəz/
- T-shirt /'tiːʃɜːt/

Footwear

- boots /buːts/
- flip-flops /'flɪp flɒps/
- sandals /'sændlz/
- shoes /ʃuːz/
- trainers /'treɪnəz/

Accessories

- belt /belt/
- cap /kæp/
- hat /hæt/
- leggings /'legɪŋz/
- gloves /glʌvz/
- scarf /skɑːf/
- socks /sɒks/
- tie /taɪ/
- tights /taɪts/

Jewellery

- bracelet /'breɪslət/
- earrings /'ɪərɪŋz/
- necklace /'nekləs/
- ring /rɪŋ/

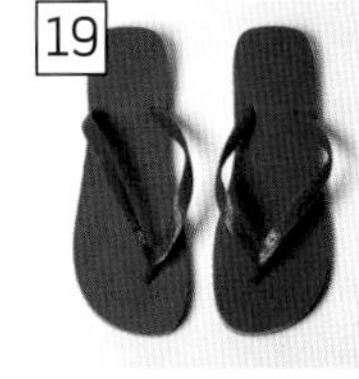

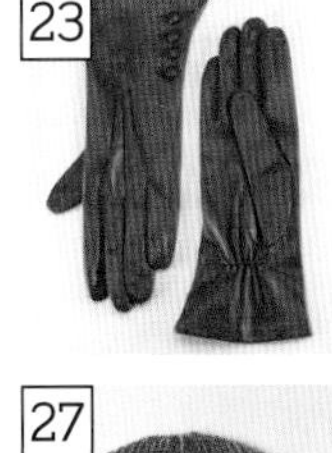

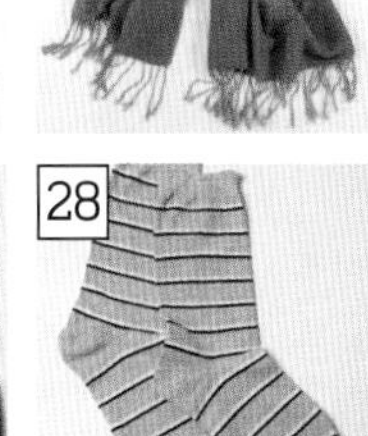

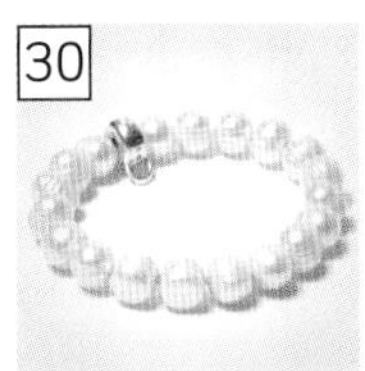

b 1 19 Listen and check.

c Cover the words and look at the pictures. Test yourself or a partner.

◀ p.8

> ***wear*, *carry*, or *dress*?**
>
> Use *wear* for clothes and jewellery / glasses, etc.
> *She's wearing a hat. He's wearing sunglasses.*
>
> Use *carry* for bags, cases, etc.
> *She's carrying a bag.*
>
> Use *dress* (with no object) to describe the kind of clothes people wear.
> *The Italians dress very well. Jane always dresses in black.*

Holidays

1 PHRASES WITH *GO*

a Match the phrases and pictures.

1 

2 

3 

4 

5 

6 

7 

8 

9 

10 

- [ ] go abroad
- *1* go away for the weekend
- [ ] go by bus / car / plane / train
- [ ] go camping
- [ ] go for a walk
- [ ] go on holiday
- [ ] go out at night
- [ ] go sightseeing
- [ ] go skiing / walking / cycling
- [ ] go swimming / sailing / surfing

b 1 31 Listen and check.

c Cover the phrases and look at the pictures. Test yourself or a partner.

2 OTHER HOLIDAY ACTIVITIES

a Complete the verb phrases.

book buy have hire rent
spend ~~stay~~ sunbathe take

stay ______ in a hotel / at a campsite / with friends
______ photos
______ souvenirs
______ on the beach
______ a good time
______ money / time
______ an apartment
______ a bicycle / skis
______ flights / hotels online

b 1 32 Listen and check.

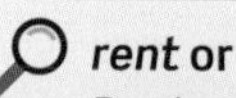

***rent* or *hire*?**
Rent and *hire* mean the same but we normally use *rent* for a longer period of time, e.g. you rent a flat or apartment, and *hire* for a short time, e.g. you hire skis, a bike, a boat, etc. With a car you can use *hire* or *rent*.

c Test yourself. Cover the verbs. Remember the phrases.

3 ADJECTIVES

a Match the questions and answers.

1 What was the weather like? It was...
2 What was the hotel like? It was...
3 What was the town like? It was...
4 What were the people like? They were...
5 What was the food like? It was...

- [ ] + comfortable, luxurious
  − basic, dirty, uncomfortable
- [ ] + friendly, helpful − unfriendly, unhelpful
- [ ] + beautiful, lovely − noisy, crowded
- [ ] + delicious − nothing special, disgusting
- [ ] + warm, sunny − very windy, foggy, cloudy

b 1 33 Listen and check.

General positive and negative adjectives
+ *lovely, wonderful, fantastic, great*
OK, not bad, alright
− *awful, horrible, terrible*

◀ p.12

Prepositions

1 *AT / IN / ON*

a Complete the chart with *at*, *in*, or *on*.

	Place	Time
1 ___	**Countries and cities** *France, Paris* **Rooms** *the kitchen* **Buildings** *a shop, a museum* **Closed spaces** *a park, a garden* *a car*	**Months** *February, June* **Seasons** *(the) winter* **Years** *2011* **Times of day** *the morning, the afternoon, the evening* (not ~~*night*~~)
2 ___	**Transport** *a bike, a bus, a train, a plane, a ship* (not ~~*car*~~) **A surface** *the floor, a table, a shelf, the balcony, the roof, the wall*	**Dates** *1st March* **Days** *Tuesday, New Year's Day, Valentine's Day*
3 ___	*school, home, work, university* *the airport, the station, a bus stop* *a party, the door*	**Times** *6 o'clock, half past two, 7.45* **Festival periods** *Christmas, Easter* *night* *the weekend*

b 1 42 Listen and check.

c Look at the chart for a few minutes. Then test a partner:

A Say a place or time word, e.g. *Paris, Tuesday*.

B Close your books. Say the preposition (*at*, *in*, or *on*).

Swap roles.

◄ p.14

2 VERBS + PREPOSITIONS

a Complete the **Prepositions** column with a word from the list.

about at for in of on to with

		Prepositions
1	I arrived ___ Paris on Friday night.	*in*
2	I was very tired when I arrived ___ the hotel.	___
3	I hate waiting ___ people who are late.	___
4	**A** What are you going to do ___ the weekend?	___
	B I don't know. It depends ___ the weather.	___
5	I'm sorry, but I really don't agree ___ you.	___
6	I asked ___ a chicken sandwich, but this is tuna!	___
7	Let's invite Debbie and Tim ___ the party.	___
8	Who's going to pay ___ the meal?	___
9	I need to speak ___ Martin ___ the meeting.	___, ___
10	I don't spend much money ___ food.	___
11	Are you going to write ___ him soon?	___
12	Don't worry ___ the exam. It isn't very hard.	___
13	She fell ___ love ___ a man she met on the internet.	___, ___
14	You're not listening! What are you thinking ___ ?	___
15	**A** What do you think ___ Shakira? **B** I really like her. I think she's great.	___

b 1 68 Listen and check.

c Cover the **Prepositions** column. Say the sentences.

> ***arrive in* or *arrive at*?**
> Remember we use *arrive in* + cities or countries and *arrive at* + buildings, stations, etc.

◄ p.23

Housework, *make* or *do*?

1 HOUSEWORK

a Match the verb phrases and the pictures.

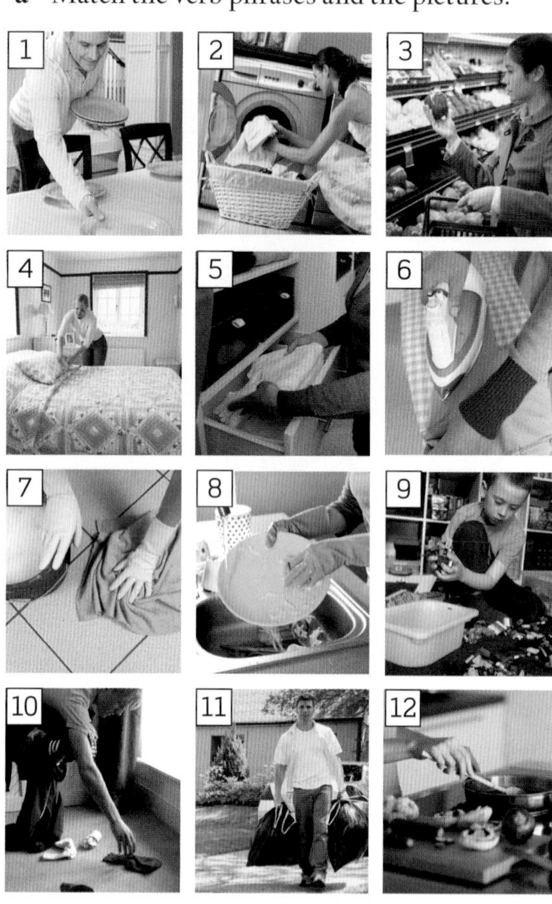

- [ ] clean the floor
- [ ] do the ironing
- [ ] do the shopping
- [ ] do the washing
- [ ] do the washing-up
- *1* lay the table (opposite *clear*)
- [ ] make lunch
- [ ] make the beds
- [ ] pick up dirty clothes (from the floor)
- [ ] put away your clothes
- [ ] take out the rubbish
- [ ] tidy your room

b 2 13 Listen and check.

c Cover the phrases and look at the pictures. Say the phrases.

2 *MAKE* OR *DO*?

a Write *make* or *do* next to the pictures.

do a course

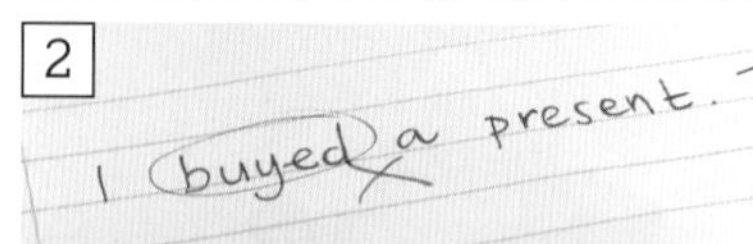

_______ a mistake

_______ an exam / an exercise / homework

_______ a noise

_______ a phone call

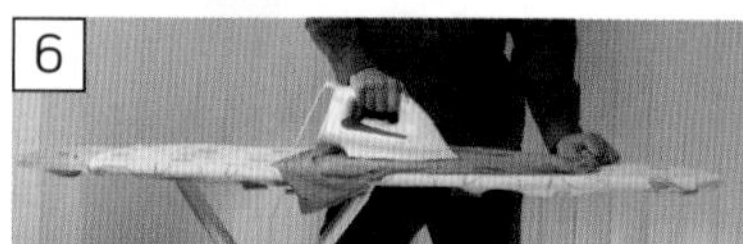

_______ housework

_______ friends

_______ lunch / dinner

_______ sport / exercise

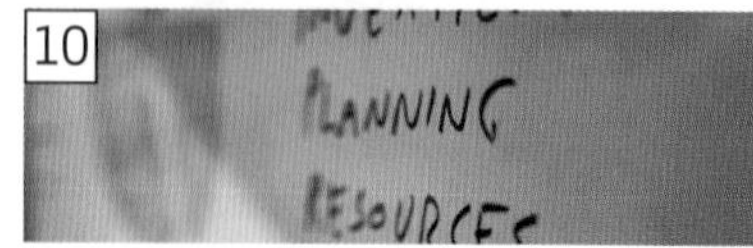

_______ plans

b 2 14 Listen and check.

c Cover the phrases and look at the pictures. Say the phrases.

d Talk to a partner.

- What housework do *you* usually do? What have you done today?
- Who does the most housework in your family?
- Do you argue about housework in your family? Give examples.
- What housework do you hate doing? What don't you mind doing? Is there any housework you like doing?

◄ p.28

Shopping

1 IN A SHOP OR STORE

a Match the words and pictures.

- [ ] changing rooms
- [ ] checkout
- [ ] customer
- [ ] receipt
- [ ] shop assistant
- *1* take sth back
- [ ] trolley / basket
- [ ] try sth on

b **2 28** Listen and check.

c Cover the words and look at the pictures. Say the words.

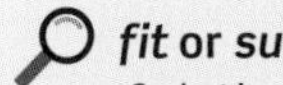

***fit* or *suit*?**

If clothes ***don't fit*** you, it means they are the wrong size (e.g. too big, too small, too tight, too loose).

If clothes ***don't suit*** you, it means they don't look good on you.

2 ONLINE

a Read the text about shopping online. Then complete it with words from the list.

account /ə'kaʊnt/ auction /'ɔːkʃn/ basket /'bɑːskɪt/ checkout /'tʃekaʊt/ delivery /dɪ'lɪvəri/ item /'aɪtəm/ payment /'peɪmənt/ size /saɪz/ ~~website~~ /'websaɪt/

Search Help

Shopping online

When you are shopping online, first you go to the [1]*website*. The first time you use a site you usually have to **create** an [2]_______, where you give your personal details. You then choose what you want to buy, and **click on** each [3]_______. If you are buying clothes, make sure you get the right [4]_______! Everything you buy goes into your **shopping bag** or [5]_______, usually at the top right of the page. When you are ready to pay you click on '**proceed** to [6]_______'. You then have to give your [7]_______ **address** where you want them to send your things, and give your [8]_______ **details**, for example your credit card number and expiry date. Many people today also buy and sell things online at [9]_______ **sites** like eBay.

b **2 29** Listen and check.

p.31

1

2

3

4

5

6

7

8

Describing a town or city

1 WHERE IS IT? HOW BIG IS IT?

a Look at the map. Then read the description of Reading and (circle) the correct words or phrases.

> Reading is a town in the *south / north* of England, on *the River Thames / the South coast*. It is about 40 miles *east / west* of London. It is a *small / medium sized / large* town and it has a population of about 250,000. It is famous for its music festival, which is one of the biggest in the UK.

b 2 46 Listen and check.

2 WHAT'S IT LIKE? adjectives to describe a town or city

a Match the adjectives and sentences 1–6.

		Opposite
☐	boring /'bɔːrɪŋ/	*exciting*
		______
☐	crowded /'kraʊdɪd/	______
☐	dangerous /'deɪndʒərəs/	______
☐	modern /'mɒdn/	______
☐	noisy /'nɔɪzi/	______
☐	polluted /pə'luːtɪd/	______

1 There are a lot of bars and clubs with loud music.
2 The air is very dirty.
3 There are too many people.
4 The buildings were all built quite recently.
5 There's nothing to do.
6 You have to be careful, especially at night.

b Match these adjectives with their opposites in **a**.

> clean /kliːn/ empty /'empti/ ~~exciting~~ /ɪk'saɪtɪŋ/ interesting /'ɪntrestɪŋ/ old /əʊld/ quiet /'kwaɪət/ safe /seɪf/

c 2 47 Listen and check your answers to **a** and **b**.

d Cover the words and look at the sentences. Remember the adjectives and their opposites.

3 WHAT IS THERE TO SEE?

a Put the words in the right column.

> ~~castle~~ /'kɑːsl/ cathedral /kə'θiːdrəl/ church /tʃɜːtʃ/ department store /dɪ'pɑːtmənt stɔː/ market /'mɑːkɪt/ mosque /mɒsk/ museum /mju'ziːəm/ palace /'pæləs/ shopping centre /'ʃɒpɪŋ sentə/ statue /'stætʃuː/ temple /'templ/ town hall /taʊn 'hɔːl/

Religious buildings	Places where you can buy things	Historic buildings and monuments
		castle

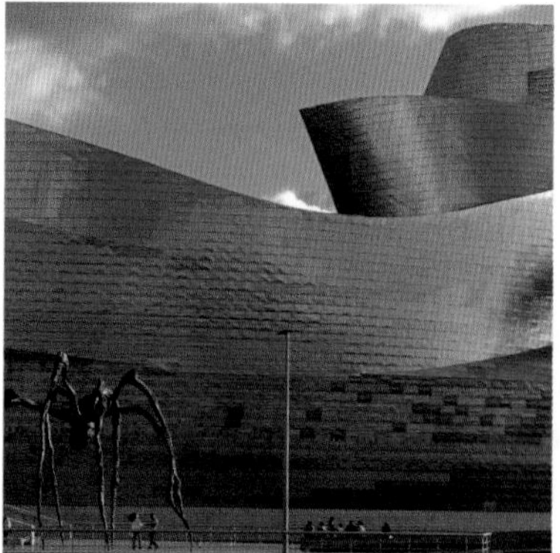

b 2 48 Listen and check.

c Which of the places in **a** are there / aren't there in your city?

There's a cathedral and some churches.
There isn't a castle.

◀ p.39

Opposite verbs

a Match the verbs and pictures.

		Opposite
	arrive (*early*) /ə'raɪv/	*leave*
	break (*your glasses*) /breɪk/	
	buy (*a house*) /baɪ/	
	find (*your keys*) /faɪnd/	
	forget (*a name*) /fə'get/	
	lend (*money to somebody*) /lend/	
	miss (*a train*) /mɪs/	
	pass (*an exam*) /pɑːs/	
1	push (*the door*) /pʊʃ/	
	send (*an email*) /send/	
	start (*a race*) /stɑːt/	
	teach (*English*) /tiːtʃ/	
	turn on (*the TV*) /tɜːn 'ɒn/	
	win (*a match*) /wɪn/	

b Find the opposite verbs in the list. Write them in the **Opposite** column.

borrow (*from somebody*) /'bɒrəʊ/
catch /kætʃ/
fail /feɪl/
get / receive /get/ /rɪ'siːv/
learn /lɜːn/
~~leave~~ /liːv/
lose (x2) /luːz/
mend / repair /mend/ /rɪ'peə/
pull /pʊl/
remember /rɪ'membə/
sell /sel/
stop / finish /stɒp/ /'fɪnɪʃ/
turn off /tɜːn 'ɒf/

c 3 2 Listen and check.

d Cover the verbs and look at the pictures. Remember the verbs and their opposites.

◀ p.44

1

2

3

4

5

6

7

8

9

10

11

12
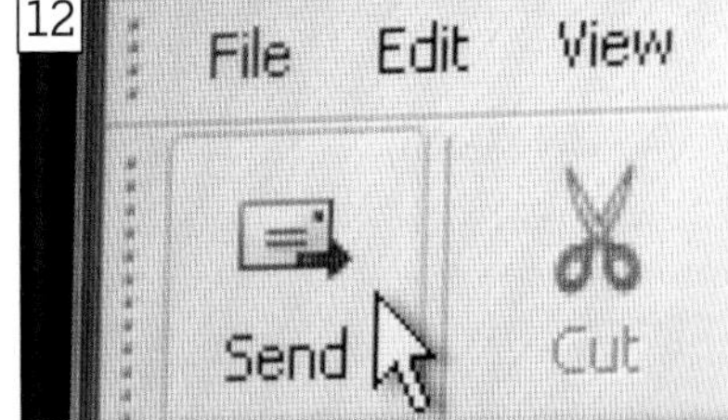

13

14

Irregular verbs

5 29

Present	Past simple	Past participle
be /bi/	was /wɒz/ were /wɜː/	been /biːn/
become /bɪ'kʌm/	became /bɪ'keɪm/	become
begin /bɪ'gɪn/	began /bɪ'gæn/	begun /bɪ'gʌn/
break /breɪk/	broke /brəʊk/	broken /'brəʊkən/
bring /brɪŋ/	brought /brɔːt/	brought
build /bɪld/	built /bɪlt/	built
buy /baɪ/	bought /bɔːt/	bought
can /kæn/	could /kʊd/	–
catch /kætʃ/	caught /kɔːt/	caught
choose /tʃuːz/	chose /tʃəʊz/	chosen /'tʃəʊzn/
come /kʌm/	came /keɪm/	come
cost /kɒst/	cost	cost
cut /kʌt/	cut	cut
do /duː/	did /dɪd/	done /dʌn/
drink /drɪŋk/	drank /dræŋk/	drunk /drʌŋk/
drive /draɪv/	drove /drəʊv/	driven /'drɪvn/
eat /iːt/	ate /eɪt/	eaten /'iːtn/
fall /fɔːl/	fell /fel/	fallen /'fɔːlən/
feel /fiːl/	felt /felt/	felt
find /faɪnd/	found /faʊnd/	found
fly /flaɪ/	flew /fluː/	flown /fləʊn/
forget /fə'get/	forgot /fə'gɒt/	forgotten /fə'gɒtn/
get /get/	got /gɒt/	got
give /gɪv/	gave /geɪv/	given /'gɪvn/
go /gəʊ/	went /went/	gone /gɒn/
grow /grəʊ/	grew /gruː/	grown /grəʊn/
have /hæv/	had /hæd/	had
hear /hɪə/	heard /hɜːd/	heard
hit /hɪt/	hit	hit
keep /kiːp/	kept /kept/	kept
know /nəʊ/	knew /njuː/	known /nəʊn/

Present	Past simple	Past participle
learn /lɜːn/	learnt /lɜːnt/	learnt
leave /liːv/	left /left/	left
lend /lend/	lent /lent/	lent
let /let/	let	let
lose /luːz/	lost /lɒst/	lost
make /meɪk/	made /meɪd/	made
meet /miːt/	met /met/	met
pay /peɪ/	paid /peɪd/	paid
put /pʊt/	put	put
read /riːd/	read /red/	read /red/
ring /rɪŋ/	rang /ræŋ/	rung /rʌŋ/
run /rʌn/	ran /ræn/	run
say /seɪ/	said /sed/	said
see /siː/	saw /sɔː/	seen /siːn/
sell /sel/	sold /səʊld/	sold
send /send/	sent /sent/	sent
shut /ʃʌt/	shut	shut
sing /sɪŋ/	sang /sæŋ/	sung /sʌŋ/
sit /sɪt/	sat /sæt/	sat
sleep /sliːp/	slept /slept/	slept
speak /spiːk/	spoke /spəʊk/	spoken /'spəʊkən/
spend /spend/	spent /spent/	spent
stand /stænd/	stood /stʊd/	stood
steal /stiːl/	stole /stəʊl/	stolen /'stəʊlən/
swim /swɪm/	swam /swæm/	swum /swʌm/
take /teɪk/	took /tʊk/	taken /'teɪkən/
teach /tiːtʃ/	taught /tɔːt/	taught
tell /tel/	told /təʊld/	told
think /θɪŋk/	thought /θɔːt/	thought
throw /θrəʊ/	threw /θruː/	thrown /θrəʊn/
understand /ʌndə'stænd/	understood /ʌndə'stʊd/	understood
wake /weɪk/	woke /wəʊk/	woken /'wəʊkən/
wear /weə/	wore /wɔː/	worn /wɔːn/
win /wɪn/	won /wʌn/	won
write /raɪt/	wrote /rəʊt/	written /'rɪtn/

Vowel sounds

	usual spelling	! but also
fish	**i** thin slim history kiss if since	English women busy decide repeat gym
tree	**ee** feel sheep **ea** teach mean **e** she we	people machine key niece receipt
cat	**a** cap hat back catch carry match	
car	**ar** far large scarf **a** fast pass after	aunt laugh heart
clock	**o** top lost socks wrong hot box	what wash want because
horse	**or** boring north **al** walk ball **aw** awful saw	water auction bought thought abroad warm
bull	**u** pull push **oo** football book look good	would should woman
boot	**oo** school choose **u*** use polluted **ew** few knew	do suit juice shoe lose through
computer	Many different spellings. /ə/ is always unstressed. <u>cle</u>ver <u>ner</u>vous a<u>rrive</u> po<u>lice</u> in<u>ven</u>tor a<u>gree</u>	
bird	**er** person verb **ir** dirty shirt **ur** curly turn	earn work world worse
egg	**e** spell lend west send very red	friendly weather sweater any said

	usual spelling	! but also
up	**u** sunny mustn't funny run lucky cut	come does someone enough young touch
train	**a*** change wake **ai** trainers fail **ay** away pay	break steak great overweight they grey
phone	**o*** open hope won't so **oa** coat goal	snow throw although
bike	**i*** quiet item **y** shy why **igh** might sights	buy eyes height
owl	**ou** trousers round account blouse **ow** crowded down	
boy	**oi** coin noisy point **oy** toy enjoy	
ear	**eer** beer engineer **ere** here we're **ear** beard earrings	really idea
chair	**air** airport stairs pair hair **are** square careful	their there wear bear
tourist	A very unusual sound. Europe furious sure plural	
/i/	A sound between /ɪ/ and /iː/. Consonant + *y* at the end of words is pronounced /i/. happy angry thirsty	
/u/	An unusual sound. education usually situation	

* especially before consonant + *e*

short vowels long vowels diphthongs

Consonant sounds

	usual spelling		! but also
parrot	p pp	promise possible copy flip-flops opposite appearance	
bag	b bb	belt body probably job cab rabbit rubbish	
key	c k ck	camping across skirt kind checkout pick	chemist's stomach mosquito account
girl	g gg	grow goat forget begin foggy leggings	
flower	f ph ff	find afraid safe elephant nephew off different	enough laugh
vase	v	video visit lovely invent over river	of
tie	t tt	try tell start late better sitting	walked dressed
dog	d dd	did dead hard told address middle	loved tired
snake	s ss ci/ce	stops faster miss message place circle	science
zebra	z s	zoo lazy freezing reason lose has toes	
shower	sh ti (+ vowel) ci+a	shut shoes washing finish patient information special musician	sugar sure machine moustache
television	An unusual sound. revision decision confusion usually garage		

	usual spelling		! but also
thumb	th	thing throw healthy south maths both	
mother	th	neither the clothes sunbathe that with	
chess	ch tch t (+ure)	chicken child beach catch match picture future	
jazz	j dge	jacket just journey enjoy bridge judge	generous teenager giraffe age
leg	l ll	little less plan incredible will trolley	
right	r rr	really rest practice try borrow married	written wrong
witch	w wh	website twins worried win why which whale	one once
yacht	y before u	yet year young yoga useful uniform	
monkey	m mm	mountain modern remember email summer swimming	
nose	n nn	need necklace none any funny dinner	know knock
singer	ng	angry ring along thing bring going	think thank
house	h	hat hate ahead perhaps hire helpful	who whose whole

voiced unvoiced

Christina Latham-Koenig
Clive Oxenden
Paul Seligson

with Jane Hudson

ENGLISH FILE

Pre-Intermediate Workbook A with key

Paul Seligson and Clive Oxenden are the original co-authors of
English File 1 and *English File 2*

Contents

STUDY LINK iChecker

Audio: When you see this symbol iChecker, go to the iChecker disc in the back of this Workbook. Load the disc in your computer.

1

Type your name and press 'ENTER'.

2

Choose 'AUDIO BANK'.

3

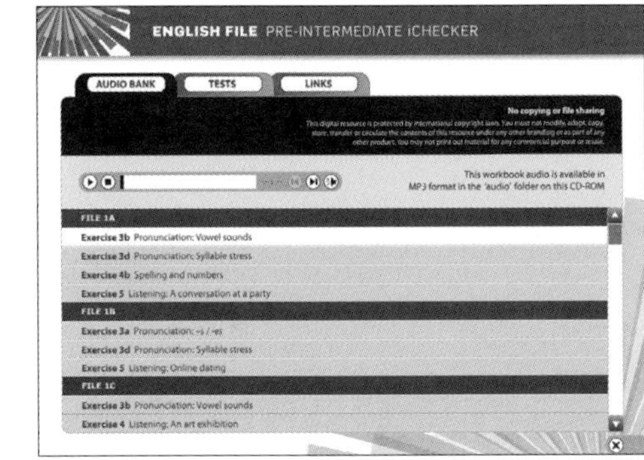

Click on the exercise for the File. Then use the media player to listen.

You can transfer the audio to a mobile device, e.g. your iPod, from the 'audio' folder on the disc.

File test: At the end of every File, there is a test. To do the test, load the iChecker and select 'Tests'. Select the test for the File you have just finished.

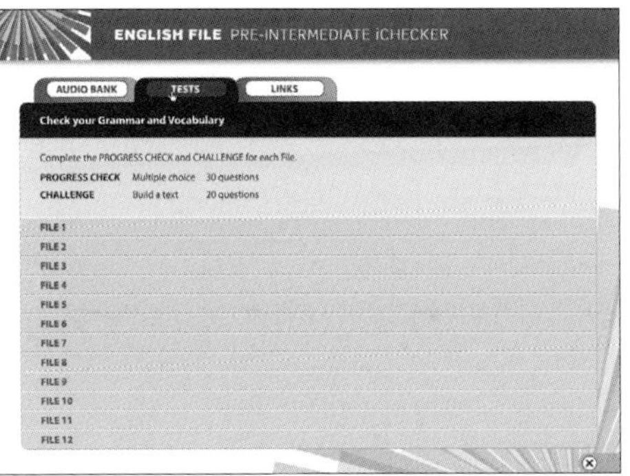

There is also more practice available online at the English File website: www.oup.com/elt/englishfile

No copying or file sharing

Today is the first day of the rest of your life.
Anonymous

1A Where are you from?

1 GRAMMAR word order in questions

a Put the word into the correct place in the questions.

1 Where you born? (were)
*Where **were** you born?*
2 Do have any brothers or sisters? (you)
____
3 What university you go to? (do)
____
4 What languages you speak? (can)
____
5 Where you study English before? (did)
____
6 What kind of music do you listen? (to)
____
7 How do you do exercise? (often)
____
8 Where did you last weekend? (go)
____

b Write questions in the present or past simple.

1 Where *do you go to university*? (you / go to university)
2 What ________________? (you / do last night)
3 What ________________? (TV programmes / your girlfriend / watch)
4 When ________________? (your birthday)
5 Where ________________? (you / from)
6 Where ________________? (your friends / go / holiday last year)
7 What kind of books ________________? (you / read)
8 Why ________________? (you / angry yesterday)

2 VOCABULARY common verb phrases

Match the verbs and nouns.

1 be born	*j*	a MTV, a TV series
2 do	☐	b in a house, with friends
3 listen to	☐	c two sisters, a pet
4 play	☐	d exercise, sport
5 read	☐	e an email, a magazine
6 speak	☐	f to the cinema, on holiday
7 live	☐	g the guitar, basketball
8 watch	☐	h a foreign language, English
9 go	☐	i dance music, R&B
10 have	☐	j in Kraków, in Poland

3 PRONUNCIATION vowel sounds, the alphabet

a Circle the letter with a different vowel sound.

1 /eɪ/ train	2 /eɪ/ train	3 /iː/ tree	4 /iː/ tree	5 /e/ egg	6 /e/ egg	7 /uː/ boot
A K (E)	H P J	G V R	M C D	N B F	X S K	Q I U

b iChecker Listen and check. Then listen again and repeat the letters.

c Underline the stressed syllables in these words.

1 in|stru|ment
2 pro|gramme
3 thir|teen
4 thir|ty
5 u|ni|ver|si|ty
6 week|end
7 ma|ga|zine
8 sis|ter
9 lan|guage
10 a|ddress

d iChecker Listen and check. Then listen again and repeat the words.

4 SPELLING AND NUMBERS

a Continue the series.

1 nine, ten, ___*eleven*___, ___*twelve*___
2 fifteen, sixteen, ______, ______
3 sixty, seventy, ______, ______
4 ninety-eight, ninety-nine, ______, ______
5 six hundred, seven hundred, ______, ______
6 three hundred and fifty, four hundred, ______, ______
7 one thousand, three thousand, ______, ______
8 ten thousand, twenty thousand, ______, ______

b iChecker Listen and write the words.

1 ___*parents*___ 6 ______
2 ______ 7 ______
3 ______ 8 ______
4 ______ 9 ______
5 ______ 10 ______

5 LISTENING

a iChecker Listen to a conversation between two people at a party. Why does Ben leave?

______

b Listen again. Mark the sentences T (true) or F (false).

1 Sandra is a nurse. *T*
2 Ben is a doctor. ___
3 Sandra likes dance music. ___
4 Sandra didn't go to the Muse concert. ___
5 Sandra plays tennis. ___
6 Ben plays football. ___

USEFUL WORDS AND PHRASES

Learn these words and phrases.

get in touch with /get ɪn tʌtʃ wɪð/
go to bed early /gəʊ tə bed 'ɜːli/
have (sth) in common /hæv ɪn 'kɒmən/
last weekend /lɑːst wiːk'end/
spend time on (sth) /spend taɪm ɒn/
somewhere nice /'sʌmweə naɪs/
How often do you…? /haʊ 'ɒfn də ju/
What kind of (music)…? /wɒt 'kaɪnd ɒv/
Where were you born? /'weə wə ju 'bɔːn/

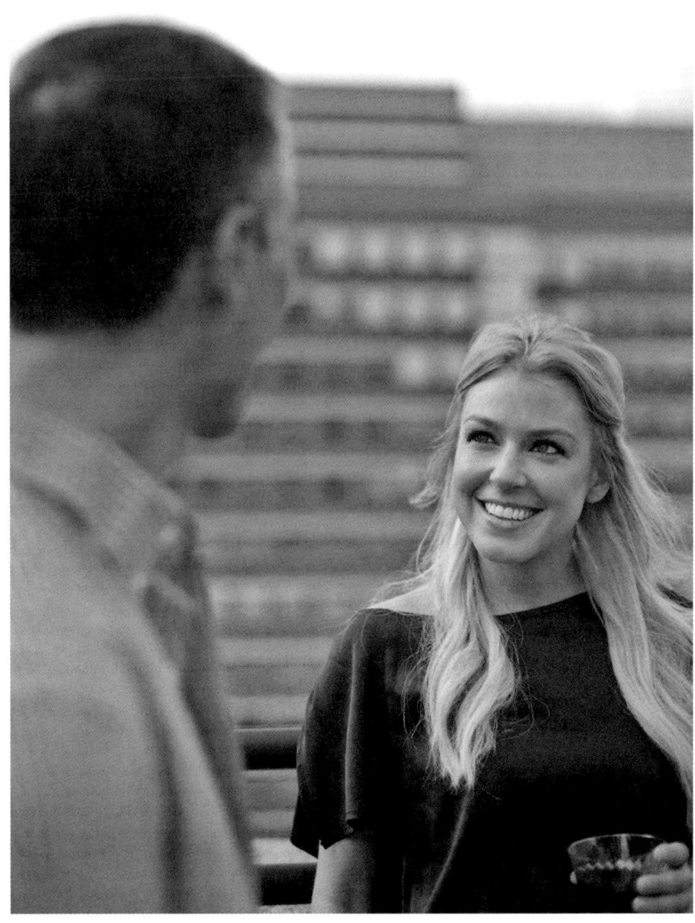

A true friend is someone who is there for you when he / she would prefer to be somewhere else.

Len Wein, American comic book writer

1B Charlotte's choice

1 GRAMMAR present simple

a Write negative sentences.

1 You get up early. *You don't get up early* .
2 It rains a lot here. ______ .
3 We live in a flat. ______ .
4 I play tennis. ______ .
5 He has a beard. ______ .
6 They go to the gym. ______ .
7 She writes a blog. ______ .

b Complete the questions with *do* or *does*.

1 When *do* you meet your friends?
2 ______ your laptop have a webcam?
3 What time ______ we need to leave?
4 ______ your mother work from home?
5 Which websites ______ you use most?
6 ______ your girlfriend like action films?
7 ______ your brother spend a long time on Facebook?

c Complete the text with the correct form of the verbs in the box.

not come earn get on study have not like live prefer not see share want ~~work~~

I am very different from my boyfriend, Jamie. Jamie [1] *works* as a vet and he [2] ______ quite a lot of money. I'm a student and I [3] ______ music at university. I [4] ______ to be a music teacher when I finish.

Jamie [5] ______ in a small house in the country, and I [6] ______ a flat with some friends in the city centre. We often [7] ______ parties in our flat, but Jamie [8] ______. He's quite shy, so he [9] ______ being with other people. I'm quite extrovert so I [10] ______ to be in a group.

I [11] ______ Jamie much because he's usually busy. But when we're together, we always [12] ______ really well. Some people say that opposites attract, and for Jamie and me, it's true.

2 VOCABULARY describing people

Appearance

a Complete the sentences.

1 Does your boyfriend have br*own* eyes or bl*ue* eyes?
2 Tanya's dad doesn't have any hair. He's b______.
3 My best friend's hair isn't str______. It's c______.
4 Andy doesn't shave. He has a b______ and a m______.
5 You aren't f______ at all. I think you're quite sl______.
6 When Jake was young, he was very th______ but now he's a bit ov______.
7 My hair isn't brown, it's r______. And I'm not short, I'm m______ h______.

b Match the questions 1–6 with the answers a–f.

1 What did you look like when you were a child? [c]
2 What does your husband look like? [ ]
3 What's your girlfriend like? [ ]
4 What does your sister look like? [ ]
5 What's George like? [ ]
6 What were you like when you were at school? [ ]

a She's tall and slim with long blond hair.
b He's very kind and quite hard-working.
c ~~I had short curly hair and I was overweight.~~
d He has short dark hair and a moustache.
e She's very clever and quite extrovert.
f I was very talkative and a bit lazy.

Personality

c Complete the opposites.

1 talkative *quiet*
2 shy ______
3 generous ______
4 friendly ______
5 hard-working ______
6 kind ______
7 serious ______
8 stupid ______

3 PRONUNCIATION final -s / -es

a iChecker Listen and (circle) the verb with a different sound.

1 S snake	2 S snake	3 Z zebra	4 Z zebra	5 /ɪz/	6 /ɪz/
works laughs (watches)	lives thinks drinks	knows rains likes	runs starts goes	leaves dresses washes	teaches cooks misses

b Listen again and repeat the words.

c Underline the stressed syllable.

1 talk|a|tive	4 ge|ne|rous	7 cur|ly
2 ex|tro|vert	5 mou|stache	8 qui|et
3 un|friend|ly	6 se|ri|ous	9 o|ver|weight

d iChecker Listen and check. Then listen again and repeat the words.

4 READING

a Read the article. What happens on 'Singles' Day' in Shanghai?

11 November is 'Singles' Day' in Shanghai, and every year a dating event takes place where all the single men and women of the city have the chance to meet a partner. Last year, it was so popular that the organizers had to close online registration because there were no more places.

Between 10,000 and 40,000 people attend the event every year. It's held in a district of Shanghai called Thames Town. At least 50 dating agencies take part. They set up stands in the town hall with billboards displaying cards with the height, birth date, education, and annual income of thousands of clients. People who did not manage to register for the event organize their own unofficial dating system by writing their names and phone numbers on bits of paper and attaching them to the fence outside the town hall.

More people take part in 'Singles' Day' every year because of the growing number of single adults in Shanghai. In the centre of the city, more than 24% of people over the age of 15 are unmarried.

b Read the article again. Mark the sentences T (true) or F (false).

1 The people who take part in 'Singles' Day' aren't married. *T*
2 Many people register for the event on the internet. __
3 All of the dating events are in the town hall. __
4 People who don't register for the event can't find a partner on 'Singles' Day'. __
5 Every year, there are more single adults in Shanghai. __

c Underline five words you don't know. Check their meaning and pronunciation with a dictionary.

5 LISTENING

a iChecker Listen to a radio programme about online dating. How many people call the programme? __________

b Listen again and match the callers with the sentences A–F.

1 Alan *C* __
2 Kate __ __
3 Paolo __ __

A He / She doesn't have time for a social life.
B He / She made a mistake.
~~C He / She had a child with the partner he / she met online.~~
D He / She married someone who was married before.
E He / She doesn't like meeting new people.
F He / She is happily married now, but doesn't have any children.

USEFUL WORDS AND PHRASES

Learn these words and phrases.

guy /gaɪ/
partner /ˈpɑːtnə/
single person /ˈsɪŋgl ˈpɜːsn/
smile /smaɪl/
sociable /ˈsəʊʃəbl/
be into (sth) /bi ˈɪntə/
feel like (doing sth) /fiːl laɪk/
get on well (with) /get ɒn wel/
go on a date /gəʊ ɒn ə deɪt/
sense of humour /sens ɒv ˈhjuːmə/

A man paints with his brain,
and not with his hands.
Michelangelo, Italian painter and sculptor

1C Mr and Mrs Clark and Percy

1 VOCABULARY

clothes

a Complete the crossword

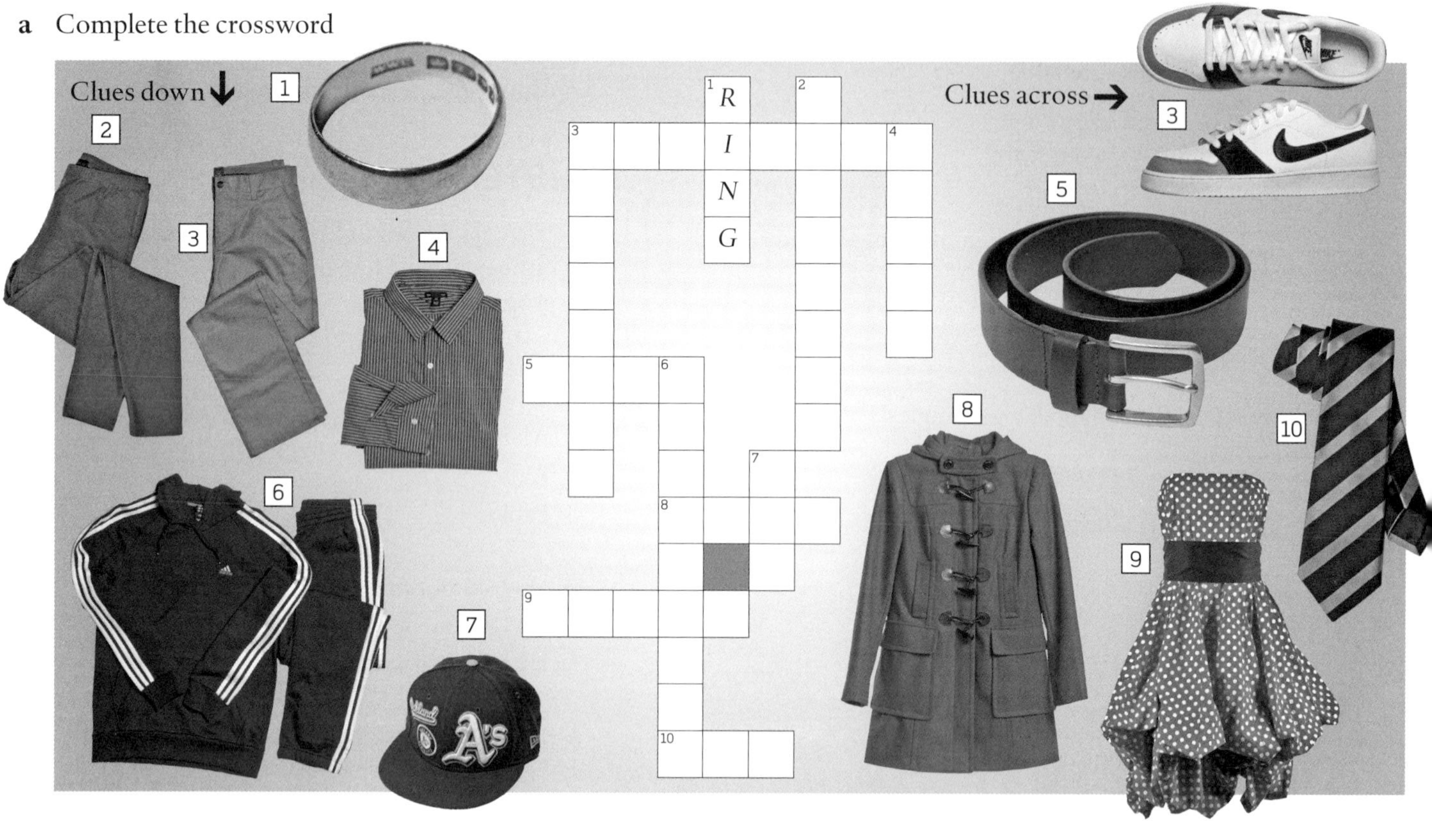

Clues down ↓ 1 2 3 4 6 7

Clues across → 3 5 8 9 10

1 down: *RING*

prepositions of place

b Look at the painting. Complete the sentences with these prepositions.

on the left ~~in~~ between behind
in front of next to

1 There are many people *in* the picture.
2 There are some boats ________ of the picture.
3 There are two small animals ________ the woman and man with an umbrella.
4 A small girl in a white dress is ________ the woman in the middle of the painting.
5 A black dog is ________ the man with a beard.
6 There is a woman ________ the two men sitting down.

2 GRAMMAR present continuous

a Look at the painting again. Read the museum guide's description of it. Write the verbs in the present continuous.

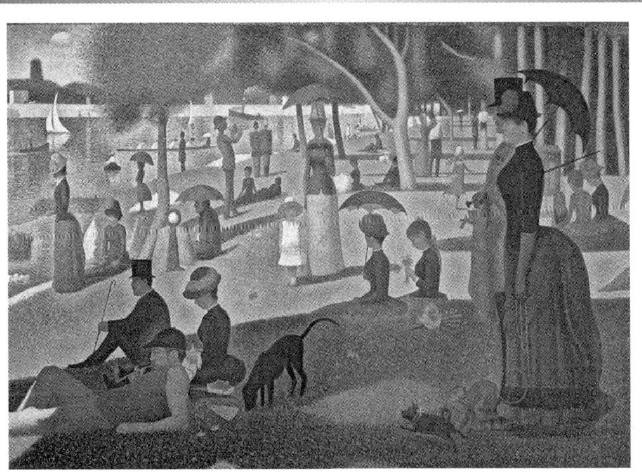

***Sunday Afternoon on the Island of La Grande Jatte,* 1884–86, Georges Pierre Seurat**

As you can see, the sun [1] *is shining* in this picture, and the people [2] ______ (relax) by the river Seine in Paris. On the right of the picture, a man and a woman [3] ______ (walk) their dogs. On the left, a man [4] ______ (lie) on the grass. He looks like he [5] ______ (relax). In the middle of the picture, two girls [6] ______ (sit) down. What [7] ______ (they / do)? Maybe they [8] ______ (wait) for some friends? Or perhaps they [9] ______ (watch) the other people? On the right, near the trees, there is another girl. She [10] ______ (play), but we can't see who with.

b Complete the sentences with the present simple or present continuous form of the verbs in the box.

drink drive like ~~listen~~ live rain sleep study wear work

1 Sorry, I can't hear you. *I'm listening* to music.
2 Charles always ______ to work.
3 'Shhhh! Be quiet! The children ______.'
4 We can't play tennis today. It ______.
5 Fiona ______ four cups of coffee every day.
6 We ______ this picture very much.
7 My brother ______ for Apple.
8 Kathy always ______ jeans at home.
9 They can't come to the theatre because they ______ for the exam tomorrow.
10 My parents ______ in a big house in the country.

3 PRONUNCIATION /ə/ and /ɜː/

a Write the words in the chart.

~~cardigan~~ fashion ~~prefer~~ sandals shirt skirt sweater trainers trousers T-shirt third world

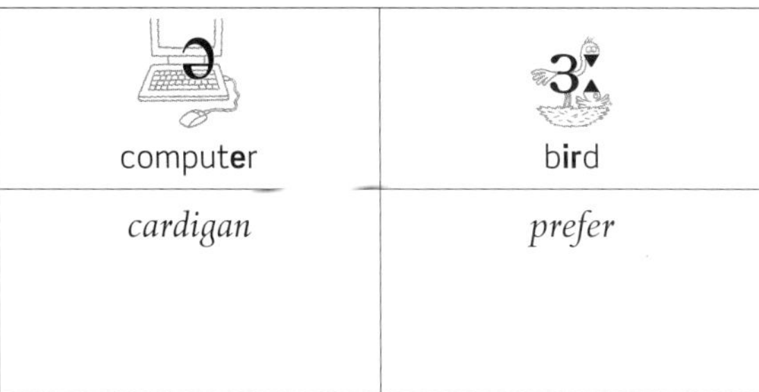

computer	bird
cardigan	*prefer*

b iChecker Listen and check. Then listen again and repeat the words.

4 LISTENING

a iChecker Listen to an advert for an art exhibition. What is special about the pictures?

______

b Listen again and answer the questions.

1 Where is the David Hockney exhibition?
______
2 What was the first picture he drew on his iPhone?
______
3 What does he do with his flower pictures?
______
4 When is the last day of the exhibition?
______
5 How much does the exhibition cost?
______

USEFUL WORDS AND PHRASES

Learn these words and phrases.

feet /fiːt/
knee /niː/
portrait /ˈpɔːtreɪt/
poster /ˈpəʊstə/
pregnant /ˈpregnənt/
relationship /rɪˈleɪʃnʃɪp/
unusual /ʌnˈjuːʒuəl/
close together /kləʊs təˈgeðə/

iChecker TESTS FILE 1

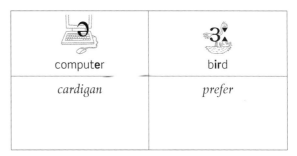

Practical English Hotel problems

1 CALLING RECEPTION

Complete the conversation with a phrase from the box.

I have a problem with the Wi-Fi.
I'll put you through to IT.
I'll send somebody up right away.
I'm sorry to bother you again.
There's a problem with the shower.
~~This is room 402.~~

A Hello, reception.
B Hello. [1] *This is room 402.*
A How can I help you?
B [2] ____________. There isn't any hot water.
A I'm sorry, madam. [3] ____________.
B Thank you.

A Good morning, reception.
B Hello. [4] ____________. This is room 402.
A How can I help you?
B [5] ____________. I can't get a signal.
A I'm sorry, madam. [6] ____________.
B Thanks.

2 SOCIAL ENGLISH

Complete the missing words in the conversation.

1 A So, here you are a*t* l*ast*.
B Yes. It's great to be here.

2 A Do you have a g__________ v__________?
B Yes. I can see the Empire State Building from my window.

3 A William is l__________ f__________ to meeting you.
B Really? Who's William?

4 A It's time to go. You m__________ b__________ really tired.
B I guess you're right.

5 A B______ t______ w______, it's great to see you again.
B Yes. It's great to see you, too.

3 READING

a Read the advert and mark the sentences T (true) or F (false).

1 The Park Central New York is in the centre of the city. *T*
2 It's near major tourist attractions. __
3 It's very comfortable. __
4 All rooms have free Wi-Fi access. __
5 The hotel's restaurant is not very expensive. __
6 The hotel has a free car park. __
7 The staff only speak English. __

Park Central New York Hotel
New York

Our facilities and services:
- in-room safe
- in-room Wi-Fi (surcharge)
- electronic check-out
- parking garage (surcharge)
- room service
- on-site car rental
- giftshop

'Great location and service'

Located in the heart of the city, the Park Central New York is in easy walking distance of Carnegie Hall, Broadway and the Museum of Modern Art (MOMA). Central Park is only three blocks away and Fifth Avenue, with its international boutiques and huge department stores, is only a ten-minute walk from the hotel. For guests who want to travel further away, there are seven subway lines located within three blocks of the hotel.

The Park Central New York offers great service, great comfort and great value. The hotel's bistro, 'Cityhouse', provides the perfect setting for dinner before a concert or a Broadway show in the evening. Guests can enjoy the reasonably priced set menu while watching the world go by on Seventh Avenue through the bistro's oversized windows. There's also a bar in the lobby where guests can enjoy a cocktail after the show.

Because of its central location, the Park Central New York is the ideal hotel for tourists visiting the city for the first time. Our multi-lingual staff on the front desk are always happy to provide tour assistance and answer any questions guests may have.

b Underline five words you don't know. Use your dictionary to look up their pronunciation and meaning.

A holiday is having nothing to do and all day to do it.

Robert Orben, American editor

2A Right place, wrong person

1 VOCABULARY holidays

a Write the phrases.

1

2

3

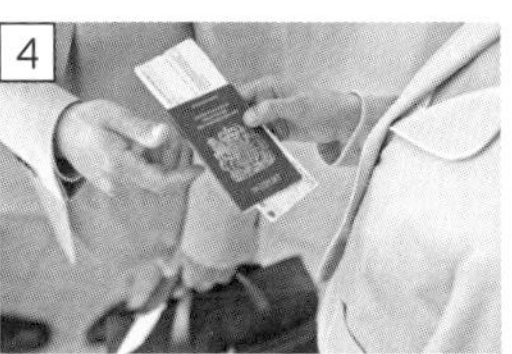
4

5

6

7

8

9

10

1 *go* camping
2 go ______ a ______
3 ______ flights on the internet
4 go ______
5 ______ skis
6 go ______ at night
7 ______ in a hotel
8 go ______
9 ______ on the beach
10 go ______ for the weekend

b Complete the sentences with an adjective.

1 We loved our room. It was very c*omfortable*.
2 The weather was warm and s______ every day.
3 There were a lot of people everywhere. It was very cr______.
4 We ate very well. The food was d______.
5 The staff in the hotel were horrible. They were very unh______, and sometimes quite rude.
6 There wasn't much in the apartment. It was very b______. It didn't even have a fridge.
7 The other people on the trip were very fr______.We hope to meet some of them again in the future.
8 The town was l______. All the houses had flowers on the balcony and were painted different colours.
9 It was cl______ and we didn't see the sun at all.
10 Our first meal was d______, so we didn't eat at the hotel again.

2 GRAMMAR past simple: regular and irregular verbs

a Write the past simple of these verbs in the correct column.

~~argue~~ ~~begin~~ arrive ask buy can choose eat feel invite rent say stay sunbathe

Regular	Irregular
argued	*began*
______	______
______	______
______	______
______	______
______	______
______	______

b Make the verbs negative.

1 We stayed at a campsite.
We didn't stay in a hotel.
2 They bought postcards.
______ any souvenirs.
3 The people were unfriendly.
______ very helpful.
4 I sunbathed on the beach.
______ by the pool.
5 We hired bikes.
______ a car.
6 He spent a month in Bangkok.
______ a week there.
7 Our room was dirty.
______ very clean.

c Complete the text with the past simple form of the verbs in the box.

arrive ask book cannot ~~decide~~ go (x2) look take want

The holiday that wasn't

Four years ago, we [1] *decided* to go away for the weekend. We [2] ______ to go to Portugal, so we [3] ______ a beautiful apartment online. A week later, we [4] ______ a taxi to the airport. We [5] ______ at the airport at two o'clock, and we [6] ______ to check in. The woman at the desk [7] ______ us for our passports. We [8] ______ in our bags, but we [9] ______ find them. So we [10] ______ home!

d Read the text in **c** again. Complete the questions.

1 When *did they decide* to go away for the weekend? Four years ago.
2 Where ______ to go? Portugal.
3 How ______ the apartment? They booked it online.
4 When ______ at the airport? At two o'clock.
5 What ______ ask for? She asked for their passports.
6 Where ______ in the end? They went back home.

3 PRONUNCIATION *-ed* endings, irregular verbs

a iChecker Listen and (circle) the verb which has a different *-ed* sound.

1 walked asked (rented)
2 argued wanted stayed
3 booked started decided
4 arrived invited sunbathed

b Listen again and repeat the words.

c Write these irregular past simple forms in the correct circle.

~~bought~~ ~~broke~~ ~~came~~ caught ~~drank~~ drove gave made rang ~~read~~ said saw sat went wrote

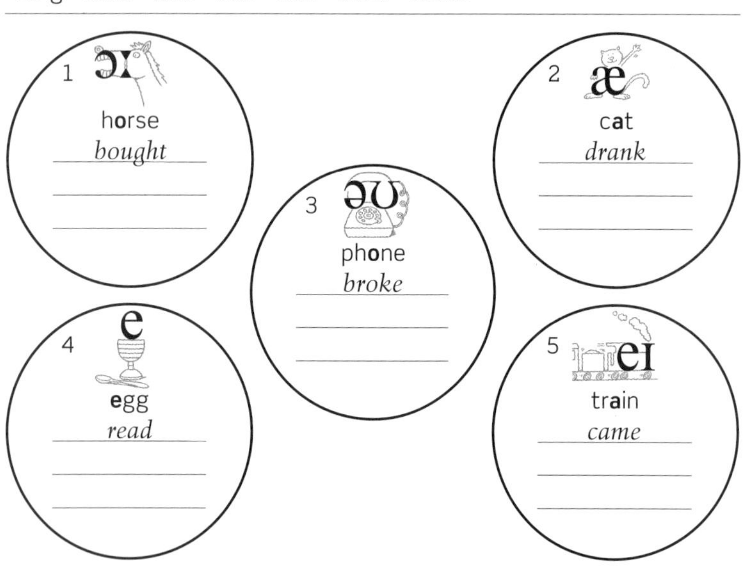

d iChecker Listen and check. Then listen again and repeat the words.

4 LISTENING

iChecker Listen to five speakers talking about holidays they didn't enjoy. Which speaker...?

a didn't have a very exciting weekend ___
b wasn't with the people he / she wanted to be with *1*
c chose a holiday destination because of the weather there ___
d went on holiday after a relationship ended ___
e didn't feel well when he / she was on holiday ___

~~Speaker 1~~

Speaker 2

Speaker 3

Speaker 4

Speaker 5

USEFUL WORDS AND PHRASES

Learn these words and phrases.

atmosphere /'ætməsfɪə/
disaster /dɪ'zɑːstə/
hostels /'hɒstlz/
complain /kəm'pleɪn/
enjoy /ɪn'dʒɔɪ/
flirt /flɜːt/
view /vjuː/
break up /'breɪk ʌp/
feel sorry for (sb) /fiːl 'sɒri fɔː/
go wrong /gəʊ rɒŋ/

Photographs are pictures taken to please the family and bore the neighbours.

Edmund Volkart, American sociologist

2B The story behind the photo

1 GRAMMAR past continuous

a Complete the sentences with the verbs in brackets in the past continuous.

1 You *were laughing* (laugh) when I took the photo.
2 It ______ (snow) when our plane landed.
3 We ______ (not drive) fast when the accident happened.
4 What ______ (he / do) when his boss arrived?
5 Why ______ (you / cry) at the party?
6 I ______ (sit) on the bus when I saw my boyfriend with another girl.
7 They ______ (live) in New Zealand when their first child was born.
8 He didn't call you because his mobile phone ______ (not work).

b Write sentences with *when*. Use the past simple and past continuous.

1 They / argue / the waiter / bring / the bill.
They were arguing when the waiter brought the bill.

2 He / fall / off his bike / cycle / home
______
______.

3 The children / play / video games / the visitors / arrive
______
______.

4 We / have / a barbecue / it / start / to rain
______
______.

5 I / finish / my report / my computer / crash
______
______.

c Complete the story with the past simple or past continuous.

Last summer I [1] *went* (go) to Los Angeles to stay with my cousin for a few weeks. One afternoon we [2] ______ (have) lunch in a nice restaurant in the centre of town when my cousin [3] ______ (get) a call on her mobile phone and went outside to talk. While she [4] ______ (speak) to her friend, I suddenly [5] ______ (notice) a man in a black hat who [6] ______ (sit) at the next table. It was the actor Johnny Depp! He was alone, and I [7] ______ (decide) to take my chance. So I got up and [8] ______ (go) to his table. 'Excuse me, could I have my photo taken with you?' I asked. He [9] ______ (say) yes, so I [10] ______ (stop) a waitress who [11] ______ (pass) by and gave her my camera. She [12] ______ (take) the photo of me and Johnny, I thanked them both, and then I returned to my table. When my cousin [13] ______ (come) back, I [14] ______ (smile).

'Why are you looking so pleased with yourself?' she asked.

'I had my photo taken with Johnny Depp.'

'Johnny Depp? Where is he?'

'He's sitting over there. Look!'

She turned around to look and then started to laugh. 'That's not Johnny Depp!'

I [15] ______ (look) at the man in the black hat – he [16] ______ (laugh) too.

2 VOCABULARY *at, in, on*

time

a Complete the sentences with *at*, *in*, or *on*.

1 The results of the election were announced _at_ 11 o'clock.
2 Mobile phones were invented ______ the 20th century.
3 Our flight is leaving ______ Wednesday at 9.30 ______ the evening and arriving ______ 12 o'clock ______ Thursday.
4 We have an exam ______ Monday morning.
5 In most countries, banks and offices are closed ______ Christmas Day and New Year's Day.
6 I hate driving ______ night, getting up early ______ the morning, and working ______ weekends.
7 Steve Jobs was born ______ 1955, and he died ______ 5th October, 2011.
8 ______ Easter we went to Portugal and we're going again ______ the summer, probably the last two weeks ______ July.

place

b Complete the sentences with *at*, *in*, or *on*.

1 He took some great photos _at_ the party.
2 I can't read a book ______ the bus or ______ a car.
3 We want to put some shelves ______ the wall ______ the living room. We're going to put all our old books ______ the shelves.
4 My family are from Ireland but we live ______ New York, ______ the 11th floor of a tall building.
5 I'll meet you ______ the bus stop.
6 The adults sat ______ chairs and the children sat ______ the floor.
7 They spent the morning ______ the museum and then went for a walk ______ the park.
8 I met my boyfriend ______ school and we split up while we were ______ university.

3 PRONUNCIATION sentence stress

iChecker Listen and repeat the dialogue. Copy the rhythm.

A **Where** were **you** at **ten** o'**clock last night**?
B **I** was at **home**.
A **What** were you **doing**?
B I was **watching** a **film**.

4 LISTENING

a iChecker Listen to a conversation between Matt and Jenny about a photo. Does Jenny like the photo? ______

b Listen again and choose the best answers.

1 The photo shows…
   a Matt's parents.
   b Matt's aunt and uncle.
   ⓒ Matt's grandparents.
2 The photo was taken…
   a in the spring.
   b in the summer.
   c in the autumn.
3 The man wanted to win…
   a some money.
   b some food.
   c some jewellery.
4 The other people in the photo were the man's…
   a neighbours.
   b friends.
   c colleagues.
5 The man on the stall…
   a took the photo.
   b asked for more money for the photo.
   c didn't like the photo.

USEFUL WORDS AND PHRASES

Learn these words and phrases.

democracy /dɪˈmɒkrəsi/
demonstration /demənˈstreɪʃn/
election /ɪˈlekʃn/
freedom /ˈfriːdəm/
hold hands /həʊld hændz/
peace /piːs/
realize /ˈrɪəlaɪz/
TV screens /tiː ˈviː skriːnz/
upload /ʌpˈləʊd/
screen saver /skriːn ˈseɪvə/

The driver is the most dangerous part of the car.
Leo Campion, French humourist

2C One dark October evening

1 GRAMMAR time sequencers and connectors

a Circle the correct words or phrases.

[1] **The summer / One summer**, I decided to travel to Peru. I flew to Lima, and then travelled to a town near Machu Picchu to spend the night. [2] **Next day / Afterday**, I climbed the mountain to visit the monument. I was quite tired [3] **when / then** I reached the top. [4] **Sudden / Suddenly**, I saw a man who was in my English class back home. [5] **Two minutes later / Two minutes after**, he came over to speak to me and he was just as surprised as I was. [6] **After that / When**, we decided to travel together. We had a great summer, and we carried on seeing each other back home. In fact, we got married two years later, and we now have a beautiful daughter called Hannah.

b Look at each group of sentences. Complete each sentence with *so*, *because*, *but*, or *although*.

1 a Linda ran to the station *because* she was very late.
  b Linda was very late ____________ she ran to the station.
  c ____________ Linda ran to the station, she was too late and she missed the train.

2 a ____________ we couldn't go out, we had a really good afternoon at home.
  b It was raining ____________ we stayed at home.
  c We stayed at home last Sunday ____________ it was raining.

3 a The tickets were really expensive ____________ they managed to sell them all in an hour.
  b ____________ the tickets were really expensive, they sold them all in an hour.
  c They sold the tickets quickly ____________ the concert was very popular.

c Rewrite the sentences using the words in brackets.

1 I didn't have any breakfast because I didn't have time. **(so)**
I didn't have time *so I didn't have any breakfast*.

2 I had a great holiday in Egypt although I can't speak Arabic. **(but)**
I can't speak Arabic ____________________.

3 I don't really like Ryan, but I went on a date with him. **(although)**
I went on a date with Ryan, ____________________.

4 I called the police because the door to my flat was open. **(so)**
The door to my flat was open ____________________.

5 Jim has a lot of money, but he's really mean. **(although)**
Jim's really mean, ____________________.

6 Mary couldn't find her wallet so she cancelled her credit cards. **(because)**
Mary cancelled her credit cards ____________________.

2 VOCABULARY verb phrases

a Match the phrases.

1 Jamie and Beth met	*d*	a	her to dinner.
2 He played		b	for her at the door.
3 She left		c	a wonderful evening.
4 He waited		d	~~in a club~~.
5 She gave		e	to a new restaurant.
6 He invited		f	the club very late.
7 He took her		g	her favourite song.
8 They had		h	him her phone number.

b Cover the right-hand column. Try to remember the sentences.

3 PRONUNCIATION word stress

a Write the words in the chart.

~~a|cross~~ ~~af|ter~~ a|gain al|though aw|ful be|cause birth|day eve|ning in|vite per|fect re|stau|rant se|cond

1 First syllable stressed	2 Second syllable stressed
after	*across*

b iChecker Listen and check. Then listen again and repeat the words.

4 READING

a Read the story. Number the paragraphs in the right order.

A lucky escape

☐ Ten minutes later, it began to rain. Soon, Liz found it hard to see out of the front windscreen. There was a lot of water on the road, so she drove more slowly. Although Liz was an experienced driver, she felt afraid.

☐ An hour later, fire fighters cut Liz out of the car. She went to hospital, but the doctors sent her home because she didn't have any serious injuries. Her head was fine and she only had a few cuts and bruises. Her son went to collect the shopping from the car and gave the loaf of bread to his mum. Now, she is going to keep it as a souvenir.

1 One day last November, Liz Douglas decided to go shopping in Glasgow. She drove to the supermarket in the city centre and spent the morning doing her weekly shop. She paid for her shopping, went back to the car park, and put the shopping bags on the back seat of the car. Then she started to drive home.

☐ However, Liz was lucky. When she braked, a loaf of bread flew out of one of the shopping bags. The car turned over, and the loaf of bread landed between Liz's head and the roof of the car. It stopped her head from hitting the car roof.

☐ Suddenly, she lost control of the car. She saw a telegraph pole in front of her and braked. She closed her eyes and hoped that the airbags in the car would inflate. Unfortunately, they didn't.

b Look at the highlighted words. What do you think they mean? Check with your dictionary.

5 LISTENING

iChecker Listen to a radio programme about people who had lucky escapes. Mark the sentences T (true) or F (false).

1. Maureen Evason was on holiday when the accident happened. *T*
2. She was in hospital for four months. ___
3. Joseph Rabadue was sitting on the floor when the accident happened. ___
4. The lorry hit the TV. ___
5. Barry McRoy was drinking coffee when the fight happened. ___
6. The DVD was in his jacket pocket. ___

USEFUL WORDS AND PHRASES

Learn these words and phrases.

anniversary /ænɪ'vɜːsəri/
brake /breɪk/
perfect /'pɜːfɪkt/
as usual /əz 'juːʒəl/
cross the road /krɒs ðə rəʊd/
High Street /'haɪ striːt/
happy ending /'hæpi 'endɪŋ/
just in time /dʒʌst ɪn 'taɪm/
madly in love /'mædli ɪn lʌv/
until the last moment /ən'tɪl ðə lɑːst 'məʊmənt/

iChecker TESTS FILE 2

I'd like to fly. Then I wouldn't have to wait in airport security lines.
Jim Morris, American baseball player

3A Plans and dreams

1 GRAMMAR *be going to* (plans and predictions)

a Complete the sentences with *going to* + a verb from the box.

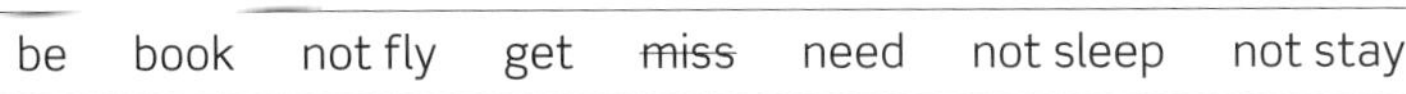

be book not fly get ~~miss~~ need not sleep not stay

1 He's *going to miss* the flight.

2 I ____________ my flight online.

3 He ____________ during the flight.

4 How ____________ she ____________ to the airport?

5 That plane ____________ today.

6 They ____________ late.

7 I ____________ in a hotel.

8 ________ we ____________ a trolley?

b Complete the dialogue with *going to* + the verbs.

Jenny [1] *Are you going to have* (you/have) a holiday this summer?
Philip Yes, but [2] ____________ (we / not / go) to the Mediterranean. [3] ____________ (we / go) to Scotland!
Jenny When [4] ____________ (you / travel)?
Philip In August. [5] ____________ (we / be) there for two weeks.
Jenny What [6] ____________ (you / do) while you're there?
Philip [7] ____________ (we / stay) in Edinburgh for a week, and then [8] ____________ (we / rent) a car and visit the Scottish Highlands.
Jenny [9] ____________ (it / be) sunny in Scotland in August?
Philip I don't know. But I hope [10] ____________ (it / not / rain) too much!

2 VOCABULARY airports

Complete the text.

Last summer, I flew to New York with my boyfriend to visit some friends. The flight left from [1]T*erminal* 1, so my brother dropped us outside the building. We went inside and looked for the [2]l____________ to take us upstairs to [3]D____________. We picked up our boarding passes at the [4]ch____________. Then we did some shopping. After that, we made our way to the [5]g____________ to board our plane. We had a good flight, but we were very tired when we landed at JFK Airport. There was a long queue at [6]p____________ c____________, and they asked us a lot of questions at Immigration. Finally, we went to [7]B____________ R____________ to pick up our bags. We needed a [8]tr____________ this time because of all our suitcases. Nobody stopped us at [9]C____________, so we went straight to [10]A____________, where our friends were waiting for us.

3 PRONUNCIATION sentence stress and fast speech

iChecker Listen and repeat. Copy the rhythm.

1 **Are** they **going** to **meet** you at the **airport**?
2 I **think** we're **going** to be **late**.
3 I'm **not going** to **forget** my **passport**.
4 **What time** are you **going** to **arrive**?
5 She's **going** to **take** the **lift**.

4 READING

a Read the text. How many airports is Beijing going to have in 2020? ____________

b Read the text again. Mark the sentences T (true) or F (false).

1 More than 54 million people use Atlanta International Airport each year. *F*
2 Atlanta International isn't going to be the busiest airport in 2020. ___
3 A new airport was built for the 2008 Olympic Games. ___
4 Beijing Capital Airport is too small. ___
5 In the future, Beijing's Metro is going to reach the new airport. ___
6 The new airport is going to have eight runways. ___

c Look at the highlighted words. What do you think they mean? Check with your dictionary.

5 LISTENING

a iChecker Listen to five conversations at the airport. Match the speakers with the places in the box.

~~Arrivals~~ Baggage reclaim Check-in
Customs Immigration

Dialogue 1 *Arrivals*
Dialogue 2 ____________
Dialogue 3 ____________
Dialogue 4 ____________
Dialogue 5 ____________

b Listen again and answer the questions.

1 What did the man eat on the plane?
2 What's the Gate number?
3 What's the friend's phone number?
4 What colour is the suitcase?
5 What did the woman buy?

The World's Biggest Airport

The world's busiest airport today is in the USA. Nearly 54 million passengers pass through Atlanta International Airport every year. However, by the end of the next decade there's going to be a new airport even bigger and busier than Atlanta. The new airport is going to be in the capital of China: Beijing.

Beijing already has two airports. The first is Beijing Capital, where an extra terminal was built for the 2008 Olympic Games. The second is Nanyuan Airport, which is mainly used by military planes . Just over 37 million passengers passed through Beijing Capital Airport last year, making it the second busiest after Atlanta. But the current airport is not big enough for all the Chinese passengers who want to travel by plane. This is why the government is going to build a new one.

The new airport is going to be in the suburb of Daxing, in the south of the city. Daxing is about an hour's drive from the city centre. The government is going to extend Beijing's Metro so that passengers can reach it more easily. There are also plans for a high-speed train line. The airport is going to have eight runways for commercial flights, and a ninth runway for military use. This is going to make it the biggest and the busiest airport in the world.

USEFUL WORDS AND PHRASES

Learn these words and phrases.

dreams /driːmz/
facilities /fə'sɪlətiz/
paradise /'pærədaɪs/
passenger /'pæsɪndʒə/
security /sɪ'kjʊərəti/
traveller /'trævələ/
board /bɔːd/
delayed /dɪ'leɪd/
free (Wi-fi) /friː/
connecting flight /kə'nektɪŋ flaɪt/

The future belongs to those who believe in the beauty of their dreams.

Eleanor Roosevelt

3B Let's meet again

1 GRAMMAR present continuous (future arrangements)

a Complete the text with the present continuous form of the verbs in brackets.

'Hi, I'm Lisa, your guide, and I'm going to tell you about the arrangements for your day trip to Paris. We [1] *'re starting* (start) our trip in about five minutes, so please make yourselves comfortable. We [2] ________ (drive) you straight to Dover – we [3] ________ (not stop) for breakfast on the way. We [4] ________ (get) the 9.15 ferry, so we're in a bit of a hurry. When we arrive in France, we [5] ________ (go) straight to Paris with no stops. We [6] ________ (not take) you to the city centre, because the traffic is terrible. We [7] ________ (stop) in Torcy, just outside Paris. We [8] ________ (arrive) in Paris at about midday, so you have all afternoon to go sightseeing and shop. We [9] ________ (pick) you up from the station in Torcy at 5.30 in the evening. We [10] ________ (catch) the ferry home at 8.45, so please don't be late. Now, any questions?'

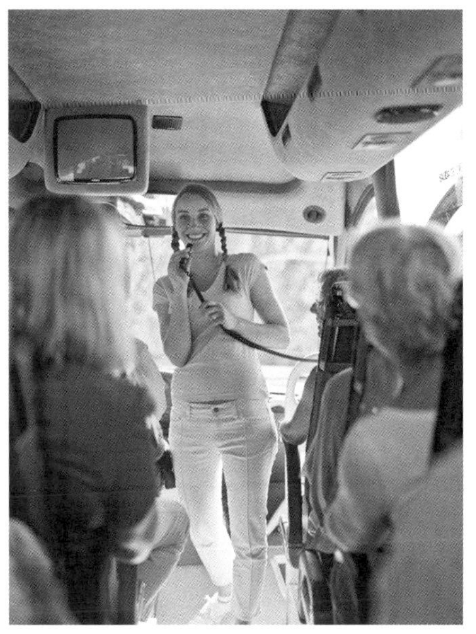

b Circle the correct verb form. If both forms are possible, tick (✓) the sentence.

1 **A** Why are you looking so worried?
B I'm sure **I'm going to get** / **I'm getting** lost.

2 **A** Do you have any plans for this weekend?
B Yes, **I'm going to visit** / **I'm visiting** my grandparents on Sunday.

3 **A** I'm going to Poland next week.
B Really? Do you think **it's going to be** / **it's being** cold?

4 **A** My brother has a job interview in London.
B Oh. Do you think **he's going to get** / **he's getting** the job?

5 **A** What time's the train?
B At 7.15. Don't worry. We **aren't going to miss** / **aren't missing** it.

6 **A** We're going on holiday next month.
B Are you? Where **are you going to go** / **are you going**?

7 **A** How do you get to work?
B I usually catch the bus, but tomorrow **I'm going to drive** / **I'm driving** because the buses are on strike.

8 **A** Your girlfriend drives too fast.
B I know. I'm sure **she's going to have** / **she's having** an accident one day.

2 VOCABULARY verbs + prepositions

Complete the sentences with the correct prepositions.

1 I completely agree *with* you.
2 We're arriving ________ Brazil at 6 a.m.
3 I'm worried ________ my flight because it's snowing.
4 They're waiting ________ Anna. She's late.
5 She spends a lot of money ________ clothes.
6 I want to speak ________ my boss after lunch.
7 Sarah's arriving ________ the airport tonight.
8 What do you think ________ the government's proposal?

3 PRONUNCIATION sounding friendly

a Number the dialogue in the correct order.

1 Would you like to go away for the weekend?
__ What about next weekend? What are you doing then?
__ Are you free this weekend?
__ I love it!
__ OK. Let's go to Devon – the countryside is beautiful!
__ Sorry, no. I'm working on Saturday.
__ Nothing. Next weekend is fine.
__ I'd love to.
__ Great. Do you like walking?

b iChecker Listen and check. Then listen again and repeat the sentences. Copy the rhythm.

4 READING

a Read the advert for a holiday. How many nights does the tour last?

Tour of the Magic Triangle: Prague – Vienna – Budapest

Visit these three beautiful capital cities and discover their historic monuments and lively atmosphere. Enjoy three wonderful cultural performances and return with unforgettable memories.

Prague

The tour starts in Prague, capital of the Czech Republic. A free bus takes you from the airport to your hotel, where you spend three nights. The price includes a tour of the city, a cruise on the Vltava River, a visit to a spa resort, and a performance at the Laterna Magika theatre. From Prague you travel first class by train to your next destination: Vienna.

Vienna

The Austrian capital has many spectacular monuments, which you can visit with the free 72-hour travel card which you receive when you arrive in Vienna. The price also includes a tour of the city, Viennese coffee and cakes at the famous Hotel Sacher, and a performance at the opera. After your three nights in Vienna you travel first class by train to your final destination: Budapest.

Budapest

You spend your last three nights in Budapest, the capital city of Hungary, where there are plenty of places to explore. The city is divided into two parts: the old historic city of Buda on the hill, and the commercial city of Pest on the other side of the River Danube. The price includes a tour of the city with a visit to the Parliament building, a typical Hungarian dinner, a performance of classical music, and the return journey from your hotel to the airport.

At only €1599, this is an opportunity you cannot afford to miss!

b Read the advert again. Answer the questions with P (Prague), V (Vienna), or B (Budapest).

In which city do customers…?

1 travel free on public transport *V*
2 have a traditional evening meal ___
3 go on a boat trip ___
4 listen to a concert ___
5 have a drink and sweet snack ___
6 go to a place to relax ___

c <u>Underline</u> five words you don't know. Use your dictionary to look up their meaning and pronunciation.

5 LISTENING

a iChecker Listen to two people, Chris and Dawn, talking about an Interrailing holiday. Which countries is Dawn visiting?

____

b Listen again and correct the sentences.

1 Dawn is going Interrailing **on her own**.
with a friend
2 Chris went Interrailing when he was **a child**.
3 Dawn is going Interrailing for **a month**.
4 Dawn's first stop in Italy is **Milan**.
5 Dawn wants to visit **the Eiffel Tower** in Paris.
6 Dawn is spending most nights **on the train**.

USEFUL WORDS AND PHRASES

Learn these words and phrases.

(travel) arrangements /ə'reɪndʒmənts/
conference /'kɒnfərəns/
news /nju:z/
fix /fɪks/
perhaps /pə'hæps/
still /stɪl/
both of us /'bəʊθ əv ʌs/
I'd love to /aɪd 'lʌv tu:/
for ages /fə(r) 'eɪdʒɪz/
How are things? /haʊ ə 'θɪŋz/

What is a rebel? A man who says no.
Albert Camus, French writer

3C What's the word?

1 GRAMMAR defining relative clauses

a Match the beginnings and ends of the sentences.

1 That's the hotel *f*
2 I need a phone
3 My mum is the only person
4 I love the picture
5 That bus is the one
6 Benicassim is the Spanish town
7 David Hockney is the artist
8 That's the restaurant

a which has a good camera.
b which my brother takes to work.
c which serves fresh fish.
d who remembers my birthday.
e who painted *Mr & Mrs Clarke*.
f where we spent our honeymoon.
g where they have a famous music festival.
h which is on the wall of your room.

b Complete the sentences with *who*, *which*, or *where*.

1 Do you know the man *who* lives next door?
2 That's the gallery __________ had the Leonardo da Vinci exhibition.
3 Are those the people __________ are selling their house?
4 Do you know a good restaurant __________ is open on Sunday night?
5 Is that the bus __________ goes to the airport?
6 We walked past the school __________ their children go.
7 She's the woman __________ everyone is talking about.
8 I took my laptop back to the shop __________ I bought it.
9 Antwerp is the city __________ I lived as a child.
10 Is there someone __________ can speak Arabic in your class?

2 VOCABULARY expressions for paraphrasing: *like, for example*, etc.

Complete the sentences for explaining words.

1 *mean* It's the o*pposite* of generous.
2 *cardigan* It's a k__________ of jumper.
3 *hire* It's s__________ to *rent*.
4 *slim* It's l__________ *thin*, but it's more polite.
5 *souvenir* It's s__________ you buy to remind you of your holiday.
6 *sunbathe* For e__________, you do this on the beach.
7 *pilot* It's s__________ who flies a plane.
8 *campsite* It's s__________ you can sleep in tents.

3 PRONUNCIATION pronunciation in a dictionary

a Match the words with their pronunciation. Use your dictionary.

1 beard *b* a /bɔːld/
bald *a* b /bɪəd/

2 quiet __ a /kwaɪt/
quite __ b /ˈkwaɪət/

3 shoes __ a /ʃuːz/
socks __ b /sɒks/

4 suit __ a /swiːt/
sweet __ b /suːt/

5 sightsee __ a /ˈsaɪtsiː/
sunbathe __ b /ˈsʌnbeɪð/

6 height __ a /weɪt/
weight __ b /haɪt/

7 shirt __ a /ʃɜːt/
shorts __ b /ʃɔːts/

8 crowded __ a /ˈklaʊdi/
cloudy __ b /ˈkraʊdɪd/

b iChecker Listen and check. Then listen again and repeat the words.

4 READING

a Read the definitions and complete them with these words.

agritourism chick lit E-waste fashionista netiquette sandwich generation staycation ~~web rage~~

More new words in English

1 *Web rage* is the angry feeling you get because of a problem with the internet.

2 A ________________ is a person who always wears the latest styles.

3 ________________ is a kind of book which tells a story from a woman's point of view.

4 ________________ is all the electrical machines and devices which people throw away.

5 The ________________ is a group of people who look after their parents at the same time as they're looking after their children.

6 ________________ is a kind of holiday where people stay on farms and help with all the work.

7 ________________ is a set of rules which explains how to be polite on the internet.

8 A ________________ is a holiday which you spend at home.

b Underline five more words you don't know. Use your dictionary to look up their meaning and pronunciation.

5 LISTENING

a iChecker Listen to a radio programme about the word game *Scrabble*. How many different names has the game had?

b Listen again. Mark the sentences T (true) or F (false).

1 Alfred Mosher Butts was out of work when he invented the game. *T*
2 The game of *Lexico* had a board and letter tiles. __
3 Butts used a newspaper to count the frequency of the letters in English. __
4 Butts gave the letters A, E, I, O, and U one point each. __
5 Butts gave 12 points to the most difficult letters to use. __
6 *Scrabble* became popular in 1948. __
7 Butts and Brunot sold the game to another manufacturer. __
8 You can buy *Scrabble* in more than a hundred different countries. __

USEFUL WORDS AND PHRASES

Learn these words and phrases.

barista /bəˈrɪstə/
gastropub /ˈgæstrəʊpʌb/
latte /ˈlɑːteɪ/
smartphone /ˈsmɑːtfəʊn/
google /ˈguːgl/
text /tekst/
tweet /twiːt/
update /ˈʌpdeɪt/
road rage /rəʊd reɪdʒ/
toy boy /ˈtɔɪbɔɪ/

iChecker TESTS FILE 3

Practical English Restaurant problems

1 VOCABULARY

Complete the sentences.

1 Can we have a t*able* for two, please?
2 What's on the m__________ today?
3 The st__________ is chicken soup or tomato salad.
4 I'll have the steak for my m__________ c__________.
5 Let's ask the w__________ for another bottle of water.
6 I don't want a d__________, but I'd like a coffee.
7 Can we have the b__________, please?

2 AT THE RESTAURANT

Order the dialogue.

A Are you ready to order? *1*
B Still. __
A Still or sparkling? __
B Yes, please. __
A And how would you like your steak? Rare, medium or well done? __
B A baked potato, please. __
A Can I get you something to start with? __
B Rare, please. *6*
A Here's your steak, madam. __
B Water, please. __
A Would you like that with fries or with a baked potato? __
B I'm sorry but I asked for my steak rare and this is well done. __
A OK. And to drink? __
B No, thank you. Just a main course. I'd like the steak, please. __
A I'm very sorry, madam. I'll take it back to the kitchen. *15*

3 SOCIAL ENGLISH

Complete the sentences with the words in the box.

a mistake any suggestions be great my day start with ~~tell me~~ to go we have

1 A So, *tell me*, Adam, what are your plans?
B Well, to __________, I'd like to see the world.
2 A I'd like to go sightseeing this afternoon. Do you have __________?
B How about going to Central Park? I could take you.
A That would __________.
3 A Could __________ the check, please?
B Yes of course. Here you are.
4 A Excuse me. I think there's __________.
B Oh, sorry. It's not __________ today.
5 A It's very late.
B Yes. Time __________.

4 READING

a Read the article and answer the questions.

1 How many restaurants are there in new York? *Over 20,000*
2 What time do restaurants serve Early Bird menus? __________
3 How much is the Early Bird menu at Cucina di Pesce? __________
4 Where is La Paella? __________
5 Which restaurants serve a Pre-Theatre Dinner Menu? __________
6 How much do they cost? __________
7 When is it cheapest to eat in a four-star restaurant? __________
8 What kind of food can you eat at Aquavit? __________

Eating out in NY

New York City has over 20,000 restaurants serving all kinds of food. However, eating out in the Big Apple can be very expensive. Here are some tips on how to save money during your stay.

Early Bird Menus

These are meals served in some New York restaurants between 5 p.m. and 7 p.m., when they would normally be empty. If you don't mind having dinner early, you can enjoy a three-course meal for between \$13 and \$25.

Cucina di Pesce (87 E.4th St) serves great Italian food on its \$12.95 Early Bird menu. If you prefer something Spanish, you can try the \$16.99 Early Bird menu at **La Paella** (214 E.9th St).

Pre-Theatre Dinner Menus

These are similar to Early Bird Menus, but they are served in the Theatre District. Most of the restaurants here offer a set menu at a fixed price ranging from \$30 to \$45. The offer is only available before the show, and it starts at 5 p.m.

Four-Star Restaurants

These are all very expensive at dinnertime, so why not have lunch there instead? That way you can get dinner quality food at lunchtime menu prices. **Aquavit** (65 E.55th St) serves fantastic Scandinavian food on a great lunch menu and **Jean Georges** (1 Central Park West) offers an excellent two-course lunch for only \$28.

b Underline five words or phrases you don't know. Use your dictionary to look up their meaning and pronunciation.

Few things are more satisfying than seeing your children have teenagers of their own.

Doug Larson, American journalist

4A Parents and teenagers

1 VOCABULARY housework, *make* or *do*?

a Complete the expressions with these verbs.

clean do lay make ~~pick up~~ put away tidy take out

1 *pick up* dirty clothes
2 ________ the beds, lunch
3 ________ your room, your desk
4 ________ the table for dinner
5 ________ the floor, the bathroom
6 ________ the rubbish, the newspapers
7 ________ the ironing, the washing up
8 ________ the clothes on your bed

b Complete the sentences with *do* or *make*.

1 He never forgets to *do* his homework after school.
2 I try not to ________ a noise when I get up early.
3 My husband doesn't often ________ lunch.
4 I'm going to ________ a course in Portuguese before I go to Brazil.
5 We always ________ housework on Saturday morning.
6 Some children ________ friends easily when they go to school.
7 When do you have time to ________ sport?
8 Sorry, I need to ________ a phone call.

2 GRAMMAR present perfect + *yet, just, already*

a Add *already* or *yet* to these sentences in the correct place.

1 I've done the washing.
I've already done the washing.
2 Have you made any plans for the weekend?
________?
3 We haven't finished lunch.
________.
4 Daniel has tidied his room.
________.
5 I've done the ironing.
________.
6 Have you been to the supermarket?
________?
7 I haven't cleaned the bathroom.
________.
8 Edward has taken out the rubbish.
________.

b Complete the sentences for each picture. Use *just* + present perfect and a verb from the list.

1 
2 
3 
4 
5 
6 

clean ~~do~~ lay win miss fall

1 She*'s just done* the washing up.
2 He ________ off his bike.
3 They ________ the championship.
4 'I ________ the floor.'
5 He ________ the table.
6 'Sorry. You ________ dinner.'

3 PRONUNCIATION /j/, /dʒ/

a Write a word containing the sound in the pictures.

1 a person at university *student*
2 the opposite of *old* ________
3 twelve months ________
4 a colour ________
5 special clothes for school ________

dʒ

6 a kind of short coat ________
7 a person between 13 and 19 years old ________
8 something that crosses a river ________
9 another word for *sweater* ________
10 get pleasure from something ________

b iChecker Listen and check. Then listen again and repeat the words.

4 READING

a Read the text. Which is the best title?

1 **Having a cleaner house**
2 **Equality in the home**
3 **Improving your relationship**

Men and women all over the world have arguments about doing the housework, and it's usually the women who lose. However, a recent study by researchers at Oxford University shows that the situation is slowly improving.

The researchers asked men and women aged between 20 and 59 to keep a diary of how much time they spent on housework each day. Then the researchers collected the diaries and analyzed them.

These showed that women in the UK today spend about four hours and 40 minutes each day doing housework. Men, on the other hand, spend two hours and 28 minutes doing the same things. Although women still spend more time doing domestic jobs, the figures show that the situation has improved. In the 1960s, women spent six hours a day on housework and men only 90 minutes.

Researchers say that women are still doing most of the housework because people still divide domestic jobs into two areas. They see cooking, cleaning, and looking after children as 'women's work', and general repairs, car maintenance, and work outside the home as 'men's work'.

So, in general, the results of the study bring good news for women. The difference between the amount of time men and women spend on housework is getting smaller every year. This means that the time will come when both sexes share domestic chores equally. However, women will have to be extremely patient, because the change won't be complete for another four decades!

b Read the text. Mark the sentences T (true) or F (false).

1 Men and women don't always agree about housework. *T*
2 Adults and teenagers took part in the study. ___
3 The participants had to write down the time they spent on housework. ___
4 The time people spend doing housework has changed since the 1960s. ___
5 Today, women do more housework than they did in the 1960s. ___
6 In general, people think it's normal for women to look after the family car. ___
7 Forty years from now, men and women will share the housework. ___

c Look at the highlighted words. What do you think they mean? Use your dictionary to look up their meaning and pronunciation.

5 LISTENING

a iChecker Listen to five teenagers talking about housework. Which speaker does the most housework?

____

b Listen again. Match the speakers with what they say about housework.

Speaker 1	*B*	A We all share it.
Speaker 2	___	~~B My mum does it all.~~
Speaker 3	___	C We pay someone to do it.
Speaker 4	___	D There's one thing I like doing.
Speaker 5	___	E I do a little every day.

USEFUL WORDS AND PHRASES

Learn these words and phrases.

carer /'keərə/
plate /pleɪt/
reputation /repju'teɪʃn/
teenager /'tiːneɪdʒə/
wardrobe /'wɔːdrəʊb/
dry (your hair) /draɪ/
knock (on the door) /nɒk/
carry on (texting) /'kæri ɒn/
switch off (your mobile) /swɪtʃ ɒf/
TV channel /tiːviː 'tʃænl/

I don't design clothes, I design dreams.
Ralph Lauren, American fashion designer

4B Fashion and shopping

1 VOCABULARY shopping

a Complete the text.

SHOPPING IN A SHOP OR STORE

I usually go shopping in my lunch break, so I don't have time to [1]t*ry* on clothes. There's always a long queue for the [2]ch________ r________, so I just take them straight to the [3]ch________ to pay. I keep the [4]r________ so I can change them if they don't [5]s________ me. Sometimes I get the wrong [6]s________, and the clothes don't [7]f________. I often [8]t________ things b________ to shops, but the [9]sh________ a________ don't seem to mind at all.

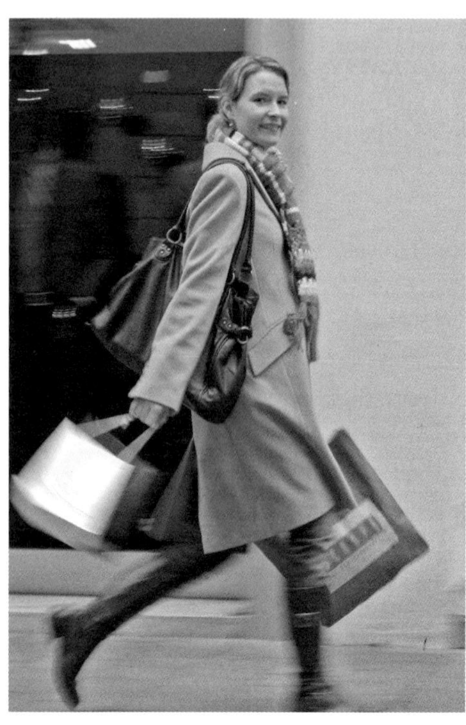

b Complete the crossword.

Shopping online

Clues down ↓

1 When you shop online, you normally have to create an a*ccount* which has your personal details.
2 Something you want to buy is called an it____________.
5 eBay is an online au____________ site, which sells things to the person who offers the most money.
7 Amazon is a popular w____________ where you can buy things such as books, computers, and clothes.

Clues across →

3 When you find something you want to buy on a website, you put it in your shopping b____________.
4 You can make a p____________ in different ways, e.g. using your credit card or Paypal.
6 When you are ready to buy something, you go to the ch____________.
8 You have to enter your d____________ address so they can send your things to the correct place.

2 GRAMMAR present perfect or past simple?

a Write sentences and questions with the present perfect. Use contractions where possible.

1 she / buy / a new jacket [+]
She's bought a new jacket.
2 I / bring / my / credit card [−]
______.
3 Anna / go shopping [?]
______?
4 your sister / ever work / as a model [?]
______?
5 you / wear / your new shirt [−]
______.
6 I / ever tell you/ about my holiday in Greece [?]
______?
7 the shopping centre / never be / so crowded [+]
______.
8 I / never use / eBay [+]
______.

b Complete the dialogues. Use the present perfect or past simple.

1 **A** *Have you ever bought* (you / ever / buy) any clothes on the internet?
B Yes, I *have*.
A What *did you buy* (you / buy)?
B I *bought* (buy) a dress for a wedding, but it didn't fit!

2 **A** ______ (you / ever / sell) anything on eBay?
B Yes, I ______.
A What ______ (you / sell)?
B Some CDs. I ______ (not want) them any more.

3 **A** ______ (you / ever / wear) any expensive jewellery?
B No, I ______.

4 **A** ______ (you / ever / lose) your wallet?
B Yes, I ______. I ______ (leave) it in a trolley at the supermarket.

5 **A** ______ (you / ever / have) an argument with a shop assistant?
B Yes, I ______. I ______ (not have) the receipt, so I ______ (not can) change some boots.

3 PRONUNCIATION *c* and *ch*

a iChecker Listen and circle the word with a different sound.

k key	1 customer account (choose)
k key	2 click proceed chemist's
s snake	3 clothes city centre
s snake	4 receive card cinema

b Listen again and repeat the words.

4 LISTENING

a iChecker Listen to a news story. What is Westfield?
______.

b Listen again and answer the questions.

1 How long has it taken to build Westfield?
Six years.
2 How much did the shopping centre cost?
______.
3 How many department stores and shops are there?
______.
4 How many cafés and restaurants are there?
______.
5 How many people work at Westfield?
______.
6 How can you get to Westfield?
______.
7 What did the reporter want to buy?
______.
8 Why didn't the reporter buy the thing she liked?
______.

USEFUL WORDS AND PHRASES

Learn these words and phrases.

bride /braɪd/
bridegroom /ˈbraɪdgruːm/
leather /ˈleðə/
sew /səʊ/
bare feet /beə fiːt/
fancy dress /fænsi ˈdres/
fashion designer /ˈfæʃn dɪzaɪnə/
high heels /ˈhaɪ hiːlz/
wedding dress /ˈwedɪŋ dres/
take off (your shoes) /teɪk ɒf/

There aren't enough days in the weekend.
Rod Schmidt, American writer

4C Lost weekend

1 GRAMMAR *something, anything, nothing, etc.*

a Circle the correct word.

1 We didn't do **anything** / **nothing** special last weekend.
2 Do you know **anything** / **anyone** about the meeting today?
3 There isn't **anywhere** / **nowhere** to go in the evenings.
4 He couldn't find his keys **nowhere** / **anywhere**.
5 We didn't know **someone** / **anyone** at the party.
6 Daniel has **something** / **anything** to tell you.
7 I phoned twice, but **anybody** / **nobody** answered.
8 We need to find **somewhere** / **anywhere** to stay in Dublin.
9 Listen! I think **somebody** / **anybody** is upstairs.

b Look at the picture. Mark the sentences T (true) or F (false).

1 There isn't anywhere to sit. *F*
2 The man on the right is eating something. ___
3 Nobody is dancing. ___
4 There's nothing on the ground. ___
5 Someone is playing with the dog. ___
6 The man cooking doesn't have anything on his head. ___
7 There isn't anybody in the swimming pool. ___

2 VOCABULARY adjectives ending *-ed* and *-ing*

Complete the sentences with an adjective ending *-ed* or *-ing*.

1 I'm reading a really in*teresting* book.
2 Going to a spa for the weekend is so r__________.
3 This film is really b__________. Turn the TV off.
4 Helen's very d__________. She's just lost her job.
5 My cousin is very in__________ in archaeology.
6 Congratulations! That's really ex__________ news.
7 The news at the moment is all very d__________.
8 We always feel very r__________ on holiday.
9 Mum, I'm b__________! I have nothing to do!
10 The dogs were very ex__________ to see us when we came home.

3 PRONUNCIATION /e/, /əʊ/, /ʌ/

a iChecker Listen and write the words in the chart.

anything ~~clever~~ ~~clothes~~ coat ~~customer~~
don't dress friendly funny gloves
goes home lunch nothing photos
something sweater website

1 e egg	2 əʊ phone	3 ʌ up
clever	*clothes*	*customer*

b Listen and check. Then listen again and repeat the words.

4 READING

a Complete the text with the activities.

Bake a loaf of bread   Play board games
Listen to some podcasts   Start a blog
Learn how to juggle   Take some photos
Meet your neighbours   Tidy your wardrobe
Organize your shelves   ~~Visit a library~~

Ten things to do during a money-free weekend

The weekend is the time when most people spend the most money. Here are some activities you can do if you want to save money.

1 *Visit a library* It doesn't cost anything to borrow a book and there may be some DVDs you want to watch.

2 ______________ Throw away any clothes you never wear, or give them to a charity.

3 ______________ Many websites have interesting interviews you can listen to for free.

4 ______________ This is a great way of spending time with the whole family.

5 ______________ You probably have the ingredients in a cupboard – the result is delicious!

6 ______________ All you need is three balls and a video showing you how to do it.

7 ______________ Invite them over for a coffee and a chat and get to know them better.

8 ______________ Decide which books, CDs and DVDs you want to keep and get rid of the rest.

9 ______________ Go for a walk with your digital camera. You'll be surprised at how beautiful your city is.

10 ______________ Not only is it fun, but writing improves your communication skills.

b Underline five words you don't know. Use your dictionary to look up their meaning and pronunciation.

5 LISTENING

a iChecker Listen to four people talking about their weekends. Where did they go?

Speaker 1 ______________
Speaker 2 ______________
Speaker 3 ______________
Speaker 4 ______________

b Listen again. Which speaker…?

1 cooked a meal ___
2 played with children ___
3 went to a different country ___
4 saw some interesting exhibitions ___
5 had an argument *1*
6 woke up early ___
7 had bad weather *1*
8 gave someone a surprise ___

USEFUL WORDS AND PHRASES

Learn these words and phrases.

survey /'sɜːveɪ/
encourage /ɪn'kʌrɪdʒ/
impress /ɪm'pres/
invent /ɪn'vent/
lie (about sth) /laɪ/
lie down /laɪ 'daʊn/
do paperwork /də 'peɪpəwɜːk/
press (the button) /pres/
tell the truth /tel ðə 'truːθ/
lift button /'lɪft bʌtn/

FILE 4

Time is the coin of your life. Only you can decide how to spend it. Don't let other people spend it for you.

Carl Sandburg, American poet

5A No time for anything

1 GRAMMAR comparative adjectives and adverbs, *as...as...*

a Complete the sentences with the correct comparative form of the adjective / adverb.

1 My new boss is *more patient* than the old one. (patient)
2 Pollution is __________ in cities than it is in the country. (bad)
3 We aren't in a hurry. You can drive __________. (slowly)
4 The summers here are __________ than they were in the past. (hot)
5 I failed the test. I'll work __________ next time. (hard)
6 It's __________ to my parents' house than it is to my boyfriend's. (far)
7 You can make the dinner tonight. You cook __________ than me. (good)
8 The Japanese diet is __________ than the American diet. (healthy)
9 A motorbike is __________ than a car. (dangerous)
10 Heathrow airport is __________ than Manchester airport. (busy)

b Rewrite the sentences using *as...as*.

1 This car goes faster than that one.
That car doesn't *go as fast as this one*.
2 Her shoes were more stylish than her handbag.
Her handbag wasn't __________.
3 My boss's office is bigger than mine.
My office isn't __________.
4 Spain played better than the Netherlands.
The Netherlands didn't __________.
5 I drive more carefully than you.
You don't __________.
6 Laptops are more expensive than mobile phones.
Mobile phones aren't __________.
7 Harry looks more relaxed than Sally.
Sally doesn't __________.
8 His shirt was dirtier than his trousers.
His trousers weren't __________.

2 VOCABULARY time expressions

Complete the sentences with these words.

in on save spend ~~take~~ waste

1 The flight to Beijing is going to *take* about 11 hours.
2 She needs to __________ more time studying.
3 I hope we arrive __________ time. My dad is meeting me at the airport.
4 Don't __________ time doing things you don't enjoy.
5 We'll __________ time if we go on the motorway. There's much less traffic.
6 My girlfriend gets very stressed when she's __________ a hurry.

3 PRONUNCIATION word stress

a Underline the stressed syllable in these words.

1 fa|ster
2 cen|tre
3 pa|rents
4 a|go
5 chil|dren
6 pa|tient
7 prob|lem
8 co|mmu|ni|ca|tion
9 tra|di|tio|nal
10 a|round
11 se|conds
12 be|tter

b Now circle the /ə/ sound.

1 fast(er)

c iChecker Listen and check. Then listen again and repeat the words.

4 READING

a Read the story.

The fisherman and the banker

An American banker was on holiday abroad. He was walking on a beautiful beach near a small village. He saw a fisherman in his boat with a few fish in it.

'Great fish!' he said. 'How long did it take you to catch them?'

'Not very long,' answered the fisherman.

'Why didn't you stay at sea longer to catch some more?' asked the banker.

'There are just enough fish here to feed my family,' answered the fisherman.

Then the American asked, 'But what do you do the rest of the time?'

'I sleep late, I fish a little, I play with my kids, and I relax. In the evening, I go to see my friends in the village. We drink wine and play the guitar. I'm busier than you think. Life here isn't as…'

The American interrupted him. 'I have an MBA from Harvard University and I can help you. You're not fishing as much as you can. If you start fishing for longer periods of time, you'll get enough money from selling the fish to buy a bigger boat. Then with the money you'll get from catching and selling more fish, you could buy a second boat, and then a third one, and so on. Then instead of selling your fish to shops, you could sell them directly to a fish factory, or even open your own factory. Then you'll be able to leave your little village for the city, and finally move to New York, where you could direct the company.'

'How long will that take?' asked the fisherman.

'About 15 to 20 years,' answered the banker.

'And then?'

'Then it gets more interesting,' said the American, smiling and talking more quickly. 'When the moment comes, you can put your company on the stock market and you will make millions.'

'Millions? But then what?'

'Then you can retire, live in a small village by the sea, go to the beach, sleep late, play with your kids…'

b Mark the sentences T (true) or F (false).

1 The fisherman needed to catch more fish. *F*
2 The American thought he was very busy. ___
3 The American wanted him to work harder. ___
4 He told the fisherman to buy more boats. ___
5 The American said that he couldn't live in New York. ___
6 The American promised the fisherman a lot of money. ___

5 LISTENING

a iChecker Listen to five speakers talk about how their lives have changed. Who…?

1 has just started working from home ___
2 has had a baby ___
3 has lost his / her job ___
4 has moved to a different country *1*
5 has retired ___

b Listen again. Which two people are happiest about the changes?

___

___

Who is the least happy?

___

USEFUL WORDS AND PHRASES

Learn these words and phrases.

abbreviations /əbriːviˈeɪʃnz/
characters /kærəktəz/
nowadays /ˈnaʊədeɪz/
story /ˈstɔːri/
irritable /ˈɪrɪtəbl/
patient (opp *impatient*) /ˈpeɪʃnt/
queue /kjuː/
stressed /strest/
stressful /ˈstresfl/
tips /tɪps/

A great city is that which has the greatest men and women.
Walt Whitman, American poet

5B Superlative cities

1 GRAMMAR superlatives (+ *ever* + present perfect)

a Complete the sentences with the superlative of an adjective from the box.

bad exciting far friendly ~~good~~ safe ugly wet

1 The traffic is awful in the town centre. The *best* way to travel around is by underground.
2 It rains a lot here in the Spring. The ____________ month is April.
3 The ____________ I've ever driven is from London to Edinburgh. It took me eight hours.
4 It was the ____________ hotel I've ever stayed in. The service was awful, so we only spent one night there.
5 The ____________ buildings are in the new town. They really aren't nice to look at.
6 The streets are very dangerous at night. The ____________ place to be is in the hotel.
7 The ____________ part of our tour was in Rio de Janeiro. We saw the first day of the carnival.
8 The ____________ city I've ever visited is Vancouver. I found the people very helpful.

b Circle the correct word or phrase.

1 That hotel has the **dirtier** / **dirtiest** rooms I have ever seen.
2 It's **the most interesting** / **more interesting** museum in Edinburgh.
3 This is the **more expensive** / **most expensive** souvenir I've ever bought.
4 That restaurant serves the **better** / **best** pasta we've ever eaten.
5 The summer is the **busyest** / **busiest** time of year.

c Write sentences with *ever.*

1 He / rude waiter / I / meet
He's the rudest waiter I've ever met.
2 That / fast car / I / drive
____________.
3 It / beautiful building / we / see
____________.
4 That / healthy meal / he / eat
____________.
5 It / good photograph / you / take
____________.
6 This / exciting sport / I / do
____________.
7 That / bad flight / we / have
____________.
8 This / interesting city / I / visit
____________.

2 VOCABULARY describing a town or city

a Complete the description of Llandudno.

Llandudno is a town in the [1]n*orth* of Wales on the [2]c____________ of the Irish Sea. It is about 35 miles [3]w____________ of Liverpool. It has a [4]p____________ of about 21,000, and is [5]f____________ as a seaside resort.

b Complete the sentences with the opposite of the adjectives in brackets.

1 Some of the buildings in the centre are quite m<u>odern</u>. (old)

2 Los Angeles is a very p__________ city – there are so many cars. (clean)

3 New York is a very s__________ city these days. (dangerous)

4 Mumbai is an extremely n__________ city. (quiet)

5 Where's the most b__________ place you've ever been to? (interesting)

6 The subway in Tokyo is very c__________. (empty)

c Circle the different word.

1	cathedral	church	shopping centre (circled)
2	mosque	temple	town hall
3	market	castle	department store
4	statue	palace	museum

3 PRONUNCIATION word stress

a iChecker Listen and <u>underline</u> the stressed syllable.

1 beau|ti|ful
2 crow|ded
3 dan|ge|rous
4 ex|ci|ting
5 fright|en|ing
6 ge|ne|rous
7 in|tere|sting
8 po|llu|ted
9 ro|man|tic

b Listen again and repeat the words.

4 LISTENING

a iChecker Listen to a radio travel programme about the Republic of Croatia. Tick (✓) the places that are mentioned in the programme.

1 Split ☑ 4 Zagreb ☐
2 Dubrovnik ☐ 5 Trogir ☐
3 Rijeka ☐ 6 the islands ☐

b Listen again and answer T (true) or F (false).

1 Zagreb is an old city. *T*
2 50,000 people live in Dubrovnik. ___
3 The palace is outside the city. ___
4 You can get a ferry to visit the islands. ___
5 The best time to visit is July and August. ___

USEFUL WORDS AND PHRASES

Learn these words and phrases.

architecture /ˈɑːkɪtektʃə/
culture /ˈkʌltʃə/
inhabitants /ɪnˈhæbɪtənts/
without /wɪˈðaʊt/
nightlife /ˈnaɪtlaɪf/
several /ˈsevrəl/
foreign /ˈfɒrən/
romantic /rəʊˈmæntɪk/
rude /ruːd/
pretend (to do sth) /prɪˈtend/

I've been on a diet for two weeks and all I've lost is fourteen days.

Totie Fields, American actress

5C How much is too much?

1 VOCABULARY health and the body

Complete the sentences with these words.

~~anxious~~ bones brain faces illness prevent skin

1 I'm *anxious* about my uncle's health because he's been ill for a long time.
2 People suffering from a serious ___________ often stay in hospital for a long time.
3 You need to cover your ___________ with sunscreen when you sunbathe.
4 You can tell they've been in the sun – their ___________ are very red.
5 When you're old, your ___________ can break more easily.
6 Coffee can sometimes ___________ you from sleeping.
7 My grandmother can't walk very well, but her ___________ is still active.

2 GRAMMAR quantifiers, *too, not enough*

a Complete the sentences with *a few, a little, much, many* or *a lot of*.

1 She's quite overweight because she eats *a lot of* sweets.
2 Can I ask you ___________ questions about your diet? It won't take long.
3 Her children don't have a healthy diet – they don't eat ___________ vegetables.
4 How ___________ sugar do you have in your coffee?
5 Could I have ___________ more tea, please?
6 I don't eat ___________ fruit – I need to eat more.
7 How ___________ hours do you spend in front of the TV every day?
8 ___________ time in the sun is good for you, but no more than 15 minutes.
9 He's in his last year at school, so he gets ___________ homework.
10 I only drink ___________ cups of coffee a day – maybe two or three.

b Circle the correct phrase.

1 I can't go to the party. I'm **too** / **too much** ill.
2 I'm not very good at basketball. I'm not **enough tall** / **tall enough**.
3 I couldn't live in the UK. It rains **too many** / **too much**.
4 I'm not going to finish my homework. I don't have **enough time** / **time enough**.
5 I can't sleep. I've eaten **too much** / **too many** chocolate.
6 I can't carry my shopping home. I have **too much** / **too many** bags.
7 I'm really unfit. I don't do **enough exercise** / **exercise enough**.
8 I'm always tired. I don't **enough sleep** / **sleep enough**.

3 PRONUNCIATION /ʌ/, /uː/, /aɪ/, /e/

a iChecker Listen and write the words in the chart.

any diet ~~enough~~ few food healthy like many much none quite too

1 ʌ up	*enough*		
2 uː boot			
3 aɪ bike			
4 e egg			

b Listen again and repeat the words.

4 READING

a Read the newspaper article. Which one of these fruits and vegetables do not count towards your five a day?

beans	☐	potatoes	☐
peaches	☐	cucumber	☐
carrots	☐	peas	☐
plums	☐	pineapple	☐

b Read the article again and write T (true) or F (false).

1 The campaign to eat more healthy food in the UK is called Six a Day. *F*
2 Fruit in a can isn't good for you. ___
3 Frozen vegetables don't count towards your five a day. ___
4 Only 100% pure fruit juice counts as a portion. ___
5 One mandarin orange counts as one portion. ___
6 You have to eat many tomatoes to get one portion. ___
7 A large spoonful of vegetables doesn't count as a portion. ___

c Look at the highlighted words. What do you think they mean? Check with your dictionary.

5 LISTENING

a iChecker Listen to two people doing a quiz about body age. How old is Alice? What is her body age?

b Listen again and complete the sentences.

1 Alice walks *quite a lot* every day.
2 She does ____________ sport or exercise.
3 She doesn't eat ____________ fast food.
4 She eats ____________ fruit and vegetables.
5 She's a very ____________ person.
6 She's ____________ stressed.
7 She sees ____________ close friends regularly.
8 She doesn't have ____________ time for herself.

USEFUL WORDS AND PHRASES

Learn these words and phrases.

bones /bəʊnz/	skills /skɪlz/
brain /breɪn/	skin /skɪn/
face /feɪs/	sunlight /ˈsʌnlaɪt/
illness /ˈɪlnəs/	sunscreen /ˈsʌnskriːn/
prevent /prɪˈvent/	anxious /ˈæŋkʃəs/

FILE 5

Five a Day

How much fruit do you eat every day? And how many vegetables? Food experts today think that we don't have enough of these foods in our diet and they say that we eat too much fat and sugar. This is why the World Health Organization has started a campaign to encourage us to eat more fruit and vegetables. The campaign in the UK is called Five a Day.

Why eat fruit and vegetables?

Fruit and vegetables are full of important vitamins and minerals which our bodies need to be healthy. Scientific studies have shown that eating a lot of them can prevent some illnesses like diabetes and obesity. Also, fruit and vegetables don't contain much fat and they don't have many calories, so they help to keep us slim.

What counts?

Nearly all fruit and vegetables count towards your five a day, except potatoes. The food can be fresh, frozen, or in a can, like peaches or peas. It can be raw, cooked, or even dried, like raisins or banana chips. A glass of 100% fruit juice with no added sugar also counts as one portion.

How much is a portion?

A portion of fresh fruit or vegetables depends on the size of the food. In the case of small-sized fruit like plums or mandarin oranges, one portion is two pieces of fruit. A piece of medium-sized fruit like an apple, an orange, or a pear also counts as one portion. With larger fruit like melon and pineapple, one portion is a 5 cm slice. We use the same method for calculating portions with vegetables. In the case of salad vegetables, a medium-sized tomato or a 5cm piece of cucumber count as one portion each. For smaller, cooked vegetables like beans and carrots, one portion is three large spoonfuls of vegetables.

Practical English The wrong shoes

1 VOCABULARY shopping

Match the prices.

1 79c	c	a	fifty-nine pence
2 €30.49		b	thirteen pounds ninety-nine
3 $3.89		c	seventy-nine cents
4 59p		d	thirty euros forty-nine
5 £13.99		e	three dollars eighty-nine

2 TAKING SOMETHING BACK TO A SHOP

Complete the dialogue.

A Can I help you, [1]m*adam*?
B Yes, I [2]b__________ this sweater yesterday.
A Yes, I remember. Is there a [3]pr__________?
B Yes, I'm [4]af__________ it's too small.
A What [5]s__________ is it?
B It's a [6]s__________. Do you have a [7]m__________?
A I'll go and [8]s__________. Just a minute. I'm [9]s__________ but we don't have this sweater in your size. But we do have this one and it's the same price. Or you can have a [10]r__________.
B Erm...I'll take this one then, please. Can I try it on?
A Yes, of course. The [11]ch__________ r__________ are over there. Is everything OK?
B Yes, this one fits perfectly.
A Good. Do you have the [12]r__________ for the other sweater?
B Yes, here you are.
A Brilliant.

3 SOCIAL ENGLISH

Order the dialogue.

A Have you had a good day? *1*
B OK. For what time? __
A Sure. __
B Can we make it a bit earlier? Say, seven thirty? __
A Why don't we go out for dinner? I could book a restaurant. __
B OK. I'll go and have a shower then. __
A Eight o'clock? __
B Oh, you know. Working! But it was OK. __

4 READING

a Read the text. Where could you…?

1 make a toy *FAO Schwarz*
2 try on a designer bracelet __________
3 buy something for when you have a shower __________
4 get a tattoo __________

Fifth Avenue Shopping:

Fifth Avenue is one of the most expensive shopping streets in the world. Most of the world's luxury boutiques are located here, including Gucci, Prada, Armani, and Cartier. It is also home to **huge** department stores like Lord & Taylor, Barneys, and Bergdorf Goodman. Most shops open daily from 10 a.m. to 7 p.m., starting later on Sundays. Here are some of the most well known:

FAO SCHWARZ

This world-famous toy store is popular with tourists and New Yorkers. The amazing Grand Hall has more than 20,000 coloured lights and there's also a giant dance-on piano **keyboard** and an enormous candy store. Big kids can have lots of fun in the **do-it-yourself** department, where they can even design their own doll.

RICKY'S

This ultra-fashionable beauty shop has been selling the latest cosmetics, hair and bath products for nearly two decades. Products range from the most expensive to the most ecological, so there's something for everybody. Upstairs, check out the fun clothing and **accessories**. You can also get temporary henna tattoos.

TIFFANY & CO

This exclusive jeweller's has occupied its current location since 1940. Customers can admire the designer jewellery on the first floor before taking the elevator upstairs to choose an **engagement** ring. You can buy elegant table, glass, and silverware on the fourth floor, and there are less **pricey** items on the third floor.

b Read the text again. Match the **highlighted** words to their meanings.

1 the set of keys on a piano __________
2 very expensive __________
3 scarves, belts, gloves, etc. __________
4 an agreement to get married __________
5 very big __________
6 the activity of making things on your own __________

A pessimist is someone who is pleased with bad experiences because they show he was right.

Heinz Ruhmann, German actor and film director

6A Are you a pessimist?

1 GRAMMAR *will / won't* (predictions)

Complete the dialogues with *will / won't* and a verb from the list. Use contractions.

not remember ~~fall~~ not sell forget not win miss

1

A I'm going climbing next weekend.
B It's very dangerous. You *'ll fall* ________.

2

A I'm playing in the tennis final tomorrow.
B The other player is very good. You ________.

3

A I'm going to study all evening.
B It's a waste of time. You ________ anything in the morning.

4

A I told Nick that it's Jane's birthday on Friday.
B You know Nick! He ________.

5

A I'm going to put my MP3 player on eBay.
B It's too old. You ________ it.

6

A I'm getting the 8.50 train.
B It's leaving in five minutes. You ________ it.

2 VOCABULARY opposite verbs

Write the opposite verb in each space. Be careful – use the correct verb form.

1 **arrive**
You won't *leave* on time.
2 **teach**
We're going to ________ English in Canada.
3 **fail**
I don't think he ________ all of his exams.
4 **Push**
________ the door to open it.
5 **mend**
I've ________ my glasses.
6 **lend**
Can I ________ a pen, please?
7 **win**
I think he's going to ________ the race.
8 **turn off**
Can you ________ the light, please?
9 **get**
I ________ more than 50 emails yesterday.
10 **lose**
I've ________ some money!

3 PRONUNCIATION *'ll, won't*

iChecker Listen and repeat. Copy the rhythm.

1 I'll **learn a lot**.
2 He'll **meet** somebody **new**.
3 **You'll** have a **good time**.
4 She **won't** get the **job**.
5 They **won't lend** you the **money**.
6 We **won't arrive** on **time**.

4 READING

a Read the horoscopes for this month. Answer the questions.

Horoscopes

AQUARIUS Jan 21–Feb 19

You'll be lucky in love this month! You'll meet someone new at work, which will be the start of something special. The colour red will bring you good fortune.

PISCES Feb 20–Mar 20

Close family will be important this month. Try to spend more time with them and they'll be very glad to see you. The colour green will bring you luck with money.

ARIES Mar 21–Apr 20

You'll have to be very careful with money this month, and avoid buying any clothes. However, you'll get a nice surprise at the end of the month. The colour blue will bring you luck.

TAURUS Apr 21–May 21

You'll have a very busy social life this month! Your friends will be taking you out all the time, and you'll make many new ones too. Orange will be your lucky colour.

GEMINI May 22–June 21

You won't have a very good month at work. Your boss will give you some bad news, but don't worry: you won't be unemployed. Work hard and next month will be better. Purple will be your lucky colour.

CANCER June 22–July 23

This will be a great month for going away! You'll win a holiday, so have your passport ready. You'll also travel a lot in your own country and you'll visit some old friends. Yellow will be your lucky colour.

1 Who will do a lot of travelling this month? *Cancer*
2 Who will have problems with their job? ______
3 Who won't go shopping? ______
4 Whose lucky colour will be red? ______
5 Who will go out a lot this month? ______

b Underline five words you don't know. Use your dictionary to look up their meaning and pronunciation.

5 LISTENING

a iChecker Listen to a conversation about horoscopes. What are Matt and Amy's star signs?

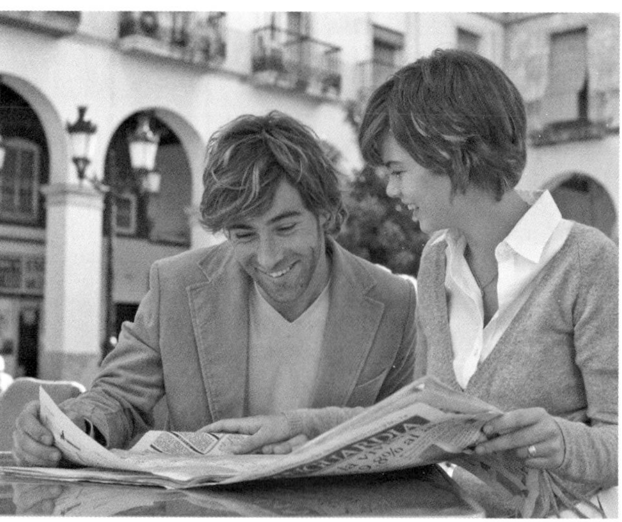

b Listen again and complete the sentences with A (Amy) or M (Matt).

1 *A* believes in horoscopes.
2 ______ doesn't believe in horoscopes.
3 ______ has a problem with someone.
4 ______ is worried about the horoscope.
5 ______ was born in January.
6 ______'s horoscope is good.
7 ______ has a meeting the next day.

USEFUL WORDS AND PHRASES

Learn these words and phrases.

optimist /ˈɒptɪmɪst/
pessimist /ˈpesɪmɪst/
(TV) series /ˈsɪəriːz/
stranger /ˈstreɪndʒə/
cheer up /ˈtʃɪər ʌp/
definitely (not) /ˈdefɪnətli/
probably (not) /ˈprɒbəbli/
I doubt it. /aɪ ˈdaʊt ɪt/
I hope so. (opp *I hope not*) /aɪ ˈhəʊp səʊ/
I think so. (opp *I don't think so*) /aɪ ˈθɪŋk səʊ/

Vote for the man who promises least – he'll be the least disappointing.

Bernard Baruch, American political adviser

6B I'll never forget you

1 GRAMMAR *will / won't* (promises, offers, decisions)

a Write sentences using the pictures and prompts. Use *Shall I / I'll / I won't*.

1 call / you tomorrow
I'll call you tomorrow .

2 lend / you some money?
______________________________?

3 have / the chicken
______________________________.

4 take / your coat?
______________________________?

5 turn off / air conditioning?
______________________________?

6 not / be late
______________________________.

b Are these sentences promises (P), decisions (D), or offers (O)?

1 I'll drive you home. *O*
2 I'll remember to tell her. ___
3 Shall I get you some water? ___
4 I'll help you clean your room, if you like. ___
5 I'll have the chocolate cake, please. ___
6 I won't tell your girlfriend. ___

2 VOCABULARY verb + *back*

Complete the sentences with these verbs.

~~call~~ come give pay send take

1 **A** Jack phoned while you were out.
B Thanks. I'll *call* him back in a minute.

2 **A** Do you want to borrow some money?
B Yes, please. I'll ___________ you back next week.

3 **A** The person you want to see isn't here. She's at lunch.
B That's OK. I'll ___________ back later.

4 **A** It's a really nice top, but it doesn't fit me.
B Don't worry. I'll ___________ it back to the shop and change it.

5 **A** Have you finished that book I lent you?
B Yes. I'll ___________ it back to you tomorrow.

6 **A** That toy car you bought on the internet doesn't work.
B Doesn't it? I'll ___________ it back, then.

3 PRONUNCIATION word stress: two-syllable verbs

a iChecker Listen and underline the stressed syllables. Circle the words which are stressed on the second syllable.

1	wo|rry	(re|lax)	(be|come)
2	de|cide	e|mail	pro|mise
3	prac|tise	li|sten	re|pair
4	bo|rrow	for|get	a|gree
5	sun|bathe	in|vite	com|plain

b Listen and check. Then listen again and repeat the words.

4 READING

a Read the text. What did Paul learn from his experience?

An expensive lesson

My name's Paul, and this happened to me when I was visiting a friend in Paris.

I was getting off the Eurostar train at the Gare du Nord station when a man came up to me. He was wearing a suit and he looked quite respectable. 'Do you speak English?' he asked. He had a French accent, but he said he was a banker from Montreal in the French-speaking part of Canada. Then he told me he had a problem. 'I'm here in Paris with my wife and our three children, and we don't have enough money for a hotel. You see, my wife tried to get money from a cash machine, but she couldn't remember our PIN number. She used the wrong number three times, so the machine kept her card. Could you help me?' I wasn't sure, so I asked to see his passport. 'My passport is with my wife. She's waiting in a café with the children. We only need €65 for the night and I promise I'll pay you back.' By this time the man was actually crying, so I thought he was telling the truth. I agreed to lend him the money and I wrote down his name, email address, and phone number in Montreal. Then we went to a cash machine and I gave him the money. He said thank you, gave me a big hug, and left. I never saw him or heard from him ever again.

I knew his story wasn't completely true. Why did a banker have only one bank card? Why didn't he tell me how he would pay me back? Were his wife and children really in the café, and did they even exist? But I was tired and in a foreign country, and I felt like I had to help him. I now know to be very careful who I talk to when I arrive somewhere new!

b Read the text. Number the sentences in the right order.

a Paul wrote down the man's contact details. __
b The man explained his problem. __
c The man's wife had his passport. __
d Paul arrived in Paris. *1*
e Paul asked for the man's passport. __
f A man started talking to him. __
g Paul didn't hear from the man. __
h Paul gave the man some money. __

c Underline five words you don't know. Use your dictionary to look up their meaning and pronunciation.

5 LISTENING

a iChecker Listen to five speakers describing problems they have had abroad. What do the speakers have in common?

b Listen again and match the speakers with the sentences.

Speaker 1 *D*
Speaker 2 __
Speaker 3 __
Speaker 4 __
Speaker 5 __

A Next time, I'll check before I go.
B I'll buy my own in future.
C I won't let anyone in another time.
~~D I won't do anyone any favours in the future.~~
E I won't go out with anyone I don't know again.

USEFUL WORDS AND PHRASES

Learn these words and phrases.

hurt /hɜːt/
previous /'priːviəs/
relationship /rɪ'leɪʃnʃɪp/
double portion /'dʌbl pɔːʃn/
ice cream sundae /aɪs kriːm 'sʌndeɪ/
get engaged /get ɪn'geɪdʒd/
get in touch /get ɪn 'tʌtʃ/
in their twenties /ɪn ðeə 'twentiz/

Only in our dreams are we free.
The rest of the time we need wages.
Terry Pratchett, British writer

6C The meaning of dreaming

1 GRAMMAR review of verb forms: present, past, and future

a Complete the dialogues with the correct form of the verbs in brackets. Use contractions where possible.

1 **A** *Are* you *going to go out* to go out tonight? (go out)
B No, I'm really tired. I'm *going to go* to bed early. (go)

2 **A** What time ________ you usually ________ to bed? (go)
B At 10.30. Then I ________ for an hour before I go to sleep. (read)

3 **A** Do you think England ________ tonight? (win)
B No, I think they ________. (lose)

4 **A** What ________ you ________ at midnight last night? (do)
B I ________ TV. (watch)

5 **A** ________ you ever ________ that you were flying? (dream)
B No, I ________ never ________ that dream. (have)

6 **A** What ________ you ________? It's 5 o'clock in the morning! (do)
B I can't sleep so I ________. (read)

7 **A** ________ you ________ well last night? (sleep)
B No, I ________ in the middle of the night, and I couldn't go back to sleep. (wake up)

8 **A** What time ________ you ________ tomorrow? (leave)
B I'm ________ at 8 o'clock. (go)

b Complete the text with the correct form of the verbs in brackets. Use contractions where necessary.

What colour are our dreams?

[1] *Do* we *dream* (dream) in colour or in black and white? People argued for many years about this question and scientists [2] ________ (do) a lot of research into this question. One of these scientists is a psychologist who [3] ________ (work) at Dundee University. Her name is Eva Murzyn, and right now she [4] ________ (study) the effect of television on our dreams. Eva [5] ________ just ________ (publish) the results of her latest study.

Sixty people [6] ________ (help) Eva with her research. They completed a questionnaire and kept a diary of their dreams. She [7] ________ (choose) people who were either under 25 or over 55. When Eva analyzed their diaries, she [8] ________ (discover) that the younger people usually dreamt in colour, whereas the older group often [9] ________ (have) black and white dreams. Eva thinks that this is because the older group [10] ________ (see) programmes in black and white when they were young. She believes that something happened to their brains while they [11] ________ (watch) TV at that time.

2 VOCABULARY adjectives + prepositions

(Circle) the correct preposition.

1 Sleeping eight hours a night is good (**for**) / **to** you.
2 She's angry **with** / **at** him because he forgot her birthday.
3 The village of Cheddar is famous **to** / **for** its cheese.
4 I'm very bad **in** / **at** drawing.
5 Be nice **to** / **at** me today because I'm in a bad mood.
6 We aren't interested **about** / **in** motor racing.
7 My little sister is afraid **of** / **to** big dogs.
8 The new boss is very different **of** / **from** our old one.

3 PRONUNCIATION the letters *ow*

a iChecker Listen and (circle) the word with a different sound.

aʊ owl			
1 brown	(know)	how	town
2 blow	snow	now	show
3 borrow	crowded	shower	towel
4 low	throw	window	down

b Listen and check. Then listen again and repeat the words.

4 LISTENING

a iChecker Listen to a radio programme about recurring dreams. Number the dreams in the order you hear them.

__ You are flying.
1 You are running.
__ You can't escape.
__ You are lost.
__ You are falling.

b Listen again and match the interpretations with the dreams.

Dream 1 [*e*] a You don't know what to do in your life.
Dream 2 [ ] b You can't change a difficult situation.
Dream 3 [ ] c Your life has improved in some way.
Dream 4 [ ] d You don't want your life to change.
Dream 5 [ ] ~~e You don't want to face a problem.~~

USEFUL WORDS AND PHRASES

Learn these words and phrases.

champagne /ʃæm'peɪn/
flowers /'flaʊəz/
owl /aʊl/
psychoanalyst /saɪkəʊ'ænəlɪst/
violin /vaɪə'lɪn/
freezing /'friːzɪŋ/
be frightened of /bi 'fraɪtnd ɒv/
dream about /'driːm əbaʊt/
be successful /bi sək'sesfl/

iChecker TESTS FILE 6

This page was intentionally left blank.

Listening

1A

Ben Great party.
Sandra Yes, it is.
Ben Sorry...hi...my name's Ben.
Sandra I'm Sandra.
Ben What do you do, Sandra.
Sandra I'm a nurse. How about you?
Ben Me? Oh, I'm a student.
Sandra A student? Really? What university do you go to?
Ben Manchester. I go to Manchester University. I'm in my second year of medicine.
Sandra Do you like it?
Ben Yes, I do. I like it very much...

Ben What do you think of the music, Sandra? Do you like it?
Sandra No, not really.
Ben What kind of music do you listen to?
Sandra I like rock music.
Ben Do you? Who's your favourite band?
Sandra Muse. I really like Muse.
Ben Me, too. Did you go to the concert last month?
Sandra No, I didn't. Was it good?
Ben Yes, it was excellent. I'm sorry you missed it.

Ben Do you do any sport or exercise, Sandra?
Sandra Yes, I play tennis.
Ben Ah, nice. I play rugby. I'm in the university team.
Sandra Are you?
Ben Yes, I am. But I play tennis, too. Perhaps we can play together one day.
Sandra Maybe. But I usually play with my boyfriend.
Ben Your boyfriend?
Sandra Yes, here he is. Wayne, this is Ben. Ben, Wayne.
Wayne Hello. Nice to meet you.
Ben Hi. Um, look at the time. Um, must go – some friends are waiting for me. Um, bye Sandra.
Sandra Bye.

1B

Presenter Hello and welcome to *Love Online*. Today, we'd like you, the listeners, to call in and tell us about your experiences of online relationships. And – oh my! – that's quick! – we already have our first caller. Hello?
Alan Hi, my name's Alan.
Presenter Hello, Alan. Can you tell us about your experience of internet dating?
Alan Yes, of course. I'm quite shy, you see, and I'm not very good at talking to girls I don't know. So one day, I registered on an online dating agency and I met Susan.
Presenter And what happened?
Alan We got on really well. In fact, after four months, we bought a house together. And now we've got a beautiful little boy called Sam.
Presenter Congratulations, Alan! Thanks for calling. Now, I think we have another caller. Hello?
Kate Hi, I'm Kate.
Presenter Hello, Kate. What can you tell us about love online?
Kate Well, I decided to try a dating site because I work long hours and I don't have time to meet new people.
Presenter So what happened?
Kate Well, I met some guys, and then I met Craig.
Presenter Who's Craig?
Kate Well, now, he's my husband. And we're very happy together.
Presenter That's great news, Kate! It looks as if it is possible to find love online. Now, who's our next caller.
Paolo Paolo.
Presenter Hi, Paolo. Did you marry someone you met on the internet?
Paolo Yes, I did, but it was the worst thing I ever did.
Presenter Oh. Why's that?
Paolo Because she didn't really love me.
Presenter How do you know that?
Paolo It was in the newspaper. There was an article about a woman who contacted men online, married them, and then left with all their money. And there was a photo of my wife next to the article, with her ex-husband.
Presenter Oh, I'm sorry to hear that, Paolo. And I'm afraid that's all we've got time for today. Join me next week for another edition of *Love Online*...

1C

And now for the latest news in the art world. If you're in Paris this weekend, you might like to visit the new David Hockney exhibition called *Fresh Flowers*. As the name suggests, most of the pictures depict flowers. However, these are no ordinary flower pictures, because Hockney uses his iPhone or his iPad to draw them.

Hockney started painting on his iPhone during the winter of 2008. At the time, he was staying at his home in the North of England where he has a beautiful view out of his bedroom window. One morning, he picked up his iPhone, and used his fingers to paint the sunrise. He was very pleased with the result, and started experimenting with other pictures. Now, he sends his friends a different flower picture every morning. They love it!

Fresh Flowers is on at the Fondation Pierre Bergé, Yves Saint Laurent in Paris until January 30th. The exhibition shows the drawings Hockney made on an iPhone, and the pictures he drew on an iPad. The gallery is open from 11 a.m. to 6 p.m. from Tuesday to Friday, and admission costs €5. Don't miss this show; it will be a bright moment in your day.

2A

Speaker 1 When I was 17, I went on holiday with my parents to Brittany, in France. My parents rented a lovely house on the beach, and the weather was great. We went for a delicious meal for my birthday, but I was miserable. I wanted to be with my friends and I didn't smile once in two weeks!
Speaker 2 A few years ago, I went to visit an old school friend, but I didn't enjoy the weekend at all. At school we got on really well, but now she has two small children so she didn't want to go out. I spent a very boring two days in her house watching TV. I don't think I'm going to visit her again.
Speaker 3 It's really hot where we live, so we always try to go on vacation where it's cool. Last year, we booked a vacation in Sweden, but we arrived in the middle of a heat wave. It was awful because there was no air-conditioning anywhere. We just sat in cafés and argued all day. We can do that at home!
Speaker 4 When I finished university, I went on a cruise around the Mediterranean with some friends from my course. We wanted to celebrate the end of our exams. As soon as we left the port, I started feeling seasick. I spent the whole week in bed, and I hated every minute of the cruise.
Speaker 5 Three years ago, I broke up with my boyfriend, so I decided to go on an expensive vacation on my own to the Seychelles. Unfortunately, the travel agent didn't tell me that the islands were popular with couples on their honeymoon. Everywhere I looked, there were people holding hands and I felt very lonely.

2B

Jenny What shall we do this afternoon, Matt?
Matt I know! Let's have a look at that box of photos my aunt gave me yesterday...Here it is...Oh, look at that!
Jenny Who's that?
Matt That's my grandfather. And that's my grandmother behind him on the right. She's the one in the flowery dress. It was just after they got married, but before they had any children. My aunt told me all about this photo a few years ago.
Jenny So, where are they?
Matt Well, as you know my dad is Spanish. My grandparents lived in the centre of Madrid, and this photo was taken in the district where they lived.
Jenny What's going on exactly?
Matt Well, there's a festival there called 'La Paloma'. It takes place in the middle of August every year, and it still happens now. There are lots of stalls selling food and also stalls where you can win a prize.
Jenny So, what was your grandfather trying to win?
Matt He was trying to win a bracelet for my grandmother. He was shooting at a target on the stall and all those people were watching him.
Jenny Do you know any of the other people in the photo?
Matt No, I don't. But I think they all lived near my grandfather.
Jenny Who took the photo?
Matt The man on the stall. The photo was included in the price. You had three chances to hit the target and you got the photo for free.
Jenny It's a lovely photo. I think your granddad was very good-looking!
Matt That's what everyone says!

2C

Presenter Hello, and welcome to the programme. Today, we're looking at lucky escapes, and Nick Williams from the news desk is here to tell us some amazing stories. Nick?
Nick Hi Gloria. Well, my first story is about a tourist who fell into a volcano. Maureen Evason was walking at the top of the Teide volcano in Tenerife, when she tripped and fell. She fell 27 metres until she hit a tree, which stopped her fall and saved her life. The rescue operation took nearly four hours, and after that Maureen spent two months in hospital before she could go home.
Presenter Lucky Maureen! What else have you got for us?
Nick Joseph Rabadue had a lucky escape when he was at home watching TV. Joseph was sitting on the floor, so his dad told him to go and sit on the sofa. Five minutes later, a lorry crashed into their living room, and threw the family television into the air. The TV then landed on the exact spot where Joseph had been on the floor before.
Presenter What a lucky escape! Do you have any more?
Nick Yes, just one more for now. One Saturday morning, Barry McRoy was leaving a café when two men came in. The men were fighting, and one of them had a gun. The man fired, and the bullet hit Barry in the chest. Luckily, he had a DVD in the pocket of his jacket at the time, and the DVD stopped the bullet. Barry McRoy is a very lucky man.
Presenter Absolutely! So, now it's time for you, the listeners, to call in and tell us about your own experiences. And here's our first caller.

3 A

Dialogue 1

Woman John!
Man Hi, Jane. You look well.
Woman You, too. How was your flight?
Man We took off a bit late, but it was fine.
Woman 1 Are you hungry?
Man 1 No, I had a sandwich on the plane.
Woman 1 Well, let's go and find the car. It isn't far.
Man 1 Great!

Dialogue 2

Ground staff Hello. Where are you flying to?
Passenger To Bristol.
Ground staff Can I see your passport, please?
Passenger Here you are.
Ground staff Thanks. Can I see your hand luggage?
Passenger Yes, just this bag.
Ground staff OK. Here's your boarding pass. The flight is boarding at 16.50 from Gate B28. You're in Group B.
Passenger Thanks a lot.
Ground staff Enjoy your flight.

Dialogue 3

Immigration Officer Can I see your passport please, sir?
Passenger Here you are.
Immigration Officer What is the purpose of your visit, Mr Green?
Passenger I'm going to stay with a friend.
Immigration Officer And how long are you going to stay in San Francisco?
Passenger For three weeks.
Immigration Officer Can I have a contact telephone number, please?
Passenger Yes. My friend's number is 415 673 702.
Immigration Officer Thank you, Mr Green. Enjoy your stay.

Dialogue 4

Woman 2 Look! There's a grey case. Is it ours?
Man 2 No, it's too big. Ours is much smaller.
Woman 2 It's taking a long time to come out...
Man 2 Yes. The first one came out really quickly.
Woman 2 Look! There it is! At last!
Man 2 You stay here with the other bags. I'm going to get it.
Woman 2 OK. I'll wait for you here.

Dialogue 5

Customs Officer Excuse me, madam. Can you come this way, please?
Passenger Yes, of course.
Customs Officer Have you got anything to declare?
Passenger No, I don't think so. I bought some chocolate in the Duty Free Shop, but that's all.
Customs Officer Can I check your bag, please?
Passenger Sure. Go ahead.
Customs Officer OK...That's fine. You can go on through.
Passenger Thank you.

3 B

Chris Hi, Dawn. I hear you're going to be on holiday next week.
Dawn Yes, I am. And I'm really looking forward to it.
Chris What are you going to do?
Dawn I'm going Interrailing with a friend.
Chris Interrailing? I did that when I was a student. I travelled around Europe with very little money, not much food, and no sleep. It was fun, but I don't want to do it again.
Dawn Ah, but you see Interrailing as an adult is very different.
Chris Really? In what way?
Dawn Well, you can travel first class now, and you don't have to go for a whole month.
Chris How long are you going for?
Dawn I wanted to go for two weeks, but work's so busy at the moment... so just a week.
Chris And which countries are you visiting?
Dawn Italy and France. We're starting in Venice, then we're going to Verona, and then Milan. We're stopping off in Paris on the way back, because I want to visit the Louvre.
Chris What about sleeping arrangements? Are you sleeping on the train like all the students do?
Dawn No, only on the night train from Paris to Venice. We have a two-bed sleeping compartment. And we're having dinner in the dining car of the train. Apart from that, we're sleeping in hotels. They're already booked.
Chris Well, it sounds like a different kind of trip to the one we went on as students.
Dawn Absolutely. It's going to be different, but I'm sure we're going to have lots of fun.

3 C

Presenter Hello and welcome to *The World of Words*. Today, we're going to look at word games, so let's start with the most popular of them all: *Scrabble*. Ricky Jones from the National Scrabble Association is here to tell us all about it. Ricky, who actually invented the game?
Ricky Well, it was an American called Alfred Mosher Butts. Butts was an unemployed architect, and in his free time he did a lot of crosswords. These crosswords gave him the idea for a game which he called *Lexico*. The game had the same letter tiles as *Scrabble*, but no board. Players used the letter tiles to make words. They scored by adding up the points on each of the letter tiles. Later, Butts introduced a board, and a set of rules and changed the name to *Criss-Cross Words*.
Presenter How did Butts decide how many points to give each letter?
Ricky He counted how many times each letter appeared on the front page of the *New York Times*. Then, depending on the frequency of each letter, he gave it between one and ten points. The most common letters, like the vowels, got only one point because they are easier to use. There are more of these letters in the game. There was only one tile for each of the least common letters, for example Q and Z, which got ten points.
Presenter So, when did Butts' original game become the modern game of *Scrabble*?
Ricky Well, in 1948, Butts met a businessman called James Brunot, who designed a new board and changed the name of the game to *Scrabble*. Then in 1952, the president of Macy's, the famous New York department store, discovered the game on holiday, and loved it so much he placed a large order. Butts and Brunot knew they couldn't produce enough *Scrabble* sets for Macy's, and so they sold the rights to the game to another manufacturer. Today, Scrabble is sold in 121 countries in 29 different languages.
Presenter What a story, Ricky! Thank you for sharing it with us.
Ricky My pleasure.

4 A

Speaker 1 Housework? Me? No, that's my mum's job. She only goes to work two days a week, so she has enough time to cook and clean and things like that. I go to school and then I see my friends, so I'm too busy to do housework. My dad goes out to work every day, so he doesn't have time either.
Speaker 2 Well, I try and help my mum when I can. I make my bed when I get up in the morning and I always lay the table for dinner. I usually tidy my room, but my mum is the one that cleans it. Apart from that, I'm not at home very much, so I don't do anything else.
Speaker 3 Oh yes, everyone in my family helps with the housework. There are four of us and we're all very busy. During the week, my mum or my dad cook the dinner, and my brother and I do the washing up. We do the cleaning together on Saturday mornings.
Speaker 4 It's true – I don't do much housework, but I love cooking. I don't have time to cook during the week, but I do all the cooking at the weekends. My mum does all the cleaning, though. She says she doesn't mind it.
Speaker 5 We have a cleaning lady who comes in every day and she does all our housework. She makes the beds, cleans the floors, and tidies our rooms – she even does the ironing! I'm not sure who does the shopping, but the fridge is always full. That's the important thing!

4 B

Presenter Those listeners who enjoy going shopping will be interested to hear our next news story. It's taken six years and 1.45 billion pounds to build, but at last the Westfield shopping centre has opened in Stratford, in East London. We sent our reporter, Juliet Redditch, over to take a look at what is now Europe's largest urban shopping centre. Juliet, what's it like in Westfield right now?
Juliet Well, Terry, there are crowds of people everywhere, especially outside the stores which have special opening offers. Some shops have called security staff to help them control the queues.
Presenter Just how big is Westfield, Juliet?
Juliet Oh, it's really very big! There are two enormous department stores, a huge supermarket, and 300 smaller shops. You can spend all day here if you want to. I haven't decided where I'm going to have lunch, but there are 70 different places to eat – it's amazing!
Presenter What effect has the shopping centre had on the local area, Juliet?
Juliet Well, this is an area where there are many people out of work. The shopping centre has created 10,000 new jobs, so it has really helped.
Presenter How did you get to Westfield today?
Juliet I came by car. There's an enormous car park with space for 5,000 cars. But you can also get here by bus, train, and by the underground – it's the best connected shopping centre in the country.
Presenter Now, Juliet, the big question is...have you bought anything yet?
Juliet No, I haven't. I was just looking around, really. I saw some trousers I liked, but I didn't buy them. There were too many people in the changing rooms to try them on!
Presenter OK, thanks Juliet, and now onto a news story of a different kind...

4 C

Speaker 1 Last weekend was really awful. My boyfriend and I went camping in the Lake District with some friends, and it rained the whole time. It was really depressing. We had to stay in the tent and play cards all day, which was OK to begin with, but then my boyfriend got bored. He started complaining about the weather, then about our friends, and finally about me! We had a terrible argument, and in the end we came home on Saturday night. I'm never going camping again!
Speaker 2 My weekend was fantastic. I took my wife to Paris, which is somewhere she has wanted to visit her whole life. We stayed in a wonderful hotel, in a beautiful old building overlooking the river. The view was incredible. We ate some really great food, and although it was quite cold, we had a very nice walk around the city. The best bit was that it was a surprise for my wife: I met her after work on Friday and we drove straight to the airport. She had no idea where we were going!
Speaker 3 I haven't got much money at the moment, so I didn't do anything special this weekend. But actually I had a really good time! I visited a local museum with some friends. All the museums here are free, and they have some interesting exhibitions about places like Egypt, Rome, and India. We then watched two of my favourite DVDs on Saturday night, and on Sunday I invited my parents to my flat and I cooked dinner for them. Not a bad weekend, really.
Speaker 4 My brother and his wife stayed with us this weekend. They have three children, and we spent the whole time playing with them. We took them swimming, we went to the zoo, and on Sunday we

went to the park. They have so much energy! And they're really noisy – especially in the morning when they wake up, which is usually around 6 o'clock. I was completely exhausted by Sunday night, but it was lovely to see them.

5 A

Speaker 1 Well, I haven't been here long, so I haven't had time to make many friends yet. After I get home from work, I spend most of the evening online chatting with friends and family back home. Twice a week, I have classes to try and learn the language. Most of my colleagues speak really good English, but I haven't been out with them yet.

Speaker 2 I guess you could say I'm a bit depressed at the moment. Time goes really slowly when you've got nothing to do. I spend more time sleeping now, and I have a lot of time to do the housework. It doesn't take all day to make the bed and clean my room, so I get quite bored. I hope I find another job soon because I really need the money.

Speaker 3 My life has changed a lot now that I don't have to leave the house to go to work. Things aren't so stressful first thing in the morning now. I just get up, make a cup of tea, and switch on my computer. It's strange communicating with colleagues online and not seeing them face-to-face. Sometimes it gets a bit lonely.

Speaker 4 Oh no, I never get bored. There's always so much to do! I like to get up early and read the newspaper while I'm having breakfast. Then I like to go for a walk and do a bit of shopping. After lunch, I go and pick up my grandchildren from school. We spend an hour in the park until their mum comes to get them. I'm really enjoying life right now.

Speaker 5 This is the best thing that has ever happened to me! She's so beautiful that I seem to spend all day looking at her! I don't have time to see friends now, so I keep in touch with everybody by phone or online when she's asleep. We go shopping together and I do more housework and cooking, but I don't get much sleep anymore!

5 B

Presenter Hello and welcome to *The Travel Programme*. Now, one of the most popular tourist destinations these days is the Republic of Croatia in the Balkans. Paula Wilcox from the National Tourist Board is here to tell us all about it. Paula, what's so special about Croatia?

Paula Oh, there's just so much to see and do there. First of all, there are historic cities like Zagreb – the capital – and Dubrovnik to visit.

Presenter Let's start with Zagreb. What is there to see there?

Paula Well, Zagreb is in the north of the country on the River Sava. It's both an old city and a modern one at the same time. There are lots of elegant restaurants and fashionable shops there, and the city has lots of museums – the most important one is the Archaeological Museum.

Presenter What about Dubrovnik?

Paula Dubrovnik is much smaller than Zagreb – the population is only about 43,000. It's in the south of Croatia on the Adriatic coast. Inside the old city walls there are palaces, churches, and a Baroque cathedral to visit. In my opinion, Dubrovnik is one of the most beautiful cities in the world.

Presenter Apart from the cities, what else would you recommend?

Paula The beaches and the islands. There are wonderful beaches on the Adriatic Sea – Croatia's coast is very long – and it has more than a thousand islands.

Presenter How can you get to the islands?

Paula Well, the best place to get a ferry is Split, another city on the coast which is larger than Dubrovnik, but also has some wonderful monuments. There are a number of ferries, which take you to many different islands, where you can do water sports or just relax on the beach.

Presenter So, when is the best time to visit Croatia, Paula?

Paula The main tourist areas are very crowded in July and August, so it's better to go in May or June, when it isn't as busy.

Presenter Thank you for that, Paula. Croatia certainly sounds like a very interesting holiday destination. Now, let's look at a different type of holiday ...

5 C

Dave Hey Alice. Let's do this quiz. It says you can find out your body age.

Alice Body age? OK.

Dave You first. So...we start with your real age, which is 35...

Alice Don't tell everyone.

Dave Sorry...then we add or subtract years depending on your answers to the questions. Got that?

Alice Yes.

Dave Right. First question. How much do you walk a day?

Alice Well, I always go for a walk at lunch time. So ... quite a lot.

Dave Quite a lot. OK, so we subtract one year, which leaves us with 34. Next question. How much sport and exercise do you do?

Alice Oh I hate sport. And I don't do any exercise. I guess that means none.

Dave No sport or exercise. Add two years. That makes 36. How much fast food do you eat?

Alice None. I don't eat any.

Dave Great! Subtract a year. We're back on 35 again. How many portions of fruit and vegetables do you eat?

Alice A lot. I have more than five every day.

Dave A lot. Subtract two years. That's 33. Next one. How would you describe yourself mentally?

Alice Um, what do you mean?

Dave Well, are you a positive person, or a negative person?

Alice Oh, right. Um, I think I'm a very positive person.

Dave OK. Subtract three years...Now you're on 30. Next question. How would you describe your stress level?

Alice Mmm, I would say I'm a little stressed...but it's under control.

Dave OK, so we don't have to add or subtract anything. You're still on 30. How many close friends do you see regularly?

Alice Mmm. A few. I don't have much time.

Dave Right...we don't add or subtract anything again. Last question. How much time do you have for yourself?

Alice Not enough. I'm always really busy.

Dave Add a year...That makes 31. Which means that you are 35 but your body is only 31. What do you think of that?

Alice 31? That's great news! Now it's your turn...

6 A

Matt What are you reading?

Amy Nothing. Just my horoscope.

Matt Really? What star sign are you?

Amy Virgo. My birthday's on September 15th.

Matt So, what does it say?

Amy It says that people will talk about me next week because of something I've done.

Matt But you don't really believe that, do you?

Amy Well, actually I do. Because I have done something that will make people talk about me.

Matt Oh. What have you done?

Amy I sent an email to my boss yesterday complaining about my new colleague. She's really lazy and she never does any work.

Matt Did you?

Amy Yes. So my boss will ask the other people in my office about this new person and he'll probably ask about me, too. So, my horoscope is right. People will definitely talk about me next week.

Matt Well, don't worry about it. I'm sure everything will be alright.

Amy I hope so.

Matt Anyway, what about me? What does my horoscope say?

Amy Let me have a look. Your birthday's January 5th, so that makes you...Capricorn.

Matt That's right....So, what does it say?

Amy It says...oh! Listen to this! It says you'll be lucky with money next week.

Matt Really? Perhaps I should go out and buy a lottery ticket!

Amy No, wait a minute. Let's think about this. You've got a meeting with <u>your</u> boss tomorrow, haven't you?

Matt Yes. Why?

Amy Perhaps she'll give you a pay rise!

Matt Oh, Amy! Really! You're taking this far too seriously! I don't believe a word of it!

Amy Well, I do. I think your boss will put up your salary tomorrow. Perhaps she'll offer you a better job!

Matt Amy, you're being far too optimistic. It's only a horoscope, for goodness' sake!

6 B

Speaker 1 I was on holiday, and I was looking round a famous palace, when a man came up to me and asked me to take a photo of him. He gave me his camera, but it wasn't working properly. When I gave it back to him, he dropped it on the floor and it broke. I picked it up and went to give it to the man, but he was gone. Then I discovered my wallet was missing.

Speaker 2 When I went abroad last year for a business trip, I didn't have time to get any local money before I left. So after I landed, I went straight to the bank to get three hundred euros. I was in a hurry because I had a train to catch. The cashier slowly counted out the notes and when he stopped, I picked them up. When I got to the train station I realized later that I only had a hundred euros.

Speaker 3 When we were on holiday, two men knocked on the door of our apartment. They were wearing uniforms and they said they were police inspectors. One of them came in to look around while the other stayed by the door. Unfortunately, while we were talking to the first man, the second man took our wallets and cameras from the bedroom.

Speaker 4 I was having a problem using the ticket machine in the metro, when someone came up to help me. He told me how much money I needed and then offered to put it in the machine for me. I counted out the money, but he said it wasn't enough. I gave him some more money and I got my ticket. Unfortunately, I paid ten times the price for it!

Speaker 5 I was waiting at a bus stop, when this beautiful woman came up to me. We got chatting, and she invited me to go to a club with her. We had a few drinks together and then the waiter brought me an incredibly expensive bill. I started to complain but then I noticed four big men at the door who were looking at me. Of course I paid the bill.

6 C

Presenter Hello and welcome to the programme. Do you ever have the same dream night after night? These dreams are called 'recurring dreams', and psychologist Dr William Harris is in the studio today to tell us all about them. Good morning, Dr Harris.

Dr Harris Hello.

Presenter Dr Harris, which is the most common recurring dream?

Dr Harris Well, top of the list is the dream where someone or something is running after you. Either it's a person or a dangerous animal, like a bull or a lion. The dream means that there is something in your life that you don't want to face. It can be a feeling, a conflict or a memory, for example, but whatever it is, it's something that you don't want to deal with.

Presenter Right. What's the next dream on the list?

Dr Harris It's the one where you are falling for what seems like a very long time. Falling is a definite sign that you are out of control. You have lost direction in your life and you don't know what to do.

Presenter Yes, I've had that dream before. Not recently, though. Anyway, what other recurring dreams are there?

Dr Harris This is another fairly common dream. You're trying to get somewhere but you get lost on the way, and you don't know where you are. People often have this dream when they're going through a period of change. It shows that they don't want to accept the new situation.

Presenter OK, Dr Harris. Have you got any more recurring dreams for us?

Dr Harris Yes, there are two. The first dream is a good one. Some people have a recurring dream that they are flying through the air. They are enjoying it, and enjoying looking down on the world below. This shows that they are feeling free, possibly because they have solved a problem they had, or they have escaped from a difficult situation in their life.

Presenter And the last dream?

Dr Harris This one isn't so good. It's a feeling of being trapped. Maybe you are in a lift that is trapped between floors and you can't get out. This dream means that there is something in your life that is making you feel unhappy, and you feel that you cannot change it.

Presenter Dr Harris, that was very interesting. Thank you for talking to us.

Dr Harris You're welcome.

Answer key

1 GRAMMAR

a 2 Do you have any brothers or sisters?
3 What university do you go to?
4 What languages can you speak?
5 Where did you study English before?
6 What kind of music do you listen to?
7 How often do you do exercise?
8 Where did you go last weekend?

b 2 did you do last night
3 TV programmes does your girlfriend watch
4 is your birthday
5 are you from
6 did your friends go on holiday last year
7 do you read
8 were you angry yesterday

2 VOCABULARY

a 2d 3i 4g 5e 6h 7b 8a 9f 10c

3 PRONUNCIATION

a 2P 3R 4M 5B 6K 7I

c 2 programme 3 thirteen 4 thirty
5 university 6 weekend 7 magazine
8 sister 9 language 10 address

4 SPELLING AND NUMBERS

a 2 seventeen, eighteen
3 eighty, ninety
4 one hundred, one hundred and one
5 eight hundred, nine hundred
6 four hundred and fifty, five hundred
7 five thousand, seven thousand
8 thirty thousand, forty thousand

b 2 exercise 3 breakfast 4 family
5 cinema 6 thousand 7 teacher
8 university 9 weekend 10 important

5 LISTENING

a Because some friends are waiting for him. / Because Sandra's boyfriend arrives.

b 1T 2F 3F 4T 5T 6F

1 GRAMMAR

a 2 It doesn't rain a lot here
3 We don't live in a flat
4 I don't play tennis
5 He doesn't have a beard
6 They don't go to the gym
7 She doesn't write a blog

b 2 Does 3 do 4 Does 5 do 6 Does
7 Does

c 2 earns 3 study 4 want 5 lives
6 share 7 have 8 doesn't come
9 doesn't like 10 prefer 11 don't see
12 get on

2 VOCABULARY

a 2 bald 3 straight, curly
4 beard, moustache 5 fat, slim
6 thin, overweight 7 red, medium height

b 2d 3e 4a 5b 6f

c 2 extrovert 3 mean 4 unfriendly 5 lazy
6 unkind 7 funny 8 intelligent

3 PRONUNCIATION

a 1 watches 2 lives 3 likes 4 starts
5 leaves 6 cooks

c 2 extrovert 3 unfriendly 4 generous
5 moustache 6 serious 7 curly 8 quiet
9 overweight

4 READING

b 2T 3F 4F 5T

5 LISTENING

a three

c 1E 2A, F 3B, D

1 VOCABULARY

a Down: 2 leggings 3 trousers 4 shirt
6 tracksuit 7 cap
Across: 3 trainers 5 belt 8 coat
9 dress 10 tie

b 2 on the left 3 in front of 4 next to
5 behind 6 between

2 GRAMMAR

a 2 are relaxing 3 are walking 4 is lying
5 is relaxing 6 are sitting 7 are they doing
8 are waiting 9 are watching 10 is playing

b 2 drives 3 are sleeping 4 's raining
5 drinks 6 like 7 works 8 wears
9 're studying 10 live

3 PRONUNCIATION

a /ə/: fashion, sandals, sweater, trainers, trousers
/ɜː/: shirt, skirt, T-shirt, third, world

4 LISTENING

a David Hockney used his iPhone and iPad to draw them.

b 1 In Paris.
2 The sunrise.
3 He sends them to his friends.
4 30 January.
5 Five euros.

1 CALLING RECEPTION

2 There's a problem with the shower.
3 I'll send somebody up right away.
4 I'm sorry to bother you again.
5 I have a problem with the Wi-Fi.
6 I'll put you through to IT.

2 SOCIAL ENGLISH

2 good view 3 looking forward
4 must be 5 By the way

3 READING

a 2T 3T 4F 5T 6F 7F

1 VOCABULARY

a 2 for, walk 3 book 4 abroad
5 hire 6 out 7 stay 8 sightseeing
9 sunbathe 10 away

b 2 sunny 3 crowded 4 delicious
5 unhelpful 6 basic 7 friendly 8 lovely
9 cloudy 10 disgusting

2 GRAMMAR

a Regular: arrived, asked, invited, rented, stayed, sunbathed
Irregular: bought, could, chose, ate, felt, said

b 2 They didn't buy
3 The people weren't
4 I didn't sunbathe
5 We didn't hire
6 He didn't spend
7 Our room wasn't

c 2 wanted 3 booked 4 took 5 arrived
6 went 7 asked 8 looked 9 couldn't
10 went

d 2 did they want
3 did they book
4 did they arrive
5 did the woman at the desk
6 did they go

3 PRONUNCIATION

a 2 wanted 3 booked 4 invited

c 1 caught, saw 2 rang, sat 3 drove, wrote
4 said, went 5 gave, made

4 LISTENING

a 2 c 3 d 5 e 4

2B

1 GRAMMAR

a 2 was snowing 3 weren't driving
4 was he doing 5 were you crying
6 was sitting 7 were living 8 wasn't working

b 2 He fell off his bike when he was cycling home
3 The children were playing video games when the visitors arrived
4 We were having a barbecue when it started to rain
5 I was finishing my report when my computer crashed

c 2 were having 3 got 4 was speaking
5 noticed 6 was sitting 7 decided
8 went 9 said 10 stopped 11 was passing
12 took 13 came 14 was smiling
15 looked 16 was laughing

2 VOCABULARY

a 2 in 3 on, in, at, on 4 on 5 on
6 at, in, at 7 in, on 8 At, in, in

b 2 on, in 3 on, in, on 4 in, on 5 at 6 on, on 7 at, in 8 at, at

4 LISTENING

a Yes.

b 2 b 3 c 4 a 5 a

2C

1 GRAMMAR

a 2 Next day 3 when 4 Suddenly
5 Two minutes later 6 After that

b 1b so 1c Although 2a Although
2b so 2c because 3a but 3b Although
3c because

c 1 so I didn't have any breakfast
2 but I had a great holiday in Egypt
3 although I don't really like him
4 so I called the police
5 although he has a lot of money
6 because she couldn't find her wallet

2 VOCABULARY

a 2g 3 f 4 b 5 h 6 a 7 e 8 c

3 PRONUNCIATION

a 1 awful, birthday, evening, perfect, restaurant, second
2 again, although, because, invite

4 READING

a 2, 5, 1, 4, 3

5 LISTENING

1 T 2 F 3 F 4 T 5 F 6 T

3A

1 GRAMMAR

a 2 'm going to book
3 isn't going to sleep
4 's, going to get
5 isn't going to fly
6 're going to be
7 'm not going to stay
8 Are, going to need

b 2 we aren't going to go
3 We're going to go
4 are you going to travel
5 We're going to be
6 are you going to do
7 We're going to stay
8 we're going to rent
9 Is it going to be
10 it isn't going to rain

2 VOCABULARY

2 lift 3 Departures 4 check-in 5 gate
6 passport control 7 Baggage Reclaim
8 trolley 9 Customs 10 Arrivals

4 READING

a three

b 2 T 3 F 4 T 5 T 6 F

5 LISTENING

a Dialogue 2 Check-in
Dialogue 3 Immigration
Dialogue 4 Baggage reclaim
Dialogue 5 Customs

c 1 a sandwich 2 B28 3 415 673 702
4 grey 5 some chocolate

3B

1 GRAMMAR

a 2 're driving 3 aren't stopping 4 're getting
5 're going 6 aren't taking 7 're stopping
8 're arriving 9 're picking 10 're catching

b 2 ✓
3 it's going to be
4 he's going to get the job
5 aren't going to miss
6 ✓
7 ✓
8 she's going to have

2 VOCABULARY

2 in 3 about 4 for 5 on 6 to 7 at 8 of

3 PRONUNCIATION

a 2 I'd love to.
3 Are you free this weekend?
4 Sorry, no. I'm working on Saturday.
5 What about next weekend? What are you doing then?
6 Nothing. Next weekend is fine.
7 Great. Do you like walking?
8 I love it!
9 OK. Let's go to Devon – the countryside is beautiful!

4 READING

a nine

b 2 B 3 P 4 B 5 V 6 P

5 LISTENING

a Italy and France

b 2 a student 3 a week 4 Venice
5 the Louvre 6 in hotels

3C

1 GRAMMAR

a 2 a 3 d 4 h 5 b 6 g 7 e 8 c

b 2 which 3 who 4 which 5 which
6 where 7 who 8 where 9 where
10 who

2 VOCABULARY

2 kind 3 similar 4 like 5 something
6 example 7 someone 8 somewhere

3 PRONUNCIATION

a 2 a quite, b quiet 3 a shoes, b socks
4 a sweet, b suit 5 a sightsee, b sunbathe
6 a weight, b height 7 a shirt, b shorts
8 a cloudy, b crowded

4 READING

a 2 fashionista 3 Chick lit 4 E-waste
5 sandwich generation 6 Agritourism
7 Netiquette 8 staycation

5 LISTENING

a three

b 2 F 3 T 4 T 5 F 6 F 7 F 8 T

Practical English Restaurant problems

1 VOCABULARY
2 menu 3 starter 4 main course
5 waiter / waitress 6 dessert 7 bill

2 AT THE RESTAURANT
2 Yes, please.
3 Can I get you something to start with?
4 No, thank you. Just a main course. I'd like the steak, please.
5 And how would you like your steak? Rare, medium or well done?
6 Rare, please.
7 Would you like that with fries or with a baked potato?
8 A baked potato, please.
9 OK. And to drink?
10 Water, please.
11 Still or sparkling?
12 Still.
13 Here's your steak, madam.
14 I'm sorry but I asked for my steak rare and this is well done.

3 SOCIAL ENGLISH
1 start with 2 any suggestions, be great
3 we have 4 a mistake, my day 5 to go

4 READING
a 2 5 p.m.–7 p.m. 3 $12.95 4 214 E.9th St
5 Restaurants in the Theatre District
6 $30–$45 7 At lunchtime
7 Scandinavian food

4A

1 VOCABULARY
a 2 make 3 tidy 4 lay 5 clean 6 take out
7 do 8 put away

b 2 make 3 make 4 do 5 do 6 make
7 do 8 make

2 GRAMMAR
a 2 Have you made any plans for the weekend yet
3 We haven't finished lunch yet
4 Daniel has already tidied his room
5 I've already done the ironing
6 Have you been to the supermarket yet
7 I haven't cleaned the bathroom yet
8 Edward has already taken out the rubbish

b 2 's just fallen 3 've just won
4 've just cleaned 5 's just laid
6 've just missed

3 PRONUNCIATION
a 2 young 3 year 4 yellow 5 uniform
6 jacket 7 teenager 8 bridge 9 jumper
10 enjoy

4 READING
a 2
b 2 F 3 T 4 T 5 F 6 F 7 T

5 LISTENING
a Speaker 3
b Speaker 2 E, Speaker 3 A, Speaker 4 D, Speaker 5 C

4B

1 VOCABULARY
a 2 changing rooms 3 checkout 4 receipt
5 suit 6 size 7 fit 8 take, back
9 shop assistants

b Down: 2 item 5 auction 7 website

Across: 3 basket 4 payment 6 checkout
8 delivery

2 GRAMMAR
a 2 I haven't brought my credit card
3 Has Anna gone / been shopping
4 Has your sister ever worked as a model
5 You haven't worn your new shirt
6 Have I ever told you about my holiday in Greece
7 The shopping centre's never been so crowded
8 I've never used eBay

b 2 **A** Have you ever sold, **B** have, **A** did you sell, **B** didn't want 3 **A** Have you ever worn, **B** haven't 4 **A** Have you ever lost, **B** have, left 5 **A** Have you ever had, **B** have, didn't have, couldn't

3 PRONUNCIATION
a 2 proceed 3 clothes 4 card

4 LISTENING
a A shopping centre
b 2 £1.45 billion
3 Two department stores, one supermarket, and 300 smaller shops
4 70
5 10,000
6 By car, bus, train, and by the underground
7 Some trousers
8 Because there were too many people in the changing rooms to try them on

4C

1 GRAMMAR
a 2 anything 3 anywhere 4 anywhere
5 anyone 6 something 7 nobody
8 somewhere 9 somebody

b 2 T 3 T 4 F 5 T 6 F 7 F

2 VOCABULARY
2 relaxing 3 boring 4 depressed
5 interested 6 exciting 7 depressing
8 relaxed 9 bored 10 excited

3 PRONUNCIATION
a 1 anything, dress, friendly, sweater, website
2 coat, don't, goes, home, photos
3 funny, gloves, lunch, something, nothing

4 READING
a 2 Tidy your wardrobe
3 Listen to some podcasts
4 Play board games
5 Bake a loaf of bread
6 Learn how to juggle
7 Meet your neighbours
8 Organize your shelves
9 Take some photos
10 Start a blog

5 LISTENING
a Speaker 1 went camping in the Lake District.
Speaker 2 stayed in a hotel in Paris.
Speaker 3 went to a local museum.
Speaker 4's brother and wife came to stay.

b 1 Speaker 3 2 Speaker 4 3 Speaker 2
4 Speaker 3 6 Speaker 4 8 Speaker 2

5A

1 GRAMMAR
a 2 worse 3 more slowly 4 hotter
5 harder 6 further 7 better 8 healthier
9 more dangerous 10 busier

b 2 as stylish as her shoes
3 as big as my boss's
4 play as well as Spain
5 drive as carefully as me
6 as expensive as laptops
7 look as relaxed as Harry
8 as dirty as his shirt

2 VOCABULARY
2 spend 3 on 4 waste 5 save 6 in

3 PRONUNCIATION
a 2 centre 3 parents 4 ago 5 children
6 patient 7 problem 8 communication
9 traditional 10 around 11 seconds
12 better

b 2 centre 3 parents 4 ago
5 children 6 patient 7 problem
8 communication 9 traditional
10 around 11 seconds 12 better

4 READING
b 2 F 3 T 4 T 5 F 6 F

5 LISTENING

a 1 Speaker 3
2 Speaker 5
3 Speaker 2
5 Speaker 4

b Happiest: Speakers 4 + 5
Least happy: Speaker 2

1 GRAMMAR

a 2 wettest 3 furthest 4 worst 5 ugliest
6 safest 7 most exciting 8 friendliest

b 2 the most interesting 3 most expensive
4 best 5 busiest

c 2 That's the fastest car I've ever driven
3 It's the most beautiful building we've ever seen
4 That's the healthiest meal he's ever eaten
5 It's the best photograph you've ever taken
6 This is the most exciting sport I've ever done
7 That's the worst flight we've ever had
8 This is the most interesting city I've ever visited

2 VOCABULARY

a 2 coast 3 west 4 population 5 famous

b 2 polluted 3 safe 4 noisy 5 boring
6 crowded

c 2 town hall 3 castle 4 statue

3 PRONUNCIATION

a 2 crowded 3 dangerous 4 exciting
5 frightening 6 generous 7 interesting
8 polluted 9 romantic

4 LISTENING

a 1, 2, 4, 6

b 2 F 3 F 4 T 5 F

1 VOCABULARY

a 2 illness 3 skin 4 faces 5 bones
6 prevent 7 brain

2 GRAMMAR

a 2 a few 3 many 4 much 5 a little
6 enough 7 many 8 A little 9 a lot of
10 a few

b 2 tall enough 3 too much 4 enough time
5 too much 6 too many 7 enough exercise
8 sleep enough

3 PRONUNCIATION

a 1 much, none 2 few, food, too
3 diet, like, quite 4 any, healthy, many

4 READING

a potatoes

b 2 F 3 F 4 T 5 F 6 F 7 T

5 LISTENING

a Alice is 35. Her body age is 31.

b 2 no 3 any 4 a lot of 5 positive
6 a little 7 a few 8 enough

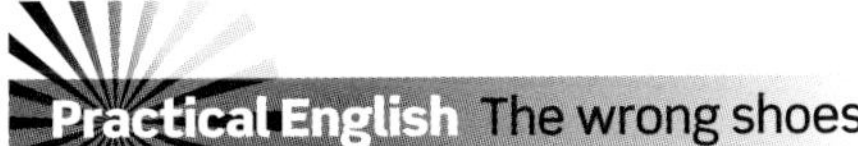

1 VOCABULARY

2 d 3 e 4 a 5 b

2 TAKING SOMETHING BACK TO A SHOP

2 bought 3 problem 4 afraid 5 size
6 small 7 medium 8 see 9 sorry
10 refund 11 changing rooms 12 receipt

3 SOCIAL ENGLISH

2 Oh, you know. Working! But it was OK.
3 Why don't we go out for dinner? I could book a restaurant.
4 OK. For what time?
5 Eight o'clock?
6 Can we make it a bit earlier? Say, seven thirty?
7 OK. I'll go and have a shower then.
8 Sure.

4 READING

a 2 Tiffany & Co 3 Ricky's 4 Ricky's

b 1 keyboard 2 pricey 3 accessories
4 engagement 5 huge 6 do-it-yourself

1 GRAMMAR

a 2 won't win 3 won't remember
4 'll forget 5 won't sell 6 'll miss

2 VOCABULARY

2 learn 3 'll pass 4 Pull 5 broken
6 borrow 7 lose 8 turn on 9 sent
10 found

4 READING

a 2 Gemini 3 Aries 4 Aquarius 5 Taurus

5 LISTENING

a Matt's star sign is Capricorn and Amy's star sign is Virgo.

b 2 M 3 A 4 A 5 M 6 M 7 M

1 GRAMMAR

a 2 Shall I lend you some money
3 I'll have the chicken
4 Shall I take your coat
5 Shall I turn off the air conditioning?
6 I won't be late

b 2 P 3 O 4 O 5 D 6 P

2 VOCABULARY

2 pay 3 come 4 take 5 give 6 send

3 PRONUNCIATION

a 2 decide, email, promise
3 practise, listen, repair
4 borrow, forget, agree
5 sunbathe, invite, complain

4 READING

a Paul learnt not to lend money to strangers.

b a 6 b 3 c 5 e 4 f 2 g 8 h 7

5 LISTENING

a They had problems with crime.

b Speaker 2 A Speaker 3 C Speaker 4 B
Speaker 5 E

1 GRAMMAR

a 2 do … go, read
3 will win, 'll lose
4 were … doing, was watching
5 Have … dreamt, 've … had
6 are … doing, 'm reading
7 Did … sleep, woke up
8 are … leaving, going to go

b 2 have done 3 works 4 's studying
5 has … published 6 helped 7 chose
8 discovered 9 had 10 saw
11 were watching

2 VOCABULARY

2 with 3 for 4 at 5 to 6 in 7 of 8 from

3 PRONUNCIATION

a 2 now 3 borrow 4 down

4 LISTENING

a 2 You are falling. 3 You are lost.
4 You are flying. 5 You can't escape.

b Dream 2 a Dream 3 d Dream 4 c
Dream 5 b

This page was intentionally left blank.

Great Clarendon Street, Oxford, OX2 6DP, United Kingdom

Oxford University Press is a department of the University of Oxford. It furthers the University's objective of excellence in research, scholarship, and education by publishing worldwide. Oxford is a registered trade mark of Oxford University Press in the UK and in certain other countries

First published in 2012
2016 2015 2014
10 9 8 7 6 5

ISBN: 978 0 19 459868 2 MultiPack A
ISBN: 978 0 19 459817 0 Student's Book/Workbook A
ISBN: 978 0 19 459797 5 iTutor
ISBN: 978 0 19 459812 5 iChecker

Printed in China

This book is printed on paper from certified and well-managed sources

ACKNOWLEDGEMENTS

STUDENT'S BOOK ACKNOWLEDGEMENTS

The authors would like to thank all the teachers and students round the world whose feedback has helped us to shape English File.

The authors would also like to thank: all those at Oxford University Press (both in Oxford and around the world) and the design team who have contributed their skills and ideas to producing this course.

Finally very special thanks from Clive to Maria Angeles, Lucia, and Eric, and from Christina to Cristina, for all their support and encouragement. Christina would also like to thank her children Joaquin, Marco, and Krysia for their constant inspiration.

The publisher and authors would also like to thank the following for their invaluable feedback on the materials: Beatriz Martín, Brian Brennan, Elif Barbaros, Gill Hamilton, Jane Hudson, Joanna Sosnowska, Wayne Rimmer, Urbán Ágnes, Anne Parry, Belén Sáez Hernáez, Edelweis Fernández Elorz, Emilie Řezníčková, Erika Feszl, Imogen Clare Dickens, Jonathan Clarke, Kieran Donaghy, Kinga Belley, Laura Villiger Potts, Manuela Gazzola, Mariusz Mirecki, Paolo Jacomelli, Pavlina Zoss, Rebecca Lennox, Robert Anderson, Sandy Millin, Sophie Rogers, Washington Jorge Mukarzel Filho.

The Publisher and Authors are very grateful to the following who have provided information, personal stories, and/or photographs: Lindka Cierach, p.30 (interview); Krysia Cogollos, p.112 (photo and description); Elif Barbaros, p.114 (Kayseri)

The authors and publisher are grateful to those who have given permission to reproduce the following extracts and adaptations of copyright material: p.14 Extract from 'The story behind the picture: American Elections 2008' by Tom Pilston, *The Times*, 17 November 2009. Reproduced by permission; p.15 Extract from 'The image that cost a fortune' by Ben Macintyre, *The Times*, 17 November 2009. Reproduced by permission; p.19 Extract from 'These people were at the museum not to admire the art, but to take snaps to prove they were there' by Marcel Berlins, *The Guardian*, 13 May 2009 © Copyright Guardian News & Media Ltd 2009. Reproduced by permission; p.39 Extract from 'Wish you weren't here' by Tim Moore, *The Sunday Times*, 06 July 1998. Reproduced by permission; p.51 Extract from 'Musical wings on my feet' by Warren Pole, *The Times*, 02 October 2009. Reproduced by permission.

The publishers would like to thank the following for their kind permission to reproduce photographs: Alamy pp.13 (Nagelestock), 19 (Lusoltaly/taking photos), 21 (Imagebroker), 29, 30 (Andrew Twort/shoes), 35 (NM Photo/shoes), 38 (Directphoto.org/Chanel), 100 and 103 (f4foto/Bethany), 114 (Ayhan Altun), 150 (nobleIMAGES/girl blue eyes, Catchlight Visual Services/girl red hair), 151 (mediablitzimages (uk) Limited/dress, Creative Control/top), 152 (Robert Stainforth/walking in wood, Tristar Photos/plane coach car, Gregory Wrona/skiing), 154 (Nicosan/shopping, mauritius images GmbH/ironing, Jochen Tack/wash floor, jacky chapman/tidy lego, Photofusion Picture Library/rubbish), 155 (allesalltag/returning garment, David Levenson/checkout), 156 (Jon Arnold Images Ltd/castle), 157 (Marc Hill/pass exam, Jim Cartwright/e-mail, AFP/win match); Catherine Blackie pp.154 (pick up clothes,) 157 (find keys); Mark Bourdillon Photography p.39 (Tim Moore); Camera Press p.15 (Rapho/Gamma/Jean-Pierre Rey); Conde Naste p.30 (*Vogue* Magazine); Corbis Images pp.150 (Sherrie Nickol/Citizen Stock/slim man in jeans), 152 (Simon Marcus/passport); Getty Images pp.7 and 100 and 103 (Alexander/Jena Cumbo, Oliver/James Whitaker), 8 (Nick Harvey), 20 (John Slater/girl with backpack, Tracy Kahn/man in jeans), 38 (Jochem D Wijnands/Little mermaid, James Strachan/Barcelona), 44 (phone), 100 and 103 (Cultura/Jessica, Michael Malyszko/Hughes, PBNJ Productions/Abigail), 111 (Getty/Image Source), 113 (Thomas Grass), 150 (Ray Kachatorian/girl dark straight hair, Brad Wilson/girl wavy hair), 154 (Doug Corrance/exam, Leander Baerenz/noise, Zia Soleil/people running), 157 (runner, Commercial Eye/girl in classroom); Image Source p.155 (empty trolley); Oxford University Press Capture Web pp.6 (Getty Images/Christopher Robbins), 12 (Photolibrary/couple, Getty Images/girls in boat), 36 (Getty Images Rene Mansi/street, David Oxberry/girl), 37 (Getty Images/Junos/timer, Karan Kapoor/boat), 39, 100, 103 (Getty/Comstock/Dixon, Sam Edwards/Kelly), 150 (Alamy/PhotoAlto/very tall man, Getty Images/Image Source/bald man, Getty Images/Jupiter Images/man with beard, Photolibrary/fat man), 151 (Alamy: Hugh Threlfall/shorts, Oleksiy Maksymenko Photography/Coat, Anatoliy Sadovskiystriped t shirt, Peter Jobst/tights), 152 (Alamy/Juice Images/couple with suitcases, family with car, Getty Images/Michael Blann/tourists, Getty Images/A. Inden/greeting people), 154 (Getty Images/Image Source/lay table, washing machine, Corbis/Monalyn Gracia/put clothes away, Alamy/Relaximages/frying), 154 (Getty Images/Noel Hendrickson/computers, phone call, Getty Images/Iris Friedrich/ironing, Getty Images/Photodisc/people chatting, Emely/make sandwich, Photodisc/planning), 155 (receipt, Getty Images/Yellow Dog Productions/customer, Corbis/Stuart O'Sullivan/Changing room, Getty Images/Fuse/girl trying on jeans, shopping basket, shop assistant), 156 (Guggenheim), 157 (Image Source/Fancy/buy house, Image Source/Nick White/TV control, whiteboard, Image Source/Blend Images/miss train; Panos p.14 (Tom Pilston); Photolibrary p.38 (gondola); Rex Features pp.30 (Kate Middleton, Nils Jorgensen/Royal wedding), 38 (Kevin Foy/pub), 45 (NBCU Photobank), 152 (Westend 61/camping, Monkey Business Images swimming), 154 (Monkey Business/bed, Burger Phanie/washing up); South West News Service p.47; Tate London p.9; Times on Line p.51 (NI Syndication/runner); p.156 Redferns (crowd).

The photograph on page 9 is reproduced by kind permission of: David Hockney. '*Mr. and Mrs Clark and Percy*' 1970–71 (Acryllic on Canvas, 84 x 120', Copyright David Hockney, Collection: Tate Gallery, London).

Pronunciation chart artwork: by Ellis Nadler

Illustrations by: Peter Bull Studios pp.101, 106, 156; Annelie Carlstrom/agencyrush pp.6, 28, 29, 46; Mark Duffin p.20 (signs); CartoonStock pp.44, 45/Tim Cordell; Alex Green/Folio Art p.20; Atsushi Hara/dutchuncle pp.102, 129, 130, 131, 135; Satoshi Hashimoto/dutchuncle agency p.153; Chris Kasch/CIA Illustration agency pp.100, 106; Olivier Latyk/Good Illustration Ltd pp.4, 5; Jerome Mirault/Colagene p.33; Cheryl Taylor/Synergy Art pp.8, 16, 17; James Taylor/DebutArt pp.25, 40, 41; Jonathan Krause pp.48, 49, 103, 107

Commissioned photography by: Gareth Boden pp.20, 22, 23 ('Lily' and 'Matthew'), 30, 31 (Lindka Cierach), 24, 151 (jeans, suit, shirt, tracksuit, trousers, all shoes, belt, tie, cap, hat, socks, earrings, bracelet, ring, jacket), 157 (shaking hands, lend money, break your glasses). MMStudios pp.151 (skirt, top, sweater, gloves, scarf, leggings, necklace), 154 (mistake), 157 (push the door)

Practical English stills photography by: Rob Judges, Jacob Hutchings, and Richard Hutchings pp.10, 11, 26, 27, 42, 43

WORKBOOK ACKNOWLEDGEMENTS

The authors would like to thank all the teachers and students round the world whose feedback has helped us shape English File.

The authors would also like to thank: all those at Oxford University Press (both in Oxford and around the world) and the design team who have contributed their skills and ideas to producing this course.

Finally very special thanks from Clive to Maria Angeles, Lucia, and Eric, and from Christina to Cristina, for all their support and encouragement. Christina would also like to thank her children Joaquin, Marco, and Krysia for their constant inspiration.

The authors and publishers are grateful to the following who have given permission to reproduce the following extracts and adaptations of copyright material: p.9 Extract from 'Fleurs Fraîches' by Heidi Ellison, 19 October 2010. © Heidi Ellison, ParisUpdate.com. Reproduced by permission; p.16 Extract from 'My loaf saver: Woman's life is saved by bag of sliced white bread as it stops her head smashing against crashed car' by Luke Salkeld, *The Daily Mail*, 26 November 2011. Reproduced by permission of Solo Syndication; p.16 Extract from 'Man's life saved by heroic DVD', www.metro.co.uk. Reproduced by permission of Solo Syndication; p.25 Extract from 'Research: women will be doing the housework until 2050' by Tim Ross, *The Telegraph*, 20 May 2011. © Telegraph Media Group Limited 2011; p.40 Extract from 'Tourist Scam Alert'. © 2012 www.ricksteves.com, used with permission.

Although every effort has been made to trace and contact copyright holders before publication, this has not been possible in some cases. We apologize for any apparent infringement of copyright and if notified, the publisher will be pleased to rectify any errors or omissions at the earliest opportunity.

The publishers would like to thank the following for their kind permission to reproduce photographs: Alamy Images pp.8 (Mediablizimages/dress), 11 (Robert Stainforth/bluebell wood), 33 (Prisma Bildagentur AG/beach), 33 (Funkyfood London-Paul Williams/ferry); The Bridgeman Art Library pp.8 and 9 (The Art Institute of Chicago); Corbis pp.11 (RCWW, Inc/typing, Simon Marcus/ passport, A.Inden/young people), 20 (Tibor Bognar/Vienna Opera house), 23 (Atlantide Phototravel/soup), 29 (Franz-Peter Tschauner/dpa/monopoly), 32 (John Warburton Lee/JAI); Getty Images pp.5 (Yellow Dog Productions), 6 (Bartomeu Amengual), 10 (Lester Lefkowitz), 12 (Kniel Synnatzschke/girl wavy hair, Brad Wilson/girl with dark curly hair, Gabe Palmer/man curly hair), 15 (Jacob Halaska), 18 (Bloomberg), 20 (Joe Cornish/Prague, Keith MacGregor/ Budapest), 23 (Dorling Kindersly/paella), 29 (PM Images/tidy up), 33 (Walter Bibikow/Zagreb, John and Tina Reid/Dubrovnik), 35 (Davies and Starr), 38 (Leon); Oxford University Press pp.8 (Oleksiy Maksymenko Photography/ coat), 11 (Michael Blann/tourists, sunbathing, Alamy/Juice Images/couple with suitcase), 12 (Getty Images/Kindler Andreas/man with scarf, Getty Images/ Alan Graf/middle-aged woman), 19 (Corbis/Ocean), 20 (Getty Images/Chase Jarvis/backpacker), 29 (Getty Images/Art Vandalay/juggling, Corbis/Plattform/ Johner Images/baking), 41 (Getty Images/Jose Luis Pelaez Inc); Reuters p.7 (Aly Song); Rex Features pp.11 (camping, Sipa Press/ski hire, Dan Callister/hotel reception), 23 (Ben Pipe/The Travel Library/New York), 26 (FI Online), 36 (Alex Segre); SWNS p.16 (SWNS.com).

The painting reproduced on pages 8 and 9 is *Sunday Afternoon on the Island of La Grande Jatte*, 1884–86 (oil on canvas), Seurat, Georges Pierre (1859–91)/The Art Institute of Chicago, IL, USA/The Bridgeman Art Library.

Commissioned photography by: Gareth Boden p.8 (ring, trousers, shirt, track suit, hat, trainers, belt, tie)

Illustrations by: Atsushi Hara/Dutch Uncle Agency pp.13, 24, 25, 39; Tim Marrs pp.22, 42; Jérôme Mireault/Colagene Illustrations pp.28, 31, 40; Roger Penwill p.37; Kath Walker Illustration pp.16, 17

Picture research and illustrations commissioned by: Catherine Blackie

Design by: Stephen Strong